PERSPECTIVES IN SOCIOLOGY

PERSPECTIVES IN SOCIOLOGY

third edition

E. C. CUFF, W. W. SHARROCK
and D. W. FRANCIS

London and New York

First published in 1979 by Unwin Hyman Ltd.
Third edition published in 1990

Reprinted in 1992
by Routledge
11 New Fetter Lane, London EC4P 4EE

Simultaneously published in the USA and Canada
by Routledge
a division of Routledge, Chapman and Hall Inc.
29 West 35th Street, New York, NY 10001

British Library Cataloguing in Publication Data

A catalogue record for this book is available from the British Library.

Library of Congress Cataloging in Publication Data

A catalogue record for this book is available from the Library of Congress.

ISBN 0-415-07920-9

Contents

Preface to the first edition

In recent years an awareness has been developing, at all levels of education, that successful learning requires an explicit focus on the nature of knowledge, on how knowledge is acquired and on the fact that there are different kinds of knowledge. Within this framework we believe that sociology can best be understood as a variety of perspectives, all of which collectively comprise our ways of understanding the social world.

The original impetus for writing this book was prompted by the first-hand experience of some of us in teaching and examining GCE Advanced Sociology courses, and the book is primarily written for 'A' level students and their teachers. Sociology at this level can degenerate into a collection of memorizable sociological findings to be regurgitated in examinations – the examination scripts of most students at 'A' level generally show insufficient awareness of the various methodologies employed to produce those findings. In subscribing to the view that sociology is better understood as being a variety of ways of thinking about the world, we hope to encourage more active learning situations, in which students can develop a deeper understanding of the nature of sociological work. We recognize that rote learning of facts might well be replaced by rote learning of perspectives, and have attempted to organize our book in a manner designed to meet this danger.

We appreciate that practising sociologists do not operate with all of these perspectives. By and large, they tend to opt for one or another in pursuing their empirical studies. We feel, however, that it would be improper in an introductory textbook to advocate our personal preferences. Instead, we have endeavoured to outline the nature of each of the various perspectives and to emphasize the strengths rather than the weaknesses of each approach. The book should therefore not be read 'developmentally', with the implication that later chapters represent more advanced sociological work. Rather, the order of chapters is organized chronologically, in so far as different perspectives often emerge as reactions to existing ones.

We have been encouraged in our approach by recent changes in the AEB syllabus, which now requires students to adopt a more critical approach. Furthermore, the recently introduced JMB syllabus for 'A' level sociology is specifically created around the notion of sociological perspectives.

Our experience as teachers of sociology in polytechnic, university and college of education settings suggests that this book will also be of value to first-year degree students. Its emphasis on the theoretical and methodological characteristics of sociology could usefully complement other introductory textbooks, many of which tend to be topic-based.

We have included some suggestions for further reading and a number of questions at the end of each chapter. The further reading highlights excerpts from some of the original work discussed in the chapter and has been generally selected for its easy availability. The questions at the end of each chapter are designed to help the reader to think about key issues and to enable him to reinforce his understanding of the text. A more extensive and demanding list of sources and references for each chapter is provided at the end of the book. We wish to acknowledge the help we have received in producing this book. Our primary debt is to the many students in our respective institutions and pupils in local schools for their comments and views on several drafts over a number of years. We are also grateful to M. A. Atkinson for his advice; to R. Anderson for his active encouragement and help at a crucial period; and to D. I. Shelton, a former colleague. Last – but far from least – we are indebted to Mrs D. Morris and her team – Mrs P. Curvis, Mrs J. Davies, Mrs J. French, Mrs E. Jones, Miss L. Mellor, Mrs J. Naylor and Mrs D. Ovington – for their excellent typing from some almost indecipherable drafts.

Preface to the second edition

Although several other introductory books in sociology have appeared since the publication of the first edition of *Perspectives in Sociology*, none of them directly explore what is involved in using sociological perspectives. Thus the distinctive characteristic of this book still remains its declared intention to examine methodological features of the perspectives themselves and to use studies in order to illustrate particular methodological concerns.

In response to suggestions by our readers, to whom we extend many thanks, we have taken the opportunity in this new edition to clarify some difficult sections, to expand others and to include some new materials. As our concern is to clarify the perspectives, not to 'cover' the topics and the most recent materials, we have not sought to 'update' for its own sake. We have, however, tried to include new materials where they help in this concern.

The methodological issues in sociology largely remain the same and for that reason we have not altered the basic structure of the book. We have, however, taken the opportunity to include some reference to current debates about the direction sociology might take in the future.

Finally, we wish to thank Jean Davies for doing all the typing in the second edition. We do not know what we would have done without her excellent work.

Preface to the third edition

We are grateful to our readers for giving us the opportunity to produce this third edition. It allows us to review what has been happening in British sociology over the ten years or more since the appearance of the first edition and to respond with some significant changes. As with previous editions, the changes are intended to reflect what is going on in the field rather than to display our personal preferences. Again, our concern is with theories and methods and not substantive topics.

The first major change is to incorporate a chapter on critical theory in order to reflect the extensive work and thinking that Marx's basic work continues to stimulate, particularly on the continent. This chapter introduces the complication of another meaning of 'structuralism': as well as referring to the way the organization of society (the social structure) can be seen to shape individual actions, it is now also used to refer to the idea that there is an underlying framework of language and meanings whose symbolic systems shape up or 'structure' what individuals can do, albeit unconsciously and unbeknownst to them. Secondly, interactionism now occupies less space, though it is still contained in two chapters, reflecting the relative marginalization of interactionist approaches relative to structuralism (in both senses of 'structuralism') in British sociology teaching. In recasting the chapters on interactionism, we have taken the opportunity to make a more concerted attempt to show the similarities and differences between symbolic interactionism and ethnomethodology. Thirdly, the chapter on research strategies has been completely rewritten to take account of the large amount of work going on in the philosophy of science relating to the approaches used in sociology. Finally, every other part of the book has been thoroughly revised and sometimes completely rewritten in a further effort to produce clarity and to respond to readers' comments for which we are, as always, extremely glad.

Over ten years other changes have occurred. The saddest is the death in 1983 of George Payne who was the originator and stimulus for this book. We remember him and miss him.

1 The nature of sociological perspectives

Introduction

In introductory textbooks on sociology the first chapter often begins by posing the question: 'What is sociology?' The authors proceed then tentatively to answer it by definitions such as 'Sociology is the study of man in society' or 'Sociology is a scientific study of social phenomena' and then go on to show the merits and, especially, the weakness of whichever particular definition is used. Starting by means of a definition may not be such a good idea, for one definition may simply lead to yet more definitions, without noticeably increasing understanding. For example, to define sociology as the study of man in society necessitates some further definitions (of 'society' – and then of the terms used to define 'society') and does nothing to help us to distinguish the kinds of study of man in society, for example, of the novelist, the biologist and the sociologist. Similarly, sociology may be a scientific study of social phenomena but so may be economics, law, history and some branches of psychology.

Even if we take a longer definition of sociology, the nature of the subject remains unclear. For example, one author says that

'we can state fairly simply what sociology is about. It is an effort to illuminate as much of human behaviour as can be illuminated within two kinds of limits: the limits imposed by a scientific frame of reference and the limits imposed by focusing attention only on two aspects – culture and "groupness"' (Bredemeier and Stephenson, p.1).

The original question 'What is sociology?' is, in effect, answered by a series of further questions: 'What is culture?', 'What is groupness?', 'What is a scientific frame of reference?' Then, in defining and describing 'groupness', terms like 'social structure', 'role', 'role-set', 'status', 'reference group', 'social system', and so on, are used. We need to ask the question 'What is . . .' of each of these terms. And we still have to deal with 'culture' and 'a scientific frame of reference'.

Clearly, in order to answer our original question 'What is sociology?' we need to know the answers to all the other questions it generates. This is tantamount to saying that we have to know about sociology if we wish to know what sociology is about! Though to some extent this statement is obviously correct -- we cannot know much about sociology until we have spent a fair amount of time studying the subject -- it does little to help the newcomer to gain useful initial insights into the nature of sociology. We suggest that such insights, which will be developed but not superseded by later studies, can be achieved from a discussion of the nature of *sociological perspectives*.

Sociological perspectives are simply different ways of trying to understand the social world. As the title of this book implies, we take the view that sociology as a discipline or subject is basically best understood by stressing that it is made up of a *number* of separate though more or less interlinked approaches. If students are introduced to sociology in terms of its being a single, monolithic approach, with a single set of terms or concepts, a uniform set of theories and a standard collection of unified findings, we feel that they are either being misled or talked down to -- albeit possibly for the best reasons. Instead, we prefer to credit students with both the intelligence and the desire to encounter the subject as it currently appears -- not rounded off and smoothed for the purpose of easy digestion. Such a single presentation leads to worse evils than oversimplifications which can misrepresent and distort; it may lead to the wrong sort of learning which emphasizes memorizing and regurgitating information. We prefer a more worthwhile learning based upon the thinking which can derive from studying something about the social world.

Further, we wish to emphasize that no sociological perspective -- or even all of them in combination -- can give us 'the truth' about the world. Sociological perspectives merely provide us with *ways* of trying to understand the world; none of them has a built-in assurance that eternal and unshakeable 'truth' will or can be provided. The danger of presenting sociology as a monolithic, uniform and standardized body of concepts, theories and findings is that students might presume that, in absorbing 'the facts' about sociology, they might also be absorbing bodies of 'truth', bodies of certain knowledge, which, once acquired, might be retained for all time.

In offering this approach to sociology not in terms of final truths, but rather in terms of ways of understanding, we are taking up a certain standpoint not only with respect to sociology, but also with respect to the nature of knowledge in general. It is with this view of the nature of knowledge in general that we wish to commence our more detailed exposition of sociology as comprised of various ways of understanding the social world.

Forms of knowledge

It is the task of philosophers to ask questions about the nature of knowledge in general. Knowledge in general may be viewed, categorised and argued about in a number of ways. One way is to regard man's attempts to think about himself and his world by means of posing a number of key questions. These questions are:

(a) What assumptions are being made, that is, what are the intellectual starting-points for such thinking?
(b) What sort of questions are being asked?
(c) In asking these questions, what sorts of concepts are being used?
(d) What sorts of methods are being used to find out about the world?
(e) What sorts of answers or solutions or explanations are given to the questions asked?

From these questions, it is possible to locate various forms of knowledge which appear to differ more or less in terms of answers to these questions. These forms of knowledge represent different ways of knowing about the world. One such list of the different forms of knowledge – other lists can be compiled because such lists are a matter of argument and debate, not of certainty – might include: literary and aesthetic understanding; religious understanding; natural scientific understanding; human scientific understanding; mathematical understanding; and, finally, philosophical understanding.

The list of possible forms of knowledge is based on differences between various approaches in terms of these questions about assumptions, methods, answers, and so on. It does *not* imply that there are not similarities between these forms of knowledge or that they are totally different. It does, however, provide us with a useful way of seeing how knowledge can be organized and ties in very well with how we tend to encounter knowledge as organized in the school curriculum.

For our purposes, we wish to focus on differences in forms of knowledge, and on one difference in particular, as it would take a book in itself to develop these philosophical views in any detail. This difference concerns the basic or 'bedrock' assumptions on which a particular form of knowledge rests; assumptions which, in the last resort, serve to justify or to underpin that particular way of understanding, thinking and studying.

We suggest that scientific approaches to understanding the world can be distinguished from other approaches in two fundamental and interrelated ways. First, an approach that claims to be scientific – irrespective of whether or not it originates in the field of natural or human science – must demonstrably have empirical relevance to the world. An empirical relevance involves showing that any statements, descriptions and explanations used or derived from this approach can be verified or checked out in the world. Thus, second, a scientific approach necessitates the deliberate use of clear procedures which not only show how 'results' were achieved, but are also clear enough for other workers in the field to attempt to repeat them, that is, to check them out with the same or other materials and thereby test the results. A scientific approach necessarily involves standards and procedures for demonstrating the 'empirical warrant' of its findings, showing the match or fit between its statements and what is happening or has happened in the world. These two criteria – empirical relevance and clear procedures – are bedrock assumptions built into any scientific approach. Further distinctions like types of methods (for example, experimental, historical, survey, interviewing), or distinctions like types of 'results' (for example, description or explanation, quantitative or qualitative), are merely embellishments – albeit important and often controversial embellishments – of these basic criteria which serve to distinguish scientific approaches or perspectives from other approaches to understanding the world.

It is not that other approaches have nothing to say about the world or even that none of their statements can be empirically tested and verified. Rather, the point being made is that their justification, their *raison d'être*, as ways of understanding the world is not solely or even largely dependent on these scientific criteria or basic assumptions. For example, no one would deny that we can learn much about ourselves and the world in which we find ourselves through reading and studying literature. We suggest, however, that novelists, poets and dramatists do not create their work in such a manner that it is consciously constructed in terms of the conventions of scientific procedures in order that its 'results' can be empirically warranted and verified by others in the field. Although novelists/writers often wish to portray human beings and their world in penetrating ways, they would wish their work to be judged not simply in terms of its 'accuracy' or 'truthfulness', but, more importantly, in terms of, for example, its structure, the feelings induced in the reader/watcher and the relationship of these induced feelings and emotions with the intentions of the writer. In short, literary and artistic approaches to the world are underpinned by their own bedrock assumptions that concern the aesthetic nature of the work. Agreement on the success or otherwise of such work is determined in terms of argument and discussion underpinned by these assumptions, rather than by an appeal to its 'scientific warrant'.

Similarly, the work of mathematicians can be usefully applied in the world in many ways. Such applications, however, do not provide the justifications and standards for good work in the field of mathematics. Instead, mathematical reasoning is evaluated in terms of rules of deductive logic which can be used both to construct and to check the systematic and coherent character of a mathematical proof or argument. Thus Pythagoras' theorem (that in a right-angled triangle, the sum of the squares on the two shorter sides is equal to the square on the hypotenuse) can be created and verified by someone sitting down with pen and paper. There is no need to go out into the world measuring off fields; or to check and recheck in a number of different test situations. Given the acceptance of some fundamental axioms (self-evident truisms) such as one plus one equals two, and given the knowledge and willingness to use rules of logic, then the proof can there and then be stated to be true or false, barring calculational errors. No further endeavours can make it 'truer' or 'falser'. In this way, then, mathematics, like art and literature, may be seen as different approaches to knowing, producing different forms of knowledge. In like manner, religious and philosophical approaches to knowledge can be characterized in terms of their respective bedrock assumptions, which can be contrasted with those of scientific approaches.

These two illustrations, however, should be sufficient to illustrate this point. Needless to say, forms of knowledge do not differ only in these respects. The nature of the bedrock assumptions clearly greatly affects the kind of work done, that is, the kinds of concepts used, the sort of questions asked, the type of methods employed and the sort of 'results' obtained. In this way, we can recognize these different forms of knowledge. We might equally recognize that because they represent different approaches to understanding, they are in no way competitive; they cannot be ranked in some sort of a hierarchy of importance. Because they are all doing different jobs, they are all equal in status as forms of knowledge. Of course, individuals may and do exercise their preferences, in terms of their interests and aptitudes, in choosing which forms of knowledge to study, and they may, for their particular purposes, even rank them in importance, but there is no way of demonstrating that any form of knowledge is better than any other. In their different ways, they all contribute to man's knowledge.

The social sciences

We have already suggested that the natural and human/social sciences are similar in respect of the underlying, bedrock assumptions which differentiate a scientific way of knowing about the world from other ways of knowing. They are similar in that both enterprises attempt to make statements about the world which can be warranted, that is, verified by empirical testing in the world. We can, however, crudely distinguish the two approaches in terms of their subject matter: the natural sciences largely deal with non-human phenomena; the social sciences deal with human action and behaviour. The distinction is crude for at least two reasons. First, some approaches in natural science do have things to say about human behaviour, biology for example. Second, some approaches in the social sciences treat human action as an object of study in the same manner as natural scientists treat plants, rocks, or atoms. This point will provide a major focus of interest throughout this book, especially in Chapter 6.

Given this rough and ready distinction between the natural and social sciences, we now concentrate on the latter. Included in the social sciences are approaches or 'subjects' such as economics, psychology, anthropology, demography, politics and, of course, sociology.

Although these approaches have in common their basic scientific justification or rationale, they differ to varying degrees in terms of the concepts they use, the questions about the world they pose, the methods they use to deal with these questions and the sort of 'results' or explanations or solutions they consider to be satisfactory. Also, in addition to their bedrock assumptions, they differ in respect of other important assumptions which tend to characterize and distinguish each of these differing approaches within the general area of social science. It is often the case that the basic assumptions, the starting-points, of one social science constitute the basic problems or questions to which another social science devotes itself. For example, sociologists usually assume that human action is culturally and not genetically shaped. Sociologists recognize that the genetic make-up of parents and forebears does result in individual differences between people and they may take them into account in a particular empirical study of the world. But they will not specifically and methodically examine and explore individual differences from the standpoint of genetics. Instead, they tend to be more interested in how individual differences may be patterned and shaped by the way a society is organized, and in examining how these differences may be differently patterned and shaped in different societies which have contrasting cultures (ways of living). On the other hand, psychologists may assume the existence and even importance of what sociologists are studying, but for their part may study human behaviour from other angles, using different concepts, asking different questions and, in turn, allowing knowledge of cultural differences to be an unexplored, taken-for-granted assumption in their approach. In short, sociologists may start off by assuming that cultural factors are the key determinants of human behaviour while psychologists may start off by emphasizing, say, the personality structure of individuals. Each of these approaches give us a different basis for developing a perspective on human behaviour and action and each of them can be equally valuable.

Concepts

The various social sciences offer us different, although interrelated, ways of trying to understand the social world. They give us particular perceptions of, ways of looking at, the social world and enable us to develop a systematic and disciplined way of trying to understand aspects of it. Here, the *concepts* which the respective social sciences utilize are of great significance. Our perceptions of the world, what we make of it, how and what questions we ask of it, what sort of answers we obtain, are shaped by the concepts we employ.

Concepts provide us with tags or labels for a thing or an idea, for example, 'boy', 'rat', 'stratification', 'ego', 'justice', 'balance of power', 'desk'. Obviously, as users of language we are all users of concepts. Clearly, concepts allow us to organize and relate our perceptions of the world, whether as sociologist, psychologist, theologian, or simply as the man in the street. They do more than this, however, for in a very real sense our perceptions of the world, the world itself, consists of our concepts. By this, we do not mean to suggest the extreme philosophical position which states that the world exists only in our thoughts and that if we shut our eyes, the world vanishes. We have only to kick the table hard when our eyes are shut to receive a painful reminder of the fallacy of this view. Rather, we suggest that though there is a world 'out there', what we make of it is highly dependent on the conceptual equipment we have developed to perceive the world. Thus we might come across a 'sharp, pointed stick' in the Bolivian jungle; and might later discover that the 'stick' is 'really' a primitive 'plough' used by the largely nomadic tribes in that area.

Let us take up a more extended example of how the world is shaped by our perceptions of it. Let us examine the phenomenon of a lady who is buying a new fur coat. An economist might see this social event in terms of, say, consumer spending patterns, supply and demand, indifference curves, savings and income and purchasing power. A psychologist might see it in terms of drives to nurturance-succourance, emotional gratification or even, if he is a follower of Freud, as repressed infantile sexuality and a 'return to the womb'! A sociologist might see the event in terms of the normative patterns of a social class or category, or in terms of ostentatious consumption and its relation to claims for social honour and prestige. And even as a layman, we must have the cultural knowledge, which necessitates the appropriate concepts, to be able to describe someone buying a new fur coat. A Trobriand islander, if suddenly transplanted to a large department store, might be as confused as to what is happening as we might possibly be to find that a sharp pointed stick is after all a plough.

In all of these instances, the phenomenon in the world, the event being described, is in a sense 'the same'. But what is made of it is greatly determined by the conceptual apparatus we employ. It is thus that concepts can be said to shape our perceptions of the world.

Clearly, the kinds of questions we ask about the world are dependent on the concepts we employ. In any social science, a range of concepts is generally employed, permitting a range of types of question to be asked. In so far as these questions and concepts are related and thereby systematized, a distinctive approach to understanding the social world can emerge. Such an approach tends to develop its own distinctive methods for answering these questions; and, in keeping with the distinctive assumptions, concepts, questions and methods of a particular social science, the answers or solutions or explanations also tend to be distinctive.

Sociology

It should, then, be clear to anyone who has followed the discussion so far that sociology, as an approach to understanding the world, can be differentiated from other approaches in that it attempts to be scientific, that is, to produce empirically warranted and verifiable statements about the social world and is basically distinguished only by its distinctive assumptions, concepts, questions, methods and answers. It has no special ability to provide the 'truth' about social life or to provide solutions for social problems. All it can provide is a number of viewpoints or perspectives on the social world which might help us to develop greater understanding. Occasionally, such understanding might provide a clearer basis for practical action in the world, but it will never provide the 'truth' as an end-product. No scientific approach can do this because, quite simply, a scientific approach necessitates open-ended inquiry. Once the 'truth' is known, then inquiry can stop and, eventually, what is known becomes a matter of belief, rather than an empirical and testable/verifiable matter. Clearly, from the above arguments, there are many kinds of 'truth' – economic, psychological, theological, philosophical, mathematical, and so on – many of which are subject to revision or modification or, in the case of the sciences, to falsification over time. Thus sociology can claim no superiority over other forms of systematic knowledge in giving understanding. The only valid reason for studying it is in terms of interest in the questions posed about the social world, and not, decidedly not, in terms of wishing to acquire *the* definitive version of the world. For students who want 'the truth', some variant of theological studies is suggested; for in such studies, basic belief or faith is a legitimate aspect of that approach to knowledge.

Students who have grasped these arguments may not be too surprised to discover that sociology itself as a field of study can be seen to comprise a number of distinct though interrelated perspectives, or ways of understanding the social world. Each of these ways can be characteristically distinguished by the basic assumptions made, the concepts used, the questions raised, the methods employed and the 'solutions' obtained. We should not, however, be alarmed at the picture of sociology which is emerging. For we have argued that knowledge is complex and multi-sided. It can be viewed as having a number of different forms which offer us different ways of seeing things. Each of these forms can be subdivided into large areas like physics, chemistry, economics and sociology. And sociology itself can be seen to be made up of a number of linked but distinctive perspectives, each of which gives us a different way of viewing the social world. To add to this complexity, we have suggested:

(1) There is no ultimate way of determining the superiority of any of these forms, any of these areas, or any of these sociological perspectives.
(2) There is no ultimate way of determining the 'truth' of any of these forms, areas or perspectives.

Thus within the complex total field of knowledge, we derive a picture of sociology which is 'not even' a single unified approach to knowledge and does not guarantee the truth of its findings. Given such information, students would surely be justified in giving up forthwith their study of sociology!

We suggest, however, that such an abandonment of sociology

would be premature. The picture of sociology does not highlight several important features which ought to be considered before making such a decision.

First, full account should be taken of the fact that sociology is not the only subject to be made up of a variety of approaches. In fact most, if not all, living subjects are like this. In history, for example, we have proponents of the statistical approach as opposed to the proponents of more literary studies. And cross-cutting this division we find that social historians vie with political and economic historians. And if history is not a monolithic subject, neither is the 'queen of the sciences', physics. Since the Einsteinian revolution in physics, the subject has met with severe difficulties in reconciling the traditional macroscopic approach with the apparently different behaviour of small particles studied in molecular physics. Similar difficulties and divisions can be found in all other subject areas. What usually happens, however, is that such difficulties do not become apparent to students until they have done several years of study. Here, we take the view that the nature of knowledge should be accurately portrayed to students at the outset. Then they may not be misled into thinking that they have captured the 'truth' only to find that this truth disintegrates into later difficulties and contradictions.

This point about 'truth' brings us to the second feature students should take into account when assessing the merits of sociology. We have argued that no subject which claims to be scientific can ever reveal ultimate truths. The acceptance of ultimate truths would mean that the scientific enterprise had come to an end because scientific inquiry requires, in principle, the scrutiny and questioning of any fact. Science must be open-ended. Open-endedness does *not* mean, however, that solutions and explanations are no good at all because they do not represent the ultimate truth. Instead, 'knowing better', where 'better' is displayed in the standards, criteria and spelled-out methodology of a subject, is not the same as knowing nothing, or knowing no more after the study of a subject than before it. Thus sociologists, from whatever perspective, would claim to produce a better understanding of aspects of the social world. Understanding is better in the sense of providing systematic and coherent and testable ways of studying the social world: ways which enable us to enhance and to develop our knowledge. Though such knowledge does not represent final truths, it may at least help us to understand better the social world.

At this stage, we can do no more than to state such claims in these rather general and abstract ways. The only way students can evaluate such claims is to examine the nature of the work done in sociology. In the succeeding chapters, we will fill out in some detail this picture of sociology as a number of different though linked perspectives. In so doing, we will give plenty of examples of the substance or content of sociological endeavours. Then, in the final chapter, we will return to these questions about the nature of sociology, asking again 'Is it worth studying?', 'Should we take seriously a subject which is made up of a number of perspectives?'

Thus, in the remainder of this book we will describe in some detail the basic perspectives which can be seen to comprise sociology. While the emphasis will be on ways of thinking about the social world, and not on 'results' or on 'findings', sufficient of the variety and range of the 'content' of the subject will be described to give students a good idea of the sorts of issues which interest sociologists and of the sorts of things they have to say about them. As we suggested at the outset of this chapter, however, we place more emphasis on the *ways* or methodologies of understanding the social world than on specific findings or results. After all, we have argued that 'results' are necessarily provisional, rather than final truths; they tend to become obsolescent over time. Consequently, we are suggesting that it would be more sensible to focus on ways of thinking sociologically in order to develop the ability and skills to be able, critically and constructively, to evaluate the ever-changing empirical results of sociological inquiry. Perhaps, too, the intellectual foundations might be laid for those students who wish to become professional sociologists and to produce warrantable findings themselves.

Brief overview of contents

In Chapters 2 and 3 we shall outline two distinctive approaches in sociology: consensus and conflict perspectives respectively. We shall see, however, that in one major respect these two perspectives have a common focus: they both stress the systemic nature of society. Although one perspective stresses the co-operative and harmonious elements in social life, while the other focuses on the coercive and divisive elements, they can both be seen to converge on some basic issues. In this way, both of these perspectives can be usefully labelled 'structuralism' in so far as they both focus on the whole society, the social structure and the relationship of its parts.

In Chapter 4, we reflect the great interest and huge amount of thinking currently being generated by issues raised by structuralist approaches (in particular the conflict perspective) by examining in some detail the work of modern continental thinkers like Claude Lévi-Strauss, Jurgen Habermas, Herbert Marcuse and Jacques Derrida. We can then see what sorts of transformations have been made to some of the long-standing social issues and the implication for sociological work.

In Chapters 5 and 6, we look at approaches to meaning and action. In Chapter 5, we look generally at these approaches and then focus particularly on symbolic interactionism. Although small group situations can be studied using structuralist assumptions, questions and concepts, meaning and action studies sharply contrast with structuralism in their stress on investigating social situations from the standpoint of the actors involved in them. In Chapter 6, we examine ethnomethodology as one of these approaches, given its focus on persons, language and social encounters. It takes issue, however, with all other approaches by claiming to study what they all take for granted or ignore, namely, the detailed study of the common-sense methods by which we all, sociologist and layman alike, make sense of our social world.

In Chapter 7 these sociological perspectives are examined and contrasted in terms of their distinctive methodologies. Throughout this book, we use the term 'methodology' to refer to a scrutiny of the basic assumptions, key questions, concepts and types of solution/explanation found in any particular sociological perspective. In Chapter 7 we continue to use the term in this way, and examine general research strategies and their relation to specific research techniques such as questionnaires, participant observation, analysis of transcripts, and so on, which appear to be differentially used in the various perspectives. We examine why this should be the case and probe into the view of man and of social reality which underpin both research strategies and techniques. Finally, in Chapter 8, we conclude by returning to some of the basic issues raised in this introductory chapter and examine what value there can be in studying sociology.

Before we embark on the main body of the book, however, it might be helpful to give an extended example to illustrate how a particular area of social life can be approached and understood in different ways through the application of various perspectives. The area chosen is one which has attracted much sociological interest – mental illness.

Perspectives on mental illness

'Mental illness' is a comparatively new concept, although the sorts of behaviour to which it is commonly applied are as old as mankind. Today it is an accepted way of describing the behaviour of some of our fellow members of society. Most of us have some idea of what it means to say that someone is 'mentally ill'. We may even know people who are 'mentally ill'. The concept, then, is not unfamiliar to us. Yet when we begin to delve further into the nature of 'mental illness', we discover that there are several ways of understanding and explaining it. It soon becomes obvious that there is no 'one truth' to be discovered about it. We discover that its nature is very much a question of how it is looked at.

One common feature we do find is that the concepts of 'mental illness' and 'the mentally ill person' are usually applied to people who exhibit behaviour which the rest of us consider abnormal. Hearing voices, talking to oneself, having deep depressions, being unable to carry on normal conversations – these are some of the 'symptoms' we see as signs of mental illness.

The explanations of these behaviours are, however, numerous and various. We consider only a few examples to illustrate how it is possible for a common phenomenon to be understood and explained in several different ways.

We know that in the Bible madness was associated with out-of-the-ordinary, or abnormal behaviour. The usual explanations offered for the condition referred to possession by evil spirits. It was generally assumed that the unfortunate madmen behaved the way they did because evil spirits had control of their bodies. It was understood that supernatural powers inflicted the condition primarily as a punishment for sin. Madness was seen as a curse of God. For example, we read in the Bible that when Saul, the King of Israel, rebelled against God's command, 'the spirit of the Lord departed from Saul and an evil spirit of the Lord tormented him'.

We also know that Hippocrates, in Ancient Greece, explained the sorts of behaviour we are referring to by reference to his 'Humoral

Theory'. He suggested that in the human body there were four humours or fluids which controlled our temperament, our emotions and moods. He considered that our behaviour was influenced by our moods and so in turn was controlled to a large extent by our bodily fluids. The fluids were known as *blood, phlegm, yellow bile* and *black bile*, and in the normal healthy body these fluids were present in particular proportions. But it was possible for excesses to develop, resulting in abnormal, unexpected behaviour. For example, an excess of black bile was considered to cause excessive melancholy, or what today we might call a state of depression.

We have in these examples ways of understanding, ways of seeing and explaining particular forms of behaviour, which would not be acceptable today to the vast majority of us, but which were considered perfectly adequate in their time. Although the type of behaviour displayed by the King of Israel, or by the depressed Ancient Greek or by the modern-day neurotic businessman could be similar, the ways their behaviour and condition have been understood is very different.

However, this is not to say the ways in which these conditions are seen and understood is merely a question of history. Rather, we are saying that the variety of explanations can be viewed as a result of different basic assumptions about the nature of the world and life within it.

Today, just as in the past, the description and explanation of abnormal or odd behaviour can take a variety of forms. It is the case that most modern explanations are more likely to be scientific, although religious and supernatural explanations, in terms of possession by spirits, are still accepted by persons with particular religious convictions.

In modern Western culture scientific explanations, that is, explanations which are fundamentally testable in some way against empirical observations, are usually more acceptable to the majority of people. There are, however, a number of explanations both within and between such scientific approaches to understanding as biology, psychology and sociology.

Generally speaking, biological approaches rest on the assumption that human behaviour can be explained to a large extent by reference to the genetic composition and chemical processes of the human body. Assumptions of this sort have led to a variety of investigations and subsequent explanations of mental illness in terms of heredity and physical defects.

Psychological theories of mental illness have been more common. Mental illness has been readily recognized as a problem of the mind and broad comparisons have been assumed between diseased bodies and diseased minds. Psychology, as the human science which focuses its study on the human mind and its mental processes, has naturally produced a variety of explanations of mental abnormality.

Within psychology, similar to most other disciplines, there are a variety of perspectives, each with its own bedrock assumptions about the psychological nature of the human being. Thus we find a variety of ways of seeing and understanding mental illness psychologically; but it is probable that the Freudian approach is the most well known and it provides us with an interesting example of a non-sociological, human scientific perspective.

The Freudian perspective on mental illness is founded on the assumption that the normal, stable personality develops through a number of stages in which the innate pleasure drive or libido is directed on to different objects. The normal personality passes through an oral phase, an anal phase and a genital phase. During this last phase an individual's sexual drives, which were previously directed to the parent of the opposite sex, are transferred to an appropriate other person. For a variety of reasons, mainly to do with inadequate familial relationships and early childhood experiences, a person may regress to an earlier stage of development or become fixed in a particular stage. Such fixations can result in abnormal behaviour. For Freudians, mental illness is seen largely as a pathological (that is, sick) condition of the personality brought about by experiences in early childhood which have hindered the normal development of the individual.

For sociologists, mental illness has been an area of investigation for several decades. Ever since Emile Durkheim demonstrated at the turn of the century how such an apparently individually motivated act as suicide can be explained by *social* causes, later sociologists have not hesitated to investigate and explain other aspects of behaviour which superficially have not appeared relevant to sociological consideration. Mental illness is one such typical area.

Following Durkheim's particular sociological tradition, some sociologists have sought the causes of mental illness in the structure of society. They, like Durkheim, have assumed that what an individual does is very much a question of what his social environment, what his society, structures him into doing. On the basis of this broad assumption, mental illness has been seen as a condition or attribute of the person like a disease or disability, produced by the person's societal environment. Consequently these sociologists have looked at the structure of various societies and particular parts of societies in order to discover what associations may exist between particular aspects of the social structure and mental illness.

An investigation typical of this approach is the study by A. B. Hollingshead and F. C. Redlich, *Social Class and Mental Illness* (Wiley, 1958). In this study the authors seek to demonstrate that in the urban community of New Haven in the United States of America the incidence and type of mental illness vary according to position in the class structure. For example, they show that while social class 1 (High Status) contains 3.1 per cent of the community's population, only 1 per cent of all known psychiatric cases in the area come from it. Conversely they show that social class V (Low Status) includes 17.8 per cent of the community's population, but contributes as many as 36.8 per cent of the psychiatric patients. They also found that neuroses are concentrated at the higher levels and psychoses at the lower levels of the class structure.

An exact, detailed account of all the facts and figures they produce is not relevant to our purpose. What is important is that we recognize that this sort of sociological knowledge, this sort of generalization, is the product of a particular approach, a particular perspective. It is only arrived at because the investigators started out with certain assumptions about the nature of mental illness and what causes it. The production of this sort of explanation is an example of the use of the 'structuralist perspective' in sociology. In this particular case, social class is assumed to be a feature of the structure of society. Members of the same social class are assumed to have similar roles in the economic order of society, similar attitudes and educational backgrounds, and similar life-styles. This broad economic and cultural similarity is assumed to differentiate large groups within the society and to produce different behaviours and conditions in the individual members of the groups. In this case, it is assumed to produce differences in the incidence and type of mental illness.

Similar broad structuralist assumptions lie behind studies which seek to discover associations between the incidence of mental illness and ecological factors such as area of urban residence. Studies of this sort imply that the style of life and the general organization of different parts of a town or city can condition individuals into mental illness.

H. Warren Durham and Robert Faris, for example, have shown that in Chicago the incidence of schizophrenia varies in different parts of the city (Phoenix, 1967). They found that areas near the centre of the city had extemely high rates compared with other areas. The highest rates for schizophrenia were in the area they called hobohemia – the area of rooming houses and foreign-born communities close to the city centre. They suggest that these areas are locations of social disorganization and as such constitute environments conducive to the development of schizophrenia. The implication clearly is that this particular form of mental illness is related to the ecological or spatial pattern of the city, which in turn produces different sorts of social organization and environment. The condition of the person is assumed to be a result of the structural organization of urban social and economic life, and in this way, this study presents an example of the use of a structuralist sociological perspective.

In contrast, the 'meaning and action perspectives' provide a rather different view of mental illness. Here, mental illness is not seen as a condition lying within the individual. Instead it is seen as a social status conferred on the person by other members of society. That is to say, instead of assuming that mental illness is something which persons can have 'within them', like a disease or incapacity which anyone can observe and recognize, it is seen as a state which is very much in the eyes of the beholder. A person is seen as mentally ill if other people say he is; the mentally ill person is one to whom that label has successfully been applied. Mental illness is seen as a label, a categorization, conferred on to particular individuals by other individuals.

This way of understanding mental illness is not founded on the assumption that society is an entity with a structure which determines, or at least very strongly influences, individuals and their behaviour. Rather, it derives from a stress on the individual actions and perceptions of persons. Members of society are seen as active agents who construct their social action on the basis of the meanings and interpretations they give to their environment. They do not simply transmit or reflect a given structure, but in fact create it by their interaction. The world has to be interpreted, has to be made sense of and has to be given meaning. 'Mental illness' and 'mental patients' are neither 'objects' nor 'conditions' which are assumed to be 'out there', to be discovered. Rather, the concern is with locating the processes by which people go about classifying others as 'mentally ill'.

Thomas Szasz (1973) has approached the study of mental illness from these basic assumptions and has attempted to show that there are some roles in society which have more power attached to them than most when it comes to the conferring of the label 'mentally ill' on to people. Although we may consider that we can recognize a mentally ill person when we are with one, psychiatrists are generally accepted as being the 'experts' in diagnosing persons in need of treatment. Szasz points out that the psychiatrist has considerable power; on the basis of his observations and analysis of an individual's behaviour, he can declare that the person is sick, that he needs treatment and that he should be put into an institution. The psychiatrist's diagnosis is likely to be accepted and acted upon by other members of society. In this way, the individual concerned becomes 'mentally ill' not simply because he does odd things, but also because the psychiatrist has put that particular label on him. If others try to apply the label, it is less likely to stick.

Some studies, starting out from these assumptions, have shown how psychiatrists and others trained to identify the mentally ill person can disagree over the interpretation and meaning of the behaviours they observe. The possibility of disagreement shows how the differentiation of the 'mentally ill' from the 'normal' member of society can be largely contingent upon the circum-stances of the social situation. An example of this work is the investigation by Thomas Scheff of the psychiatric screening pro-cedures used in a Midwestern state in America to determine whether mental patients should be released. Scheff (1964) has shown how the diagnosis of a person as mentally ill, requiring involuntary confine-ment, can be affected by the financial, ideological and political position of the examining psychiatrists. He shows how these factors tend to predispose the court-appointed psychiatrists to assume that the subject is ill. The situation is defined as one in which the subject is presumed from the outset to be mentally ill and the psychiatrists then go on to interpret the behaviour and records of the patient on the basis of their prior definition of the situation. Scheff argues that without this prior definition, the records, behaviours and responses to the psychiatric tests can be interpreted differently.

Meaning and action perspectives also focus on the individual's conception of himself. That is, they assume that individuals have to interpret and give meaning to their own actions as well as those of others. It assumes that our self-conception influences whatever actions we may construct, and that this self-image is largely a result of the interpretations of other people's reactions to what we say and do. These assumptions have led to investigations into how people labelled as mentally ill see themselves and how, for example, the conferring of the label 'mentally ill' can subsequently produce abnormal behaviour by an individual because he constructs actions which he recognizes others expect of him.

Thus we can see that the kinds of sociological analyses and explanations of mental illness produced by sociologists using meaning and action perspectives differ considerably from those produced by the sociologists using structuralist perspectives. The events and behaviours in the world that both are observing may be 'the same', but because they start from different bedrock assumptions about the nature of the social world and make use of different conceptual frameworks, they produce different sociological analyses.

The questions which shape their research strategies and the actual methods of investigation they use tend to differ because they start from different views of the nature of the social world. Sociologists making structuralist assumptions such as Hollingshead and Redlich, or Dunham and Faris, tend to use questionnaires and survey methods, quantifying their data into statistical tables to produce analyses involving a heavy reliance on mathematics. Interactionists, however, are more likely to use methods of direct observation. They try to see the world from the same points of view as the mental patients, doctors and officials they are studying. Their research approach often involves living with their subjects over a prolonged period of time and sharing their day-to-day experiences. Neither the structuralist nor the meaning and action way of seeing, investigating and explaining mental illness is necessarily more correct than the other. They simply represent different ways of seeing the world sociologically.

Another variant of a meaning and action approach is known as ethnomethodology. Ethnomethodology can be seen as yet another sociological perspective because it asks questions and investigates the social world on the basis of different assumptions and using a different conceptual framework.

The ethnomethodological approach assumes that the social

world is being constantly created by members of society and that, for them, this continuous creation is largely unproblematic. It is unproblematic because it is seen as the result of members using their common sense. Through the use of their taken-for-granted, common-sense knowledge about how the world works and how they can get around it in acceptable ways, the members of a society are seen to be actually creating the society. But although ordinary members of society have no fundamental problems in living and achieving their daily social lives, the ethnomethodologist suggests that this everyday, mundane social activity is the product of complex methodic practices. He assumes that members of society do in fact continuously accomplish the social world through the use of common, albeit sophisticated, methods. Much of the effort to uncover these methods is directed to the analysis of transcriptions of natural conversations, on the argument that members constitute their social encounters in, by and through such talk.

Thus the ethnomethodologist is not likely to investigate mental illness as a specific topic for study, given his concern with the more general and formal analysis of members' methods. Nevertheless, when his materials for analysis have reference to mental illness, the ethnomethodologist's approach can be illuminating. For example, Roy Turner (1968) has suggested that former mental patients can be faced with particular problems when taking up conversations with acquaintances. His focus of study is in the way persons 'resume contact' after having been discharged from the mental institution. Turner suggests that in *any* subsequent encounter between *any* two persons, it may be the case that the parties to the conversation do some work of recognition. He argues that when persons engage in this 'resuming' work they offer identifications of themselves and the persons they are talking to, and in so doing they are suggesting a relationship between them. These identifications can be, and usually are, offered without explicitly announcing that one is a friend, or a long-lost acquaintance. For example, by saying, 'Hi Chuck, how did it go last night? I sure wish I could've made it,' as the opening utterance in an encounter the speaker is, without spelling it out word for word, probably identifying himself and the person he is talking to as 'friends'. Turner adds that part of this resuming work may involve bringing the parties to the conversation up to date, that is, filling each other in on newsworthy items which have happened to them individually since they last met. In the case of an encounter involving a 'former mental patient', however, Turner illustrates how troubles in everyday resuming work can be generated. For example, it may require the 'former mental patient' to accept unwanted identification. After all, it is likely that such an individual wants to forget that he has been mentally ill; he may consider his 'former state' is as irrelevant to his current life as a broken leg. But when resuming involves bringing the parties up to date, it is often difficult to avoid the topic of his recent experiences. Turner appeals to his materials and to our common-sense knowledge of the social world to suggest that the identity 'former mental patient' is one which persons who have not been mentally ill are most likely to use, in preference to any other, when they are doing resuming work with someone they know to have been mentally ill. Thus, the ethnomethodologist, by analysing conversational materials, can show us how interactional troubles can be generated and managed in everyday encounters. In particular, Turner's work illustrates how such analysis can illuminate some interactional problems involving persons who have been 'mentally ill'.

The 'post-structuralists' offer us yet another way of looking at mental illness. We have already mentioned Thomas Szasz. He argued that the institution of psychiatry is an invention of relatively recent origins. Its early growth coincided with an end to the persecution of witches but this was no mere coincidence. The practice of calling people 'insane' has replaced that of calling them 'witches' but plays much the same role, namely, that of stigmatizing and controlling people who are a lot of trouble to others. Further, the idea that insanity is 'mental illness' means that the social control of people who are difficult for others to cope with has been disguised as a form of medical treatment. In thinking in terms of medical treatment we feel that we are trying to help people 'get better' when in reality we are just trying to stop them being nuisances.

Though not drawing his ideas from the same sources, Szasz's arguments here parallel those of 'post-structuralists'. However, whilst Szasz is mainly engaged in criticizing the psychiatric profession, the post-structuralists have no desire to single psychiatrists out as a notable example of the abuse of power. They are interested, rather, in the criticism of modern society and in exposing the extent to which it is pervaded by the exercise of social power. We might think the psychiatric profession is essentially benign but Szasz suggests otherwise: we think we are helping people but really we are repressing them. The post-structuralists think this situation applies generally in the modern world and attempt to show how many of the things we regard as positive, helpful institutions, for instance, really involve the workings of social power. Their purpose in examining mental illness is not to treat it as an isolated case but to use it as an example of the general processes whereby our society is being made ever more repressive, so much so that it can be described as 'carceral' or essentially entrapping.

The fact that we do not feel imprisoned by society, but on the contrary pride ourselves on how much freedom we have, does not count against the post-structuralist case. Rather, it serves to demonstrate how we are trapped within the structure of our ways of thought. From our place within our ways of thought we take the fact that we think the way we do entirely for granted, forgetting that the terms in which we think are not ones we have made up for ourselves. We have inherited them. We acquire them simply through learning the language, unaware that a very great deal of which we are unconscious has been 'built into' the categories we use and, therefore, into the very ways we talk about things. These categories did not make themselves up, but were created in specific times and places, in specific social and institutional circumstances. We will only really understand what is built into the categories if we take an historical view and examine the actual conditions under which they were created.

One of the things we do to some people who are 'mentally ill' is to lock them away in 'asylums'. We did not, however, always lock such people up and so the practice of separating the 'insane' from the rest of us must have an origin. Post-structuralist Michel Foucault suggests that the practice of locking the insane up may owe much to the fact that there were, in late medieval Europe, places available in which such people could be contained. The disappearance of leprosy from Europe meant that the buildings which had been put up to accommodate and segregate lepers were vacated and could be used to contain the insane. Thus a quite specific condition, the availability of places of segregation, gave rise to our modern conviction that it is natural to make actual physical separation between those who are of 'right mind' and those who are 'insane'. The development of our ideas is formed by such specific contexts. The particular interest of the practice of incarcer- ating the insane to Foucault is that this physical separation of the

insane from the rest of us provided the condition for an increasingly
sharp separation in our ideas between 'reason' and 'unreason'. The
idea of 'reason' plays a very important part in our civilization, and
we generally make a distinction between dealing with people by
reason and dealing with them in terms of power. Nowadays we
think that getting people to see what to do through reasoning with
them is preferable to trying to control their actions. Foucault thinks
this opposition is false, that getting people to follow the dictates of
'reason' is one way of controlling them. When people think they
are acting solely on the basis of their own reason they are really
being regulated by social power.

Conclusion

In this introductory chapter, we are stressing that whatever topic or
problem is being investigated, there is no *one* way of approaching
it. In fact there are multiple approaches. As an aid to understanding, we have 'tidied up' some of the main ones, which we term
'sociological perspectives'. Lest, however, we go too far in this
direction, thereby misleading the reader not only about the nature
of sociology, but also about the academic world, we have drawn
attention also to the fact that within each of the major approaches
we find lively argument, disputes and controversies. Alternatively
put, there are competing *versions* about the significance of this
concept, or that method, or this or that reading of a seminal text
(whether by Marx or Durkheim or Weber or Parsons or Lévi-
Strauss or Habermas ...). These competing versions make for
lively and vigorous debate which, over time, results in some of
them becoming outmoded, old-fashioned and even obsolete. Our
discussion charts some of these superseded versions and our readers
are cordially invited to nominate which current ones are likely to
meet a similar fate, which issues will come to look purely historical
and which ones seem likely to run and run and run.

Further reading

The first three titles are current examples of alternative ways of presenting
sociology.

Anderson, R., Hughes, J., and Sharrock, W., *Classic Disputes in Sociology* (Unwin Hyman, 1987).

Giddens, A., *Sociology* (Polity Press, 1989).

Worsley, P., *The New Introducing Sociology* (Penguin, 1987).

Grusky, O., and Pollner, M. (eds), *The Sociology of Mental Illness: Basic Studies* (Holt, Rinehart & Winston, 1981) contains a wide variety of useful readings on mental illness.

Questions

1 What do you understand by a 'way of understanding' or 'perspective'?
2 In what ways can scientific approaches to understanding the world be distinguished from other approaches?
3 Illustrate how the use of different concepts can influence our perceptions and understandings of some object, event, or social interaction.
4 How is it the various social sciences can be so 'different' from each other, yet still be scientific?
5 Compare and contrast any *two* sociological approaches to the study of mental illness.
6 How does the work of (a) an investigative reporter and (b) a novelist differ from that of the sociologist?
7 Try making a list of the key concepts in a sociological article of your choice.

2 Structuralism as a perspective: I, consensus

Introduction

Within sociology it is possible to identify a broad approach founded on the assumption that our actions are to a very large extent structured by our social environment. What values and attitudes we have, what activities and relationships we produce, are seen to be the result of, or at the very least to be greatly influenced by, the organization and structure of the society in which we live. Such an assumption gives rise to a perspective we have called structuralism.

Within this broad approach, however, it is possible to identify two varieties of structuralism, each differentiated by the particular combinations of assumptions and the conceptual frameworks they use in their analyses of the social world. These two varieties are commonly known as the consensus and conflict perspectives. In this chapter we shall consider consensus as a perspective; we deal with conflict in Chapter 3.

The consensus perspective and the problem of order

Most sociology in one respect or another can be seen as a contribution to our understanding of the ordered, patterned and predictable nature of the social world. However, the notions of 'order' and 'predictability' to which sociologists generally refer are not those which would imply that social relationships and events are fixed or inevitably predetermined. Rather the conception of order referred to derives from the observation that by and large both our expectations of our own behaviour and our expectations of the activities of others are generally fulfilled in our experience. That is not to say that we know exactly what others may do in any given situation, but we generally have a good idea of the range of probable actions. We know, for example, that it is very unlikely for a grocer to start cleaning our shoes when we ask him for a tin of sardines. Just think how frightened we would be to leave our beds and our homes if we could not be fairly sure how the various people we meet are likely to behave!

A focus on the ways in which the 'ordered' nature of social life is organized is something all sociological perspectives have in common. Where the perspectives tend to differ is in their conceptualization of the nature of the achievement and management of social order. Each perspective tends to give a different emphasis and attention to those aspects of social life it considers contribute most to social order.

Those sociologists who have developed that approach in sociology we are calling the consensus perspective have explicitly focused on the 'problem of order' at a societal level, that is, they have tended to concentrate on the order of total societies. Their theoretical and empirical analyses have generally been based on the assumption that societies can be seen as persistent, cohesive, stable, generally integrated wholes, differentiated by their cultural and social-structural arrangements. This assumption has generated a conceptual framework and mode of analysis which for the last few decades has been called structural functionalism. However, as we shall see, the development of this conceptual framework and mode of analysis has generated much argument and considerable differences in emphasis. We begin our consideration of the consensus perspective with two early sociologists who had considerable influence on the development of the subject, Auguste Comte and Herbert Spencer.

Early precursors: Comte and Spencer

Auguste Comte (1798–1857) is generally seen to be the founder of sociology as a subject. Although his work is no longer regarded as useful as a whole, several of his leading ideas are important as they continue to colour some sociological thinking. Firstly, societies should be studied using the same methods as in the natural sciences: this approach is known as positivism. Secondly, societies should be studied as wholes, as systems of interrelated parts. Thirdly, as befits a science, the laws governing how society holds together (social statics) and how it changes (social dynamics) should be discovered. He went on, fourthly, to characterize the course of history, seeing society as moving through a number of stages, with each stage being characterized by particular types of society and moving from one dominated by religious ideas to one dominated by science.

Herbert Spencer (1820–1903) had similar concerns. Like Comte, his overall approach has long been outmoded, but some of his ideas persist. Firstly, his work is notorious for making a strong analogy between society and an organism, an animal, for example, arguing that they have much in common: they both grow, evolve, develop different, more specialized functions and adapt to change. Secondly, society, being like an organism, is a system made up of parts. He went on to identify the 'institutions' of society needed to fulfil the vital fuctions or 'needs' necessary to keep the organism 'alive' and 'well'. Finally, like Comte, albeit in different terms, he also classified societies in terms of their level of organization, their complexity, and hence their stage of development.

Today, however, the main claim to fame for both these thinkers is the stimulus their work provided for Emile Durkheim to carve out a general approach which is still an influential part of modern sociology.

Durkheim: basic concepts and theories

The development of functionalism

There is no doubt that Emile Durkheim (1858–1917) made a considerable contribution to the development of sociology in his own time, nor can there be any doubt that his contribution is still an influential force on the theory and practice of sociology today. However, although he claimed to be speaking for all sociology, taking it for granted that there was *one* sociological approach and *one* set of methods for doing research, it is more accurate to see his work as representing a major contribution to the development of the consensus variation of the structuralist perspective. In particular, he developed further the mode of analysis in sociology which today is generally called functionalism; and he outlined in more detail than Comte or Spencer a general research strategy to be used in the investigation of social phenomena.

The moral nature of society

Following Comte, societies were 'systems', as far as Durkheim was concerned, made up of interrelated social elements. But, most importantly for Durkheim, these social systems were *moral* entities. Although it is true that both Comte and Spencer had implicitly noted this characteristic of a society, it was Durkheim who emphasized it. For him it was a fundamental assumption; he believed it to be an irreducible characteristic of a society.

Durkheim argued that all human associations give rise to expectations of patterns of conduct. As persons associate, that is, develop relationships, with others they tend to develop common ways of perceiving, evaluating, feeling and acting. These new patterns of values, perceptions and action then give rise to expectations and constraints on how persons should or ought to behave. Thus as persons associate with each other, so there emerges a 'collective consciousness' which in turn constrains them and obliges them to behave in particular ways.

We know from our own experiences that it is quite common for people to talk of moral pressures coming from society. We speak of activities which society does not allow. We also speak of society having to protect itself against those who break its rules, and of wrongdoers having to pay their debt to society. Contained in these observations and ideas is the notion that society somehow exists over and above us. It was this notion which Durkheim appeared to be drawing on when he suggested that a society was a 'moral reality', a 'moral entity'. In his view, this moral reality included the collective values, the order of priorities on which the members of the society are agreed. He made the assumption that for any group of people to live together co-operatively, they must have some basic common agreements on what their priorities are as a group, and on how they ought to behave to each other and arrange their relationships.

Durkheim argued this case when criticizing the ideas of earlier social and political philosophers and in particular the theories of Thomas Hobbes. Hobbes had suggested that societies were formed by men coming together and agreeing, or making a contract to live side by side in peace, rather than continuing to fight one another.

He argued that men agreed to stop their 'war of all against all' and to organize themselves into a state, with ruling government, in order to ensure their collective self-preservation. According to Hobbes, men agreed to give up their freedom to fight each other, in pursuit of their own individual desires, in return for the security that the new state would provide in its control of, and protection against, the force of particular individuals.

Durkheim's argument was that for men to come together at all to make a contract, they must already have some common agreement on the value of such a contract and some common agreement to be bound by the unwritten rules of a contractual situation. This prior agreement represented for Durkheim a framework of order which is the essence of society. If men could make a contract with each other they were already members of a society because they held certain values in common. Thus a fundamental consensus or agreement on basic values becomes synonymous with an understanding of the concept 'society'.

Durkheim's emphasis on the moral nature of social relationships appears in all his work. For example, in his book *The Division of Labour in Society,* which he subtitled *The Study of the Organisation of Advanced Societies,* he claims that the division of labour itself is a moral phenomenon, rather than an economic one. In the study he focuses on the moral, legal and political problems of societies as they change from simple, traditional, agrarian systems to modern industrial societies. He suggests that each of these two types of society is characterized by different forms of social solidarity and by different social systems of morality.

Earlier Comte had argued that the division of labour would bring increased conflicts, as individuals and groups developed and protected their own interests. Spencer had suggested that the division of labour would bring greater interdependence through increased differentiation and if anything make modern industrial societies less vulnerable to collapse and disintegration than simple societies.

Durkheim takes something from both of them. He agrees that simple or primitive societies have little division of labour. He suggests that they have a segmental structure, that is, they are made up of similar units such as families or tribes. There is only a limited number of roles to be played by each group. Consequently, it is their *common* roles, practices, expectations and beliefs which bind them together. They experience what Durkheim calls a 'mechanical solidarity' because each part of the society is comparable to all the other parts. Each part can be seen in this sense as a microcosm of the wider society. In short, men are bound together by common values, based on shared and common experiences.

As the division of labour increases and new roles are required, there is an increasing differentiation of units or groupings. At the same time the uniformity of beliefs and moral ideas decreases, but the society does not disintegrate; instead a new form of solidarity, a new form of moral order develops to supplement the weakening influence of common values. This Durkheim calls an 'organic solidarity'. It is characterized by the interdependence of different elements, within a general acceptance of the need for differentiation. The differences are accepted and indeed become expected. For example, modern man comes to expect to depend on the unseen coalminer, the power worker, the Christmas card maker and the farmer. Thus the nature of the moral consensus changes. Commonly shared values still persist because without them there would be no society, but they become generalized, as they are not rooted in the totality of commonly shared daily experiences. Instead of specifying the details of action, common values tend to be a more general underpinning for actual social practices. It is in this sense that the division of labour can be seen as a moral phenomenon.

Durkheim argues that the change develops through the stages of an increase in population leading to an increase in the density of social interaction, leading in turn to competition and conflict which threatens the social cohesion. The creation of a division of labour becomes necessary to ensure the continuance of order. The differentiation brings with it an interdependence. In effect he is suggesting that a new form of social solidarity, a new form of morality, becomes necessary to prevent society from collapsing and disintegrating. This amounts to saying that as the nature of the moral consensus changes, so the nature of the society changes.

In this account of the division of labour in society, we can see Durkheim's acceptance of the systematic nature of society. Like Comte and Spencer before him, he is implicitly using an equilibrium model of society. Society is seen as a stable, orderly system which experiences change and which adjusts or adapts to the changed situation in some way to re-create a new order, a new state of equilibrium.

The concept of equilibrium is important in the consensus approach. In general, societies are assumed to be orderly and stable until some event or change occurs. When this happens, it is assumed that societies produce more changes as part of a process of adaptation to the new situation in order to re-establish an equilibrium. The use of this concept does, however, produce a tendency to reify society, that is, to give it the characteristics of a real object, to assume that it has a life or existence of its own. The roots of this assumption lie in assuming that society is like a living organism, and although as we have said, Spencer himself did not believe that society *was* an organism (he merely treated it *as if* it were one), there were others at the time who did.

Durkheim probably saw society as a special kind of organism. It was like no other. He claimed that society existed *sui generis*. That is, society existed in its own right as a separate independent entity. He was more prone to reifying society than either Comte or Spencer and possibly more so than any influential sociologist since. For example, in *Education and Sociology*, in a lecture delivered in 1902, he defines 'true education' as being a certain number of ideas, sentiments and practices that everyone, regardless of social category, has to have. He then goes on to say that 'not only is it society which has raised the human type to the dignity of a model that the educator must attempt to reproduce, but it is society, too, that builds this model, and it builds it according to its needs' (Durkheim, 1956, p. 122).

This view of society resulted in Durkheim making a very clear – too clear, say his critics – distinction between psychology and sociology, the study of the individual and the study of society. It becomes even clearer when we turn to the methods, or 'rules', which Durkheim advocates for making a scientific study of society.

Rules for investigating society

In his *Rules of Sociological Method*, Durkheim primarily described the methods to be used in the study of society, but he also spent some time describing the nature of the phenomena to be studied.

The subject-matter for sociologists, the phenomena they were to study in a scientific way, were 'social facts'. 'Social facts' were different from any other facts; they were the very fabric of society, which arose out of human relationships and human association. For example, he views a rate of suicide for a society as a distinct order of reality. A rate of so many suicides per thousand of population cannot be reduced to individual suicides or cases without losing the essential meaning of a *rate*. A rate per thousand is a collective phenomenon; it is a *social* fact.

Durkheim saw a direct connection between the social nature of a rate and the suicide statistics for different societies. Although the rates may vary from one society to another, some societies having high rates, some having low rates, each individual society seemed to have a similar rate from year to year. This observation suggested to Durkheim that suicide rates emanate from the social conditions of a society. He saw the rate in any one society arising out of the underlying structure of social life of that society; out of the ways people interacted with one another, their attitudes and feelings about things, for example, the nature of their religion. Different social structures generated 'suicidogenic' currents of differing strength and intensity, thus producing different rates of suicide. These rates are the result of collective action, they are the end product, the symptom, so to speak, and as such represent social facts.

Fashions are another example of a social fact. Fashions like long hair, mini-skirts, or platform shoes cannot be reduced to individual cases without losing the essential meaning of fashion. A fashion is a collective phenomenon; it is something which involves the collective action and sentiments of many persons.

Durkheim argued that in their emergent existence, that is, over and above, or external to any individual case, social facts constituted a distinctive and separate reality. It was a *social* reality, the reality of a society. It was the reality that sociologists alone should study.

These 'separately existing' phenomena exercised constraints on individuals. They had a coercive influence over people. For example, we can feel 'out of it', or even guilty or behind the times when we are 'out of fashion'. Similarly, some unfortunate individuals are driven to suicide by the pressures and strains a society generates.

In *Rules of Sociological Method*, Durkheim outlined a set of procedures for doing sociology. No one had provided such a clear set of methodological directives in the same detail before, and they still greatly influence the way many sociologists conduct their research today. His main aim was to make sociological research as objective and scientific as possible. His own work shows, in practice, what difficult aims these are. He said the investigator should eradicate all his preconceptions, that is, he should approach the phenomenon under study with as open a mind as possible; he should try to forget his biases. He should concentrate on the external characteristics of social facts, that is, on those characteristics other investigators will clearly be able to see, like rates of suicide. He should not use his own subjective interpretations. By concentrating on these observable and external characteristics, the researcher will be able to produce clear unambiguous definitions of the social facts he is investigating.

Social facts, according to Durkheim, are of two different kinds, and their differences need to be taken into account in any sociological study. There are 'normal' social facts and 'pathological' social facts. Social facts are normal when they are widespread or general in a society. For example, because crime is found in all societies in one form or another, it is a normal social phenomenon. The way in which he used the concept 'normal' implied that those social phenomena which could be so labelled were necessary for the operation of a 'healthy', well-ordered society. As crime can be found in all societies, it is 'normal', which in turn means that it is an integral part of any healthy society.

However, Durkheim also suggested that though some social facts may be general in a society, they may not really 'fit the conditions for that society'. It is possible, for example, for a social phenomenon to be out of date because it belongs to a past form of society. Therefore he modified the simple condition of generality with the condition that the social fact had to be 'bound up with the general conditions of the collective life' of that particular type of society, at that particular stage in evolution or development of that type of society. By his use of the concepts 'normal' and 'pathological', Durkheim appears to be coming close to making value judgements about what is 'good' or 'bad' for a society. By his qualifying conditions he also appears to be implicity using Spencer's 'organic analogy', suggesting that certain social facts can be healthy or unhealthy for particular societies.

He continues his analysis of social facts by suggesting that some system of classifying societies is required in order to determine whether social facts are normal or pathological. Following Spencer, Durkheim suggested that societies can be categorized according to their degree of composition or organization. At one end of the scale there is the 'simplest' form of society, the horde. Moving along, there is, in increasing complexity, the clan (two hordes), the tribe, the city, and so on. In each classification, further distinctions can be made between societies according to their degree of 'coalescence', that is to say, according to the extent that their component parts fuse together to produce an integrated arrangement of institutions. Ideally, the classification of societies was also required as a precondition for the use of the 'comparative method', which Durkheim saw as the most useful procedure for establishing sociological proofs. He was very concerned that sociological theories should be testable, and as experimenting with total societies was impossible, the comparative method should be used as a method of quasi-experiment, a method of indirect experiment. In making his investigations, the sociologist should compare his findings from one society with those of other societies of the same and of different types. To carry out a further investigation he should examine a social fact in as many different types of society as possible.

Finally, in *Rules*, Durkheim outlines the nature of sociological explanation as he sees it. He suggests that in explaining social facts, investigators should (*a*) find the causes of social facts, and (*b*) find the functions of social facts, that is, the part they play in helping to maintain an orderly society. In the search for causes, the sociologists should look for antecedent social facts, that is, those social facts which precede and seem to produce the particular social facts under investigation. In the search for functions, he should look to 'the "general needs" of the social organism'. We illustrate his approach by looking at two of his major studies, *Suicide* and *The Elementary Forms of the Religious Life*.

Suicide

In choosing to study suicide, Durkheim aims to show how sociologists can handle what pre-eminently appears to be subject matter concerning the individual and, therefore, the province of the psychologist. We have already referred to his way of seeing suicide as a *sociological* phenomenon, a social fact, in that different societies seem to have their own distinctive *rates* of suicide. Here we focus on how Durkheim actually goes about studying them.

Suicide is by far Durkheim's most positivistic study, that is, he goes farthest in it towards applying the methods of the natural sciences, and it has long been regarded as a model of sociological research in this tradition. Thus he begins with a definition of suicide as 'every case of death resulting directly or indirectly from a positive or negative action performed by the victim himself and which he knows will produce this end' (Durkheim, 1970). This 'objective' definition is intended to show clearly the phenomenon to be investigated and can clearly include cases not normally seen by the layman to be suicides, for example, a soldier in battle. He states his problem: how to explain the stability and predictability of suicide rates in any particular society. He goes on to examine non-social causes such as neurosis, heredity and weather conditions and can find no link between them and suicide rates. Then he turns to social explanations and finds that the nature of the social structure *is* linked to suicide rates. Thus he can conclude with law-like generalizations:

(a) Suicide varies inversely with the degree of integration of religious society.
(b) Suicide varies inversely with the degree of integration of domestic society.

These law-like statements seem therefore to be testable hypotheses; other social scientists can take them up and try them out. Given, however, that sociologists cannot and should not do experiments on society, what can they do? In *Suicide*, Durkheim showed the way. He analysed statistics. In so doing, he utilized measurement and quantification in his work, both being attributes strongly associated with 'being scientific'. He also employed the 'comparative method'. This method consists simply of making comparisons, but doing so stringently, endeavouring always to compare like with like and, essentially, trying to eliminate or negate a relationship, rather than looking for favourable evidence to 'prove' it.

Already we have seen how Durkheim looked at non-social factors before turning to possible social causes. In seeking social causes of suicide rates, he is not content simply to show an association between two factors, or 'variables', such as religious affiliation and suicide rate. Protestants may generally have higher rates than Catholics, but this association, or 'correlation', may be distorted by a third variable like 'nationality'. Consequently, Durkheim looks at suicide rates for Catholics and Protestants *within* the same society, for example, in France or in Switzerland. In this way he 'controls' for nationality, he holds it 'constant'. In effect, Durkheim makes 'quasi-experiments' by manipulating his variables through the medium of statistics. For social scientists, with many of the issues they want to study there is no viable alternative.

This approach foreshadows what has now come to be known as 'multivariate analysis'. In *Suicide*, he bombards the phenomenon under study with more and more tests, more and more variables, more and more checks. He pursues it relentlessly. For example, there *is* an association between marital status and suicide rate, but is it reduced or intensified by gender, or by the age of the parties involved? Is the assocation different for widows? Given that he has held constant nationality and religion by focusing on one area of one country, his probings have become very refined, involving and relating to multiple variables.

We cannot here take the analysis further to show how Durkheim comes up with four types of suicide which underpin and explain the reaons for the constancy and predictability of suicide rates within a particular society. Neither can we reproduce more of the many detailed arguments and findings. We should note, however, that, as laid down in the *Rules*, he looks for and claims to find the *causes* of suicide rates in social facts such as the level of cohesion as measured and indicated by statistics like divorce rates, religious affiliation and family size. He has less to say about the *functions* of suicide, suggesting little more than a small amount of suicide is 'normal' to a 'healthy' society, but too much suicide indicates an 'unhealthy' or 'pathological' society.

Religion

If *Suicide* is Durkheim's most positivistic study, then *The Elementary Forms of the Religious Life* must count as the least. Firstly, he argues that a law can be based on one well-made experiment and this claim allows him to use anthropological work from one limited area as a basis for generalizations about religion in general. Secondly, he concerns himself almost exclusively with the functions of religion for society rather than resorting to quantified causal analyses using multivariate analysis. Nevertheless, *Elementary Forms* has stimulated many sociologists to take up the major issues it contains, only some of which we touch on here.

Briefly, he suggested that religious activity is found in society because it has a positive function; it helps to maintain the moral unity of society. He analysed religious activity in a primitive tribe on the assumption that all societies have some basic characteristics in common and that understanding of religion in such a simple society would lead him to an understanding of the essential features of religion in any society.

Drawing upon accounts of Australian Aboriginal tribes he concluded that the function of religious ceremonies was to reinforce the solidarity of the members of a society. The ceremonial activity helped to show them that although they lived separate and scattered lives in their different clans, they were all a part of the same society with the same fundamental moral rules, expectations and obligations constraining them. Within the tribes, the clan is the basic unit of social life and each clan has a 'totem'. The totem, which is usually the name of an animal, such as a lizard, is like a coat of arms, or an emblem, that is, a symbol which is considered sacred and has very special meanings for those who take it as their totem. This totem is a tangible means of expressing men's feelings that the society in which they are members is bigger and better than each individual. It serves to remind individuals of their tasks and connections with the whole tribe and how much they value those links. These feelings are reinforced by the whole tribe periodically assembling for feasting and dancing and religious ceremonies; each individual experiences feelings of joy, high emotions, which he can only obtain in the whole collectivity. The individual feels acted upon by outside and valued forces and he feels solidarity with his fellows. The totemic emblem, then, reminds him of the uplifting force of society.

Obviously the Aborigines do not themselves see the emblem as representing society. They feel they are worshipping it in its own right. It is Durkheim, the sociologist, who recognizes its wider and hidden significance: the function it has for maintaining the moral order of Aboriginal society.

In his analysis and functional explanation, Durkheim compares the totem of a clan with the flag of a nation. National solidarity depends on sentiments of patriotism in the minds of the individual members of the nation. For national solidarity and patrtiotism to be maintained, some collective expression is required from time to time. Rituals pertaining to flags, monarchs, state leaders, and so on, all help to serve this function. These rituals enable the members of the nation to focus their feelings on to the collectivity of which they form a part and thus help to maintain its existence by reinforcing their social solidarity.

In summary, then, the main thrust of Durkheim's major book on religion concerns the functions rather than the causes of religion.

Throughout his work, he tends to distinguish two sides to man's nature, the individual and the social. He is in no doubt that the social side is man's 'better part' and the part that is the proper concern of study for sociologists. This view comes over clearly in *Elementary Forms* where he is constantly stressing the important function of religion in binding individuals into society. By not pursuing in any depth the causes of religion, he avoids the possibility of venturing into the 'individual side' and hence into the field of the psychologist.

Conclusion

Durkheim's thinking is clearly structuralist. The phenomena to be studied are *social facts*, that is, some emergent phenomena which only arise from man associating with man. These phenomena cannot be reduced to psychological or biological factors. Although Durkheim assumed that men may have the same basic human nature and psychological characteristics, he was not interested in studying them. What interested him was the fact that, despite these probable similarities, men developed different social relationships and social arrangements in different societies. To explain any of these social facts, we look for the functions the facts fulfil in the maintenance of the social system in which they are found. In looking at the antecedent social facts, the furthest we can go is to the 'internal constitution of a social group', that is, to the qualities and conditions of social life characteristic of any particular social group. It is the social organization – the nature of social ties and social solidarity of any group – which is the fundamental reality beyond which the sociologist need not investigate. Once he gets into psychological or biological factors, he is no longer doing sociology.

Durkheim's work has provided a rich and varied basis for further development. Unlike Karl Marx, as we shall see in the next chapter, he no longer has disciples and followers who refer to his writings for authentication and authorization. Yet his work cannot be ignored, for he has raised issues and dilemmas which are far from settled and has used methods of research which many sociologists highly value in modernized form. For us, the key issue is the problem of order in society: how can the orderly, patterned nature of society be satisfactorily explained? We have seen the way Durkheim approaches this problem.

We now turn to other thinkers who follow broadly his method of explaining and characterizing social order in terms of a consensus model of society. The chief of these modern sociologists is Talcott Parsons, a major figure in his own right, although Robert Merton, whose work we also discuss, is also of some stature as a 'structural-functionalist'. We also briefly outline some empirical work in this field and conclude with a description of recent attempts to revivify the whole approach.

Parsons: basic concepts and theories

Normative consensus

In *The Structure of Social Action* (1937) Talcott Parsons (1902–79) claimed that he could detect a convergence in the work of four major social theorists: the sociologists Max Weber and Emile Durkheim; the sociologist/economist Vilfredo Pareto and the economist Alfred Marshall. All four, starting from different positions, were coming to the same conclusion: the ends which people in society pursue are not randomly distributed.

In the context of a history of social thought, which for some three hundred years had been dominated by the assumption that ends were randomly distributed, this change was momentous. Hitherto the dominant philosophy about human conduct had been utilitarianism, which saw individuals as pursuing their own satis-factions and being concerned solely to work out the optimal way in which to get them. The consequence of seeing things this way, however, is that social life seems to work out differently than it should. The logic of the utilitarian view is that everybody should be in flat-out struggle over scarce resources. Yet we actually find co-operation and mutual accommodation. Utilitarianism treated people's ends as random. It simply assumed that people wanted whatever they did want, without asking where these wants come from. Consequently, the ends of any one individual would be only randomly related to those of any other. Parsons argued that the four theorists had changed this assumption. They saw that the ends which an individual pursues are *socially* derived; individual wants are not randomly assorted, rather, they are related. Individuals learn to want what they want from the society they live in. Only certain sorts of wants are recognized and approved in any given society. There is, therefore, a large measure of agreement about the things people want in any society. For example, in modern society almost everybody wants to become better off materially, but this want is not widespread in all societies.

Further, Parsons went on, his chosen theorists saw that people did not organize their conduct purely in terms of considerations of maximum efficiency, concerned only with how best to get what they wanted. Their choice of means toward the ends they sought was *morally* regulated. They oriented their action to considerations of right and wrong, what they ought and ought not to do. Often, they eschew the most technically efficient ways of getting something if these are morally disapproved. Agreement on general ends is fundamental to the organization of action and conduct, Parsons concluded. People in a society like ours may want different specific things (some wanting a new car, others a bigger house) but these will tend to be variants on a more general theme (in this case material betterment). The agreement has, moreover, a normative character: agreement is on what sorts of things it is morally acceptable to want, and there is agreement too on the procedures by which people can go about getting the things they want. This emphasis upon socially shared agreement is the hallmark of the 'consensus' approach and shows why Parsons is regarded as a key figure in its development.

The general theory of action

On the basis of the arguments in *The Structure of Social Action* Parsons launched a most ambitious scheme, namely, to provide a 'general theory of action'. This would provide a general framework of analysis which would include all the main social science disciplines, such as psychology, economics and government, with sociology being only one element in the scheme.

Actual organized patterns of social life involve the interrelation of three main dimensions: culture, personality and social system. Social life involves shared ideas and the means of expressing them. These are 'cultural' things, involving those shared ideas we have mentioned above to do with what kinds of ends are desirable and what kinds of means are allowable. These ends are called 'values' and the rules governing how to achieve them are called 'norms'. Equally important to social life are means of communication, that is, the language and other symbolic systems. These too are cultural.

Social life is carried on by individuals with 'personalities', that is, dispositions and inclinations, thoughts and feelings. This personality element motivates the actions of individuals. Above all else, social life involves the relationships between individuals. These social relationships contribute the 'social system' element.

In any actual society, then, there will be 'interpenetration' of three elements: culture, personality and social system. Care must be taken not to separate these three elements for more than analytical purpose for they interpenetrate in practice, as we have already indicated. For example, social systems and personalities are shaped by culture, whilst culture (shared ideas) has to be rooted in individuals (personalities) and social relationships (social systems). Parsonian analysis, therefore, is concerned with how these three elements interrelate, or to put it more formally, how they 'integrate' into the working pattern found in any social setting. Within the general project of the analysis of action, sociology specializes in the analysis of the organization of the social system.

Analysing the social system

Social life is made up of units. Not only the whole society, but also parts of it, such as the school, the business and the family, can all be considered as social systems. By 'social system' we mean something surrounded by a boundary, enabling us to distinguish an inside from the outside or environment. By considering social units as social systems we can ask what the conditions are which keep the unit together in the face of its environment and what the conditions are for its continuing survival? By asking such questions Parsons earned his title as a 'functionalist'. More precisely, he asks about the ways in which the features of society contribute to sustaining its organization, that is, how the parts of the system serve the requirements of the whole.

There are two conditions any system must meet in order to survive: it must relate effectively to its environment; it must maintain its own internal integrity. Parsons further breaks down these two vital conditions into four 'functional imperatives', which any system must satisfy. These are:

(1) *Adaptation.* Any society (or other smaller unit) must be able to mobilize resources to get things done. It must extract the necessary facilities for collective action from its environment.

At the level of the society, for example, there is the need to extract resources such as food, shelter, etc, from the physical environment.

(2) *Goal attainment.* Social units have things to do, goals to realize. For example, a school has to produce educated and trained people, and must organize itself to get this done in relation to the environment. The system or unit must, therefore organize to ensure people achieve the goals set for it.

Adaptation and goal attainment therefore refer to the first condition for survival, the need for social units to relate to the environment from which they draw facilities and into which they inject 'outputs' of their achievements. For example, the schools produce the educated and trained people needed by the rest of the society – here society is 'the environment' of schools. The next two imperatives have to do with the second condition, namely, the system's internal regulation.

(3) *Pattern maintenance and tension management.* Any social unit will only get things done, fulfil its goals, if its members are loyal to those purposes and motivated enough to put in the effort, thereby providing 'pattern maintenance'. Even if people are loyal and motivated, they will become stressed and unable to cope if they are kept unrelentingly at full stretch. There must, therefore, be ways (rest and recuperation) of preventing the build-up of tension, or of releasing it when it does build up.

(4) *Integration.* Social units involve relations among individuals and among sub-units (for example, departments in an organization). In relations there are possibilities of strain and conflict, so there must be ways of regulating relations amongst parts and preventing difficulties getting out of hand. Diagrammatically, Parson's scheme is set out in Table 2.1.

Parson's scheme is designed for the analysis of social systems generally, from large, encompassing societies to small face-to-face social groups. Any distinct social unit *must* have features of its organization which satisfy the above requirements – otherwise it would not exist as a distinct unit. Analysing at the level of the society – here modern industrial society – we can see that the four functional requirements are handled in specialized ways. Alternatively put, the organizational forms for meeting these are 'differentiated out'. For example, the primary function of the economy is to produce and distribute the material resources that people need to

Table 2.1 Society as a Social System

	INSTRUMENTAL FUNCTIONAL IMPERATIVES		
ADAPTATION	GOAL ATTAINMENT	PATTERN MAINTENANCE/ TENSION MANAGEMENT	INTEGRATION
ECONOMY	POLITY	KINSHIP	CULTURAL AND COMMUNITY ORGANIZATIONS
Major sub-system made up of INSTITUTIONS (e.g. factory system, banking system)	Major sub-system made up of INSTITUTIONS (e.g. political parties, state bureaucracies)	Major sub-system made up of INSTITUTIONS (e.g. nuclear family, marriage)	Major sub-system made up of INSTITUTIONS (e.g. schools, churches, media organizations)
Each institution is made up of SETS OF ROLES Specific norms giving concrete behavioural prescriptions define roles. These concrete norms are underpinned by	Each institution is made up of SETS OF ROLES Specific norms . . .	Each institution is made up of SETS OF ROLES Specific norms . . .	Each institution is made up of SETS OF ROLES Specific norms . . .
. . . underpinned by	. . . underpinned by	. . . underpinned by	. . . underpinned by
	FUNDAMENTAL VALUES		

live their lives and carry out their social responsibilities, and this is mainly done by organizations whose sole business is to manufacture goods.

The primary work of the 'polity' (i.e. institutions of government) is organizing the achievement of collective goals. The problems of pattern maintenance and tension management are mostly handled by the family. Within it, children are brought up in the culture and ways of the society (thereby providing pattern maintenance); and the relations of affection, companionship, joint participation in leisure, etc. amongst the members provide comfort, consolation and relief (thereby dealing with tension management).

Community and cultural institutions, such as organized religion, education and mass communication, serve the function of integration. For example, they serve it by getting different parts of the society to recognize and reaffirm their solidarity by disseminating shared culture and reinforcing that culture through ritual celebration of its values. In the event of their failure with some individuals or parts, there are mechanisms of 'social control' which operate to handle behaviour which departs from these agreed ends and standards, thereby disrupting social relations. The police and courts play prominent roles here.

In many societies, however, we will not find specialized social agencies like courts, businesses, parliaments, and so on. In societies of the sort anthropologists have traditionally studied, kinship groups are the main organizational feature of the society and everything is done through kinship – economic activity, political business, the socialization and education of the young, religious rituals, control and punishment of offenders. The four functional requirements *must* be satisfied in such a society, but they are not met by specialized means.

Parsons was often chided for ignoring social change, but he tried to answer this criticism in his later work, using ideas close to those of Durkheim. Thus he treated much change as a process through which an intially undifferentiated handling of everything through kinship is changed through the progressive emergence of specialized social organizations which take over functions previously handled by kinship. Consequently, he rebuts the view that the isolated nuclear family of modern Western societies has lost all functions. It is simply not true; the family has become purely specialized in certain vital functions, child rearing and providing

personal and emotional support, and has relinquished other functions to other agencies, such as the schools and the church.

Equilibrium and social integration

The idea of 'equilibrium' belongs with that of system. For some
systems, we can – theoretically, at least – conceive of conditions
under which a given system will be in 'equilibrium', meaning it
will show no disposition of any kind to change. We stress, though,
that this conception is a theoretical possibility only, for actual
societies will not meet such conditions.

Parsons tried to construct a simple model of the way equilibrium
could develop in social relations through the idea of 'shared
expectations'. We have described the importance of values and
norms to social organization, but have not said how they ensure
that social organization 'works'. Parsons argues that the rules of the
society, its norms of proper conduct, become the expectations of its
individual members. People's interrelationships work because the
parties to them know what to expect of one another. They see one
another as occupants of some status, that is, position, in the society,
for example, as 'teacher', 'parent', 'friend'. The concept 'role' refers
to what people in a status are supposed to do. For example, teachers
should work in classrooms, should give lessons, while 'pupils'
should, correspondingly, listen to what the teacher says and answer
his questions. If teachers and pupils in a classroom have appropriate, that is, matching, expectations as to how they should
respectively behave, then their relationships should run smoothly.

People learn expectations from one another, especially during
childhood, and the process of learning how to behave is called
'socialization'. In this way, people come to be attached to the social
rules, to feel that they and others *ought* to behave in ways
standardly expected. They come to feel that occupying a certain
status entitles them to be treated the way occupants of that position
generally are. If they are not so treated they are likely to be upset
and, moreover, to show that they are upset. If they are treated as
they expect and feel entitled to be, then they will be gratified and
will show it. Parsons makes a simple assumption: people are
sensitive to one another's approval and disapproval. They find the
approval rewarding, disapproval punishing and will seek the one
and strive to avoid the other. Thus, if person A treats person B in a
way that does not fit with B's expectations, then B will respond

negatively; A, the offender, will be hurt by the negative response and in future will not depart from the standard expectations. People 'sanction' one another's conduct with positive or negative responses, and such sanctions inhibit any tendencies to depart from expectations. If two people share expectations and conform to them in their conduct the pattern of their relationships will be stable. Any departures from the pattern will be met by negative sanctions, whilst conformity to it will be rewarded with positive sanctions. On the scale of society, therefore, we can see that the punishments meted out to offenders are, for Parsons, symbolic, expressing the society's disapproval of those who depart from its rules, just as prizes and honours symbolize its approval of those who have fulfilled the rules' requirements.

Of course, we can only theoretically conceive a society in stable equilibrium where expectations are thoroughly disseminated and exactly shared, and where everyone is consistently and wholly obedient to them. Real societies depart from this model. At the very least, there will be people who are 'inadequately socialized', who, for some reason, do not learn or do not become attached to the main norms and values. Further, there will be gaps and discrepancies between different parts of the society, resulting in people having expectations which are conflicting and cannot all be satisfied. Hence deviants are produced, that is, people who in one way or another depart from shared expectations. Correspondingly, mechanisms of social control are required to contain and counteract tendencies towards deviance.

In fact Parsons does not think stable equilibrium is the most appropriate concept for understanding society. 'Moving equilibrium' is more apt. The human organism changes all the time in developing from baby into an adult, but throughout the changes it retains its unity and identity, and it is the same with societies too. Societies change, but they develop without disintegrating. We see that though our society has changed much since 1760 it is still, in crucial ways, the same society. There have of course been disruptions and disturbances along the way, but these have not come close to destroying the society as a whole, as they have done in some other cases. Thus, the equilibrium of a social system, when its parts fit together as near perfectly as possible, is 'moving' not 'stable'.

A Parsonian approach to examining features of social organization, then, leads us to look at the ways in which parts of the relevant social system fit together to see if they are compatible with each other. Are there incompatibilities? If so, what are the consequences? Can any tensions and conflicts that incompatibilities create be contained or do they destabilize the whole unit?

Parsons argues that, within limits, there have to be compatibilities between, for example, the family and economic structures of a society. The traditional family of China placed value upon family relationships above all else, and even crimes of violence could be condoned if they were committed in order to avenge wrongs done to one's family. Such strong family tradition would not be compatible with the highly mobile, individualized, competitive economy found in the modern United States. Here family life and loyalty are considered important, but they can be outranked by the demands of economic efficiency. For example, businessmen will often put the needs of their work above time with their family. If the small, geographically mobile, nuclear family is better suited to the needs of an industrial society than the type found in traditional China, which is an extended, geographically immobile kinship network, it still does not follow that the requirements of the family and the economy in modern society are in complete correspondence. There are tensions between them. The family is an organization based upon sentiment and solidarity, in which people value one another because of who they are, not because of what they do. The economy, however, has no room for sentiment and people are judged primarily in terms of what they can do, how competent they are at their work. There has to be a means for people brought up in the protective world of the family to make a transition to the competitive world of work, given these are very different environments – even potentially conflicting ones. Parsons suggests that the school system acts as such a means in providing a mechanism which can minimize this potential conflict.

In school, the child learns that favouritism is not appreciated and that people are rewarded mainly for what they can do and for what they can achieve. The young pupils also come to notice that as they progress through the education system from infant to primary, from secondary schools to further education, they come across more and more specialization. In the infant school, they may have only one teacher, who is like a mother to them in many respects; in the secondary school and thereafter they are not only taught by specialists, but they are even likely to go to counsellors for specialized advice on their emotional problems.

In this way, the educational system can be seen as acting as a bridge between the potentially conflicting relationships and expectations encountered in the family and economic systems. As a bridge, it can be seen as helping to maintain the equilibrium of society by giving members of society an opportunity to learn how to adjust to and cope with conflicting expectations in societally approved ways.

Pattern variables and types of society

The importance Parsons places on norms and values is brought out by his concept of 'pattern variables'. This concept provides the basis for a classificatory schema for categorizing the norms and values of any society. Furthermore, Parsons claims that this schema for pattern variables can serve to display a society's measure of equilibrium and integration. He suggests that any value, role, norm, institution, sub-system of society, or even the whole society can be classified via this schema; and that the fundamental importance of values is shown in the way they set the limits to the range of norms and other features of social systems. In particular, the sociologist can derive a measure of 'fit' between norms and values in any society by using this classificatory schema for pattern variables. The schema is shown in Table 2.2.

Parsons suggests that the fundamental value system of a modern, industrial, bureaucratized society can be characterized by the pattern variables in B, and the fundamental value system of, say, a small tribal society may be characterized by the pattern variables in A. At a very general level of comparison, we see a link between Parson's two sets of pattern variables and Durkheim's mechanical and organic forms of solidarity. Parsons suggests his schema goes further; it identifies the potential conflicts of values and norms, which society must overcome in order to maintain its equilibrium, that is, to achieve its integration and stability. For example, in our society the family can largely be characterized by pattern variables A, while institutions found in the economic and political sub-systems can be broadly characterized by pattern variables B. But as there is an interchange of personnel between these system parts, a potential conflict arises. It has to be coped with by society through some integrating mechanisms for managing such tensions, in order to ensure the required degree of equilibrium for the maintenance of order.

Table 2.2 Parson's Concept of Pattern Variables

Pattern variables A	Pattern variables B
Characteristic of 'expressive' values and norms, i.e. an emphasis on emotional satisfaction.	Characteristic of 'instrumental' values and norms, i.e. an emphasis on achieving goals, and accomplishing tasks.
Ascription Emphasizing the qualities or attributes of actors, i.e. who they *are*.	**Achievement** Emphasizing the performance of actors, i.e. what they *do*.
Diffuseness Emphasizing broad relationships dealing with a range of purposes and interests, e.g. the relationship between a mother and a child.	**Specificity** Emphasizing limited relationships for specific purposes, e.g. the relationship between a doctor and a patient.
Particularism Emphasizing the organization of particular relationships with particular actors, e.g. 'being loyal to one's mother'.	**Universalism** Emphasizing the organization of interaction according to general principles, e.g. treating every one equally before the law.
Affectivity Emphasizing the gratification of emotions.	**Affective neutrality** Emphasizing the deferment of gratification, i.e. disciplining oneself.
Collective orientation Emphasizing collectivism, i.e. pursuing shared interests.	**Self-orientation** Emphasizing individualism, i.e. pursuing private interests.

One such mechanism is that of role specialization. As we have already seen, the family tends to develop into an 'isolated' nuclear structure in which most members are insulated from participation in extrafamilial institutions. Typically the adult male plays what Parsons calls the 'boundary-role' as he moves back and forth between family and non-family institutions. He also tends to concentrate on instrumental, task-oriented functions. The adult female tends to stay at home and specialize in expressive functions.

Similarly, the school can serve an integrating function by gradually socializing the child (who in his family situation has been experiencing the values and norms classified under pattern variables A) into roles and thereby norms and values which can be classified under pattern variables B. The school as an institution meets some of the problems of integration for the social system and thus helps to maintain an adequate equilibrium. The concept of pattern variables helps us to analyse and understand the nature of the possible relationships between various institutions and highlights the interdependence operating between the various elements of a social system.

Conclusion

Parsons has been much criticized not only for his sociology, but also for being hard to read. We hope, though, that we have shown that some of his basic ideas are essentially simple and can be stated clearly. Naturally, he has been criticized by those who reject functionalism as a mode of analysis, and we shall consider their views shortly. Finally, he has even been criticized by fellow functionalists.

A main critic was Robert Merton. Parsons and Merton were the two dominant influences in American sociology of the 1950s. Merton regarded Parsons's theory as too ambitious, as attempting to be much more comprehensive than is possible in the state of contemporary sociology. He called for more modest and pragmatic theorizing, making limited claims and producing 'middle range' theories. Merton argued that such theories can be systematically linked to the findings of specific studies unlike Parson's great generalities. Like Parsons, Merton was convinced of the utility of functional analysis, but took a very different view of its present state and immediate prospects.

Merton: functional analysis

Merton feels that functional analysis is a promising approach which has not been worked out as well as it might have been. Merton proposes to think through and systematize the useful ideas in functionalism. For example, he distinguishes between 'manifest' and 'latent' functions of institutions. Manifest functions are purposes which are served by features of society where it is apparent to the members of society what those purposes are. For example, the function of bookshops to sell books. There are, however, features of social organization which are neither intended nor understood by the society's members. The things people do may have consequences they do not intend, and some of these consequences may meet the needs of social organization without the members of society being aware that they do. These are 'latent' functions. Merton gives the example of the rain dance of the Hopi Indian tribe. The dancers have a purpose, the bringing of rain, which is the manifest function, but the sociological observer, who may well doubt that dancing *can* bring rain, can argue that involvement in this dance creates feelings of mutual solidarity amongst the Hopi. As reinforcing the solidarity of the tribe is not the intended or acknowledged purpose of the dance, such a positive consequence for Hopi society must be counted a latent function. A major task for the sociologist is to try to identify these latent functions and a legitimate concern is to trace the consequences that functions have for the adaptation or adjustment of the system in which they are implicated.

There are, however, dangers: functionalism must avoid some quite contestable assumptions. Merton cites:

The functional unity of society

This assumes that any particular element of society, if it is functional, must be functional for the maintenance of the *whole* society. Such an assumption, once current amongst anthropologists, may have been valid for small-scale societies, but is not for complex and highly differentiated communities. Though not functional for the whole society, some practice or arrangement may none the less be functional for a part of it. For example, it would be wrong to say that religious ceremonial promoted solidarity throughout the society of Northern Ireland, but it would be true to say that it contributes to the solidarity of subgroups within it.

Universal functionalism

Functionalism amongst anthropologists originated in part in the attempt to deal with supposed 'survivals'. In alien societies, observers found activities which appeared to have no practical value. There was a tendency to explain them as survivals from an earlier time when they must have had a use that is now obsolete. Clearly this view did nothing to explain the survival of the practice. If it had no use, why did people continue with it? Its continuance required some explanation: it might be useful, it might have, to use

Merton's term, a latent function. The danger with this line of argument is in carrying it to extremes, insisting that everything must have some latent function. This will result in strained interpretations. For example, Merton cites Clyde Kluckholn's argument that the buttons on a man's coat sleeve are not useless, but function to preserve the familiar feeling of tradition.

Merton suggested that not everything need have a function. Indeed, some things may have, so to speak, a negative function and be 'dysfunctional'. They can have disrupting, damaging consequences for the system. Functional analysis, done properly, must keep a balance sheet on a practice. We should record both positive and negative aspects, total them and then make an overall assessment of the functional character of a practice.

Functional indispensibility

Because certain things, 'functional imperatives', have to be met by society it does not follow that there is only one way of getting them done. It is too easy to suppose that if we have a condition or prerequisite of social survival, such as the production of food, and if a form of organization meets that prerequisite, then that form is indispensible. There are many different types of social arrangement which can meet a given end. For example, hunting, slaving, barter, money and industrial economies all meet the need of economic production and distribution. Merton urges us to consider the possibility of functional alternatives, substitute ways of fulfilling an identified function. To assume that an established practice is necessarily the best way of meeting a social prerequisite simply earns the functionalist approach its reputation for being conservative, for justifying the way things are and failing to consider that they may be otherwise.

Applications of functional analysis

Merton on political corruption

The 'political machine' in some American cities is notorious for its corrupt character. It provides a test case for functional analysis, being something which is widely regarded as unnecessary and even socially harmful. Such analysis, however, reveals that it makes a positive contribution to social organization. Merton argues that the political 'boss', by exchanging favours for votes, runs a system that has positive functions for the community. He argues that the political machine achieves the following:

(1) For the socially deprived, it satisfies wants which are not adequately met by the 'legimate' social structure.
(2) For business, especially big business, the political boss provides political privileges which bring immediate economic gain. Business firms seek political deals which enable them to stabilize their situation and to meet their objective in maximizing profits.
(3) The political machine provides jobs and career prospects for people who were socialized into poor and disadvantaged backgrounds. Those who work for the machine can have a chance to realize the 'American dream' of getting ahead.
(4) The machine supports illegitimate businesses, for example, drug-trafficking, prostitution, illegal gambling. These enterprises provide services similar to those of legitimate businesses in that both types of business supply goods and services in response to a demand.

Thus the machine cannot be eliminated until a suitable functional alternative is devised which fulfils these functions.

Functionalism has been regularly criticized for being unable to explain social conflict and tension and particularly for being unable to show how disruptive tendencies can be systematically built into a society. To answer this criticism, Merton provided his 'anomie' account of deviance. It is not a general account of deviance, but an attempt to explain its presence and character in American society and to do so by treating much deviance as a product of a discrepancy between the structural and cultural elements of that society.

Most people, including readers of this chapter, would probably agree that American society is thoroughly materialistic. If they do, then they have accepted the premiss of Merton's argument, which is that in American society there is extensive agreement on a central end of monetary success. The oft-cited 'American Dream' is that anyone can get to be rich. Furthermore, there is wide-reaching consensus on the norms regulating pursuit of this end: financial success should be the product of honest hard work. The value of pecuniary success and the norm of honest work provide the cultural element. The 'social structural' element has to do with the organization of social relations: American society is a stratified society. This structural fact is in tension with the cultural elements, for though everyone may be motivated to get rich, and are enjoined to do so through diligence in work, realistically, those lower down the social scale will not be able to succeed or even hope to succeed. In the face of this gap between wanting to get rich and having unrealistic prospects, people will be forced to adapt and, depending on their circumstances, will respond in different ways. For example, some will stick with the goal but will resort to illegitimate means, such as gangsterism, a response Merton terms 'innovation'. Others will give up the ambition for success but go through the motions of pursuing it. This response Merton labels 'ritualism' and also counts it as a deviant response. In this way Merton provides a demonstration that functionalist analysis can treat deviance as a 'built-in' product of the system's organization.

Kai Erikson: deviance and system maintenance

Merton makes two attempts at showing how deviance can be analysed with functional tools. Political corruption is shown to be functional, and other forms of deviance are examined as products of a system which has a less than fully integrated organization. Another attempt to show deviance as positively functional is Kai Erikson's (1966) account of 'crime waves' in New England society. He considers different instances of panic about deviance, the one cited here being the witchcraft hysteria in Salem Village in 1692.

In this episode young girls behaved in strange ways that were regarded as showing them possessed by the devil. They were invited to identify those who had bewitched them. At first, they only picked out three people, but then went on to accuse many more. Several people were brought before the courts and put to death. Eventually, however, the hysteria died down as the girls lost their credibility by virtually accusing people at random, including those who were so well respected as to be beyond suspicion.

Erikson treats the periodic obsessions of these communities with crimes in a classically Durkheimian fashion, claiming it has to do with the marking of social boundaries. A society, if it is to be a unit, must have an inside and an outside. The boundary between the social inside and outside is a moral one, with those who regard one another as upright citizens on one side, and those they reject as criminals and outcasts on the other. When these boundaries are under threat, concern about crime intensifies. Erikson argues that in the relatively newly established Puritan communities of the New World the settlers felt alone in the world, bewildered by the loss of their old destiny and not yet able to develop a strong sense of their new one. By focusing attention on certain kinds of offences, the communities were defining their own particular standards, making plain for all to see the limits of what was acceptable and valued in their way of life. Hence those accused of witchcraft were, as we have suggested, those who were not 'above suspicion' of consorting with the devil, that is, they were persons who had in some way or other alienated and offended their fellows and could thus be seen as capable of witchcraft.

Davis and Moore: a functionalist theory of stratification

A functionalist theory of stratification has been proposed by Kingsley Davis and Wilbert Moore and by Parsons. Like so many forms of analysis arising from the use of the consensus perspective; the approach derives from the work of Durkheim.

Like crime, social stratification is recognized as a common feature of all societies. It is therefore seen as a 'normal' characteristic of society and is assumed to be serving some positive function or need for society.

However, Davis and Moore (1967) make the further assumption that some of the tasks required by a society are more important than others. In particular, the tasks of administration and of governing the society are assumed to be very important. They also assume, along with Parsons, that it is necessary for a society to provide structural arrangement to motivate its individual members to fill certain positions in society *and* to motivate them to perform the duties attached to those positions. If all the positions and tasks were equally easy to fill and perform, and were all equally important to the survival of society, and if all the members of a society were equal in their abilities and talents in relation to the required tasks, there would be no problem. But such is not the case. Talents *are* differently distributed. Therefore a society *must* have some kinds of inducements or rewards available in order to encourage those with the most suitable abilities to fill the most important positions.

These inducements usually take the form of high rewards, both of goods and prestige, for the important jobs in society. They can also carry with them a not inconsiderable amount of power. The consequence is that the wealth, prestige and power society has provided for these positions make those who hold them into a privileged class.

In this way, Davis and Moore explain why social stratification must exist in all societies and, in particular, in any modern complex society. The division of labour inevitably produces inequality of reward because without these inequalities of reward, the continuity of the division could not otherwise be guaranteed. Social inequality is generated by, and is functional for, society. Not only does every society 'need' it, but social inequality can also be seen to be empirically present in all known societies. Social inequality is, therefore, both universal and necessary in society.

Smelser: a consensus approach to social change

Functionalists are regularly accused of being incapable of analysing social change. Neil Smelser (1959) tried to respond to this challenge by studying a key development in the formation of modern society which was at the core of the industrial revolution of the late eighteenth and early nineteenth century, namely, the growth of the Lancashire cotton industry during the period 1770–1840.

He suggests that this period can be seen as a series of adjustments occurring in society, in contrast to the period before 1770, which was relatively stable and represented a period of equilibrium. He claims that a new sort of equilibrium was achieved in the years after 1840. He suggests that certain initial conditions led to the industrial structure being unable to meet productive requirements and it was through a process of structural differentiation, which he describes in terms of a general sequence of identifiable stages, that a new and 'better suited' structure emerged. He follows this up by suggesting that the same general process and sequential stages of adaptive structural differentiation can be seen to have taken place in the family as it became unable to perform its functions adequately as a result of the changes in the economy. He follows this further by analysing and describing the growth of processes of structural differentiation within a variety of institutions such as trade unions, savings banks, friendly societies, and so on. These are seen as providing in part the necessary specialist agencies to mediate between the family and the economy, since family life had become segregated from work.

His analysis claims that throughout this period the various parts of British society were constantly adjusting to one another, thus demonstrating their interdependence and their collective tendency to produce an equilibrium.

In the elaboration of his model of structural differentiation, Smelser suggests that the value system is the primary source for evaluating possible structural change in society. The value system supplies the standards for legitimizing and approving new arrangements and expectations. The value system thus limits the directions and degrees of change. He admits that values can change, but they generally change much more slowly than social structure. Thus to a large extent, the fundamental value system remains constant during a single sequence of differentiation and so, for that particular period, the criteria for assessing the performance of any unit of the structure do not vary.

From functionalism to neo-functionalism

Functionalism has not wanted for critics, as the defensive responses of Merton and Smelser show. It has been criticized for being virtually an ideology justifying society being the way it is because everything is for the best in the best of all possible worlds. It allegedly treats society as though it were a perfectly integrated, harmonious whole, devoid of all conflict. Such criticisms were not really accurate, for as we have indicated, Parsons appreciated that the fully integrated society was a theoretical limit, not a real possibility and sought to provide for possibilities of social strain, conflict and change. The way in which he dealt with them, and the attempts of others, like Merton and Smelser, still failed to satisfy many critics. These critics were influenced mainly by Marxist or Weberian conceptions, which treat conflict and power struggles as more essential to social organization than agreement (they are discussed in Chapter 3). Since they did not give much significance to social classes and to class conflict, functionalist doctrines were necessarily condemned by Marxist critics for overestimating agreement in society and failing to appreciate the extent to which classes differ in culture and values. Moreover, functionalist views give too much emphasis to cultural matters, to agreement and difference in ideas, and do not recognize the extent to which social relations are rooted in economic and political considerations. Consequently, social relations are permeated with differences of interest. The primary protagonists of economic interests are social classes.

As a result of criticism, functionalism fell into disrepute, but there have been recent attempts to rehabilitate it. This 'neo-functionalism' accepts, as we shall see, many of the criticisms but provides, none the less, an attempt to rehabilitate Talcott Parsons's general approach.

Alexander: the principles of neo-functionalism

Jeffrey Alexander (1985) emphasizes the heuristic, or exploratory, nature of the strategy, and a willingness to accommodate to other orientations in sociology, especially those, like 'conflict theory', which in the past saw themselves as totally opposed to functionalism.

He concedes that his own examination of Parsons's work does not entirely exempt the latter from charges of conservatism, idealism or an excessively theorectical approach, though the extent to which Parsons is prone to these faults has been exaggerated. Alexander singles out some of the positive prominent ·features of contemporary neo-functionalist work:

(1) Functionalism provides a descriptive potrayal of society as a relatively self-contained system which is organized through the interaction of its parts, but without any suggestion that there is any overriding principle or force directing the system as a whole.

(2) The ideas of system equilibrium and system integration are used as analytical tools to describe features of society, though without assuming that participants' actions are directed to achieving either of these conditions. Alexander says that integration is a possibility and that deviance and social control are facts, thereby making quite clear that there is no naive assumption that actual societies are fully integrated.

(3) An assumption of the interpenetration of culture, personality and social system is an elemental feature of the mode of analysis, and some measure of integration of these is a necessary feature of reality. As well as a concern with the interaction of

institutions in providing for the integration of the social system, functionalism must also analyse the organization of the culture and the processes of socialization. Naive assumptions about the extent of integration *within* culture, personality and social system, as well as between them, must be avoided. Integration is not automatic or unproblematic: within and between the elements there are tensions which create strain and provoke change.

(4) Change is not only a product of strain and tension. Indeed, change can often produce strains and tension. There is a long-term evolution of Western societies through the progressive differentiation out of previously undifferentiated features in the cultural, social personality systems. These changes have moved the society as a whole from one *relatively* integrated level to another, and have become reintegrated at a higher level of adaptability.

Smelser: reconsiderations on social change

Neil Smelser's analysis of social change in the Lancashire cotton industry has been cited as a reminder that there was nothing to prohibit Parsonian functionalism from dealing with either change or conflict. Since it was first published, reflection and further study have brought Smelser to accept objections to the effect that his analysis *did* underplay the extent of conflict and did not necessarily understand its true character.

Briefly, Smelser had analysed the social conflicts in the process of industrialization in the Lancashire cotton industry in terms of the above-mentioned model of social change, emphasizing in this case the way in which the differentiation out from the family of work and education as specialized activities were sources of tension and conflict because they threatened the authority of the father within the family. His re-examination concerns his account of the development of education.

Whilst basically retaining the Durkheimian view of socialization and education as the means of transmitting culture to new generations, Smelser acknowledges it is likely to be an idealization of any society. It is almost certainly an over-idealization in times of change to suppose that there is a single, agreed and integrated set of cultural ideals which are relayed through education. Ideals will compete with one another and he continues

insofar as society has developed specialized institutional structures – economic, legal, political, etc. – those structures will, to
varying extents, have been the structural basis for participating
groups (classes, estates, ethnic groups, etc.) that are politically
significant in the competition over the values, symbols, and
ideologies that are consistent with and legitimize their own
claims over resources. Because socialisation in general and
education in particular specialize in the generation and reproduction of these kinds of cultural items, it follows that the content,
style and mode of transmitting them will be items on the social
agenda that generate group conflict. Furthermore, because the
educational process... is involved in the transmission of systems
of morality from generation to generation, it also follows that
conflicts over educational issues are likely to take the form of
conflicts over principles, or even conflicts over the definition of
the sacred. (Smelser, in Alexander (ed.) 1985, pp. 116–17)

Smelser stresses the extent to which education can mean different
things to different groups and interests, so that people will want to
control it on their own behalf. He also emphasizes the extent to
which groups and interests compete over that valued resource, the
young, so that, for example, business, the military and religions all
try to get a grip on education.

In general, Smelser had been thinking of society working as a
single, co-ordinated unit which encountered and attempted to solve
problems. This view led him to think of change as involving the
movement from the development of a problem to the reaching of a
solution, involving an intervening period in which matters were
disorganized because the problem had not been resolved. His
conception of change as differentiation meant that a situation in
which things were not working satisfactorily gave rise to pressures
for change. These pressures furthered specialization in social functions, and resulted in a process of disturbance, during which the
system handled and contained conflict. The eventual outcome was
the production of a more differentiated social structure, better
adapted to the system's needs. In retrospect, the following
revisions seem called for:

(1) Relax the assumption of a constant dominant value system
    throughout the process of differentiation. Recognize a number
    of value positions. One of these might be dominant, but there

will be conflict and competition between it and its rivals. Hence, the definition of the initial situation as 'unsatisfactory' will not necessarily be uniform. For example, in the case of the UK in the Industrial Revolution a dominant, benevolent paternalism was challenged by radicalism, religious dissent and utilitarian rationalism.

(2) Anchor talk about dissatisfaction in specific groupings rather than in a general way. For example, the fact that the UK was heterogeneous in terms of its religious, regional/ethnic and occupational/class composition should be taken into account, and so should the role of the leaders of groups in formulating the views of those groups. Consequently, the resulting reforms of the education system were a product of the interplay of the perceived values and interests of these diverse groups.

(3) Recognize the partisan nature of 'the authorities'. Smelser had originally seen dissatisfactions which originated the process of differentiation as ones to which 'the authorities' would respond. Thus he treated 'the authorities' as though they were above the political process and as though they acted on behalf of the whole society. Now he recognizes that those in government were themselves partisan participants in the process and that there were struggles amongst groups inside government, as well as in the wider society.

(4) Treat social life as a political competition. The idea of society as an instrumental, problem-solving organization, with the process of educational reform resulting in more effective functioning of the system, had been overplayed. Now Smelser sees that 'the creation of new educational structures is *also* a political victory, compromise, or defeat (or all three) worked out in the context of group conflict' (ibid, p. 122). In short, social life involves more of a power struggle.

These revisions represent substantial concessions to the critics of functionalism, particularly to those 'conflict theorists' who maintained that there had been an overestimation of the extent of value consensus and that agreement on values was in any case given too much importance relative to group interest. Both conflict theory and 'symbolic interactionism' (see Chapter 5) take the view that social life is an intrinsically political affair and that social outcomes are the result of interplay between a diversity of groups and interests. The symbolic interactionists give particular prominence to the 'rule-making' procedure, and the way a diversity of factors contribute to the process of the formation of educational policy and reform.

Turner and Maryanski: reservations about neo-functionalism

Have the modifications and concessions made functionalism more acceptable, or have they in fact constituted its final dissolution? Jonathan Turner and Alexandra Maryanski say they have done the latter, that the new line actually follows the 'Kingsley Davis ploy'. Davis (1959) had tried to defend functional analysis by arguing that there was nothing special about it, that it was really the method that all sociologists use, that is it treated society as an organization of interacting parts, which is, as we have seen, just what Alexander singled out as the key feature of this supposedly new functionalism. Turner and Maryanski agree that Alexander is right in his characterization of the neo-functionalist position, but that what he and his associates are doing is eliminating that which is actually distinctive about functionalism, which is the analysis of the interaction of system parts *relative to a notion of system needs*. For functionalists, the way system parts contribute to the integrity and continuance of the system as a whole is supposed to explain why those parts are the way they are. Neo-functionalism, however, is not really attempting to explain these matters, aiming only to describe the way system parts interact. Turner and Maryanski applaud the abandonment of the assumption of system needs as an explanatory device; the extent to which explanations can legitimately be made in terms of such needs has always been very problematic. Indeed, it has been the main weakness of functionalism.

Nevertheless, at a methodological level, perhaps the idea of system needs can play a useful role by providing a frame of reference within which comparisons of different social systems can be made. Without it the description and comparison of social systems proceeds on an *ad hoc* basis with virtually every researcher deciding in what terms to characterize a system or in what respects to compare it with others. To avoid the problem caused by talking about 'needs' Turner and Maryanski suggest that the concept 'basic problems' be used. Here they follow a suggestion from the anthropologist Walter Goldschmidt (1966) of using a list of basic problems that social systems confront to provide a common frame of reference for comparing different systems. Goldschmidt provides such a list to enable comparisons of societies with respect to certain central activities:

> (1) Delineation of rights to sexual access, including the public presentation of those rights and sanctions against breach. (2) Provision for the nurture of infants and care of pregnant and lactating mothers, including the definition of rights and obligation... (3) Provision of a defined social status and identity for each child. (4) Provision of education and indoctrination of the child... (4) Provision of an identification object for both parents through which they may project themselves into the future through sociologically established descendants. (Goldschmidt, p. 93)

If Turner and Maryanski are correct, then this attempt to revivify the Parsonian, functionalist tradition has instead finally denatured it. All that is left is a use of the notion of social units as systems, an idea which is by no means unique to functionalism. However, there are those who argue that functionalism is by no means dead, even if it would be better if it was. The explanation of the nature of system parts in terms of the needs of the system is often practised by those who do not explicitly identify themselves as functionalists, or who might even claim that functionalism is an anathema. For example, Jon Elster (1985) has criticized Marxist analysis from a Marxist point of view as often basically functionalist, and Marxists certainly do analyse many social institutions as contributing to the meeting the survival needs of the capitalist system. G. A. Cohen (1978) has also argued that Marxist analysis is often functionalist but has defended this mode of analysis.

Conclusion

In this chapter we have been illustrating the view that how a sociologist approaches the study of social life will depend on the theoretical and conceptual assumptions he or she makes about society and social behaviour. We have suggested that one variety of structuralism may be called the consensus perspective because it is based on the assumptions that: (*a*) consensus on basic values is the main feature which holds a society together and keeps it orderly; and (*b*) a society can be viewed as an integrated system of interdependent parts. We have also suggested that this perspective produces explanations of particular processes or structural arrangements found in society in terms of the functions they fulfil for the maintenance of the total society, or any particular sub-system within it.

From this perspective, societies are viewed as integrated wholes which structure and coerce the persons within them. New members have to be moulded into the cultural expectations, the norms and roles, the society requires for its persistence. The concepts of consensus, equilibrium, system, functions, functional prerequisites, interdependence, solidarity and integration form the core of this perspective and guide the form of inquiry by suggesting particular problems and offering particular answers. These answers may be described as functionalist or consensus theories.

Of course, this characterization of the consensus perspective is somewhat idealized. It probably describes best the pioneering work of Durkheim and also many anthropological studies. For, as we have seen, there are a number of other competing versions within the approach, as well as full-bodied attacks on it from without.

The different versions 'within' reflect disagreements about the use and interpretation of key concepts and assumptions, for example, the 'needs' or 'imperatives' of the system, the nature of consensus and the degree of integration and stability of society. We suggested that Parsons, though much maligned, did much to modify crude functionalism, and Merton tried to give the approach what he thought were the appropriate means of making it more empirical. Indeed, a large number of empirical studies using the approach have been made and we have cited those of Merton himself, Erikson and Smelser. Yet, as Smelser himself admits in his reconsideration of an earlier study, its basic problems have continued. In fact, his criticisms can be seen to be a part of wider attempt to revivify the structural functional approach, which labels itself neo-functionalism.

Here we come to the attacks on structural functionalism 'from without'. By far the greatest onslaught on the approach comes from Marxists and we have seen how the neo-functionalists try to accommodate such criticisms. Their concessions, although far-reaching, do not appease those who would wish to go even farther, substituting conflict for consensus as the basic and essential key to the workings of society. Both approaches share important concepts – system, the relationships of parts of the system, the way systems 'pressure' or 'structure' individual actions – and can therefore both be characterized as 'structuralist'. Yet this difference in the basic starting assumption, conflict or consensus, appears to result in the production of different descriptions of society, especially in respect of social change. We now turn to consider why this should be so.

Further reading

Alexander, J. (ed.), *Neofunctionalism* (Sage, 1985). Contains Jeffrey Alexander's 'Introduction' and Neil Smelser's 'Evaluating the model of structural differentiation in relation to educational change in the Nineteenth Century.'

Davis, K., and Moore, W., 'Some principles of stratification', in R. Bendix and S. M., Lipsett *Class, Status and Power*, 2nd edn. (Routledge, 1967).

Durkheim, E., *Rules of Sociological Method* (Macmillan, 1982).

Erikson, K., *Wayward Puritans* (Wiley, 1966).

Giddens, A. (ed.), *Emile Durhheim, Selected Writings* (Cambridge University Press, 1972).

Hamilton, P., *Talcott Parsons* (Horwood, 1983).

Merton, R., *Social Theory and Social Structure* (Free Press, 1957). Contains the essays 'Manifest and latent functions' and 'Social structure and anomie'.

Parsons, T., *Social Structure and Personality* (Free Press, 1964). Contains 'The school class as a social system'.

——, and Bales, R. F., *Family, Socialisation and Interaction Process* (Routledge, 1965). Contains Parsons's essay 'The American family'.

Smelser, N. J., *Social Change in the Industrial Revolution* (Routledge, 1959).

Thompson, K., *Emile Durkheim* (Horwood, 1982).

Turner, J., and Maryanski, A., 'Is "neofunctionalism" really functionalism?', *Sociological Theory*, vol. 6, 1986, pp. 110–121.

Questions

1 What do you understand by the problem of order?
2 What are the characteristics of the consensus approach to the problem of order?
3 How did *either* Durkheim *or* Parsons contribute to the consensus approach?
4 What are the advantages and disadvantages of seeing society as an organism?
5 Do you think Durkheim's functional analysis of religion has any relevance for the analysis of ritual behaviour in modern society?
6 Why do you think some anthropologists have found the functionalist approach so useful to their studies?

7 What do you understand by the concept 'functional imperatives' of society? Can they be scientifically proven?
8 What is meant by 'a society in a state of equilibrium'?
9 Outline a possible functional analysis of some institution in society, other than education.
10 Do you think Merton's attempt to clarify functional analysis succeeds in making the approach more scientific?
11 How can both deviant behaviour and social stratification be seen as positively functional for society?
12 In your view, what are the positive benefits of using a consensus sociological approach to studying the social world?
13 What are (*a*) the strengths (*b*) the weaknesses of structural functionalism as an approach to understanding the social world?
14 Does the neo-functionalist movement help or hinder attempts to revive structural functionalism?

3 Structuralism as a perspective: II, conflict

Introduction

Conflict or consensus? In sociology there has been a tendency for theorists to take one side or the other, to see society as being better characterized and described primarily in terms of clashing interests or in terms of shared agreements. Generally, conflict theorists regard themselves as radical critics of existing society and view consensus theorists as appeasers of the existing system, the *status quo*. On the other hand, consensus theorists dismiss conflict approaches as merely political – an attempt to argue for a new society in terms of a set of values which masquerade as 'science'. Each group of theorists tends to see their approach as more accurately describing the way society works. In this chapter we will try to show that these two approaches are not diametrically opposed, but have much in common. Yet they differ sufficiently to enable us to distinguish two distinct sociological perspectives.

Conflict as a perspective: the contribution of Karl Marx

Although Karl Marx (1818–83) died a hundred years ago, his work is very much alive today and in fact constitutes the main body of conceptual and theoretical work within conflict theory. As anyone living in the twentieth century knows, his thought has had immense influence in shaping practical policies; Marxism is a living, powerful and practical body of thought and doctrine which shapes the destiny of millions of men and women. A substantial part of this body of thought provides sociologists with a systematic and rigorous way of analysing society and forms the core of the conflict perspective. We will, therefore, devote most of this chapter to Marx's sociological work as a 'conflict theorist' and then show

how his work continues to give theoretical direction and significance to the work of later sociologists. To do so properly, we need to provide some detailed background of nineteenth-century capitalism as an essential backcloth for understanding Marx's theories and concepts.

A sociological description of nineteenth-century capitalist society

By 1850 the social systems of European countries were changing and none at a faster rate than Britain which became the first industrial capitalist society in the world. We look at this society, largely using the basic approach for describing a whole society outlined in Chapter 2. A more detailed colouring of the description can be found in the *Condition of the Working Classes in England*, written in 1848 by Marx's close collaborator, Friedrich Engels.

Economy

Despite a trebling of population between 1750 and 1850, the proportion of workers employed in agriculture was dropping rapidly. The 'surplus', non-agricultural population was fed by means of a big increase in the productivity of land due to improved (though as yet non-mechanical) agriculture techniques and, by 1800, an increase in food imports. Industrial employment was provided by an expansion of domestic or cottage industry where rural workers used handicraft skills in their own homes to produce simple goods like woollen cloth and iron nails. Limitations and bottle-necks in the supply of various simple commodities such as spun cloth stimulated the introduction of new industrial technology. At first the new water-powered machinery was located in rural areas where there were suitable falls in water levels; then, when steam power was introduced, industry moved to the towns, resulting in a massive increase in their physical size and the number of people living there. The now familiar phenomenon of industrial urbanization was clearly visible in Britain in the mid-nineteenth century.

These trends naturally brought about changes in the occupational structure of British society. Traditional work opportunities both on the land and in cottage industry declined rapidly in scale and importance. The work in the new town factories was largely 'semi-skilled' and could be done by the women and children who comprised the bulk of the workforce. New skills and trades were also developing (for example, machine-making, fitting) and some existing industries were quickly expanding (such as coal-mining).

The nature and sources of wealth were transformed by industrialization. Land was being replaced by industrial capital as the major source of wealth, that is, factory buildings and the expensive machines they contained. Industrial capital could yield larger returns (profits) because land and farm rentals were difficult to alter and depended on the vagaries of weather and crop production.

Polity

The rapid growth of industrial capital made its owners, the new industrial capitalists, major contenders for political power in Britain. They had to dispossess the traditional power-holders, the landed aristocracy and the rich merchant capitalists, who made their money through farming, trade and banking rather than from the direct control of industrial production. Then the industrial capitalists could ensure that government policies and laws concerning prices, taxation, employment, imports and exports, and new industries did not interfere with their interests. There is no question that they matched their economic dominance with impressive political achievements. Examples are the dismantling of traditional controls concerned with fair prices and the employment of apprentices; the 1832 extension of the franchise to include only well-off property-holders; the persistent checking, harassment and stunting of the trade union movement through Parliament and the courts and the use of the agreed forces; the unwillingness to yield ground on the employment of women and young children, and on working conditions (in particular the length of the working day); the successful shifting of the increasing costs of government on to the shoulders of the poor by using mainly indirect taxes levied on basic commodities, rather than direct taxes related to incomes. In fact, the success of the industrial capitalists in shaping the social system to conform to their interests is epitomized by the social, economic and philosophical ideology which served to legitimate and to justify their power position and which came to be known as *laissez-faire*.

Laissez-faire has its intellectual roots in the economic writing of Adam Smith. In his *Wealth of Nations*, Smith argued that the best way to maximize individual wealth and happiness was for governments to abstain from intervening in economic affairs and to let individuals 'get on with it'. The 'laws' of supply and demand would ensure that poor judgement was met with bankruptcy, good judgement by fat profits. The public would not suffer high prices for very long because fat profits attract new firms into an industry, the supply of the commodity produced by that industry would increase and prices (and profits) would revert to a reasonable level. On the face of it, leaving economic affairs in the hands of countless individuals would seem to invite anarchy. On the contrary, Smith argued, the market mechanisms of supply and demand, if not hampered by government controls, would ensure that economic affairs were conducted in an orderly manner that would ensure rapid increase of the nation's wealth. It seemed to him that 'an invisible hand' guided the destinies of men. Thus free enterprise, competition, the economic freedom of the individual and the profit rate as *the* criterion of economic success and efficiency were all extolled both to the detriment of more traditional forms of collective enterprise and also the government's traditional duty of securing economic justice in the form of a minimum wage or of fair price policies. By 1850 the British polity had fully absorbed *laissez-faire* doctrines and the government was reduced to two functions, foreign policy and the internal policing of society.

The agencies of the polity – Parliament, the courts, the judiciary, and the local magistrates, the armed forces and the unreformed civil service – were in no sense bodies representative of the whole population. Members of Parliament, judges, justices of the peace, army officers and influential civil servants were recruited from the prosperous and propertied sections of society. The rare recruit coming from the propertyless masses, the majority of the population, had to identify with the interests of the dominant minority to achieve social mobility and success.

Kinship

Urbanization had profound repercussions on the pattern of family relationships that make up the institution of kinship. Clearly, the move to the towns to find work in the new factories necessitated the abandonment of a rurally based life-style where agricultural work and pursuits were intermingled to varying degrees with cottage-based industrial work. Most town families ceased to be economic units of production, no longer being able to produce goods like woollen cloth for the market or to grow foodstuffs for themselves. Instead they became solely units of consumption whose purchasing power was earned by selling their labour mainly in the new factories. Such employment tended to disrupt and to disorganize stable family life because women and children, being paid much lower wages, tended to be preferred to adult males by the industrial capitalists. For the capitalists were constantly trying to cut costs, especially labour costs, in an effort to bring down prices, beat their competitors and capture the market for their goods. With a working day of about sixteen hours, with the women and children in a family working in one factory and the adult males working (or looking for work) elsewhere, the home came to be no more than a dormitory for six days in the week. And as the home tended to be jerry-built, overcrowded and ill-lit, with atrocious sanitation and other 'amenities', most workers in their sparse leisure time tried to seek entertainment and diversion elsewhere.

Thus families tended to be less secure economically. They were now entirely dependent on the vagaries of the employment market for work and income and could no longer fall back to some extent on the produce of their own land or gardens. Moreover, they no longer had the support of neighbours and 'extended kinfolk', such as uncles, cousins and grandparents. And the local community might well have been underpinned by the local church and local large landowner or 'squire' taking some responsibility for local welfare. Conditions in towns in the first half of the nineteenth century militated against the development of new-style local town communities.

Families were also insecure in their internal relationships. The traditional division of labour and allocation of responsibilities within families, which shaped the nature and content of husband–wife, parents–children and child–child role relationships, were obviously disrupted by the small time spent together as a family unit, by the husband's loss of the role of chief bread-winner, by the wife's need to return to work as soon after childbirth as possible. Given the long hours of work, the geographical separation of home and work, the ever-present threat of unemployment, the world of work, the economy, dominated the family life of the factory workers to an unprecedented extent.

Values

Values are concerned with standards of acceptable and unacceptable behaviour, notions of right and wrong conduct and, therefore, ways of seeking to justify or to legitimate behaviour. Different societies can be compared and contrasted in terms of the distinctive variety and range of values incorporated in bodies of religious, philosophical, political and other systems of thought. These values help to shape the workings of such major institutions of society as the economy, the polity and the family. In saying this, we are not necessarily agreeing with the consensus theorists that the regularities and uniformities and orderliness of social life stem from the agreement of all members of society on a basic set of shared values (that is, a common value system). We are simply saying that values do play a part in shaping the actions of members of society in that they may be used as a resource for explaining, justifying and even motivating action. Consequently, it is important to be aware of the nature and range of values which are available to provide such a resource in a given society.

In nineteenth-century capitalist society the structural changes in the economic, kinship and political institutions of society outlined above were paralleled by equally far-reaching and significant changes in values. Whereas in pre-capitalist societies social action was largely justified and conducted within a framework of tradition, in the new capitalistic British society notions of rationality, of rational action, were becoming more and more influential and pervasive in the social structure. A good reason for engaging in social actions like, for example, obeying the political authorities, or cultivating the fields in a certain manner, or bringing up the children in a certain way, could no longer be accepted, taken for granted and justified on the grounds of tradition, that is, it had always been done like this. Instead, rationality involves a search for reasons and criteria to demonstrate that of all the alternative ways of doing anything, the 'best' way or means has been chosen. Thus, the relative stability of traditional thinking was replaced by rational thinking – the perpetual quest for best means to achieve a given end of goal – thereby tending to open up social life to more scrutiny and questioning than hitherto. Traditional practices could no longer serve as a bulwark against the rapid change that can result from an unchecked appeal to reason, an unceasing search for criteria, for good, clear and logical grounds for action. Consequently, there was a growing opening up of goals and standards as well as of means.

In Britain, indeed throughout Western Europe, standards of value and goals of action were in process of being reshaped. Views of society and the natural world were changing. People could no longer view themselves in a time-honoured order, where, for example, social position, occupation and authority were 'given' and the range of possible changes in them were limited for all but a tiny handful of people. By 1850 there had been drastic changes in the social position of individuals and widespread and sweeping changes in the very structure of society. Underlying these changes was the growing conviction that the forces that shaped both the natural world and society could be understood and ultimately mastered. Coupled with this faith in reason was the growing stress on individuality, the importance of the individual in society.

These beliefs had to come from somewhere; they were rooted in recent experiences. Thus, economically and technologically, the inimical and unpredictable forces of nature were being mastered and, as we outlined above, major changes in the economy were taking place. Such changes consisted not only of massive increases in total production and in the reorganization of the labour force, but also in major shifts in values and attitudes.

In most societies there have been small groups of businessmen who have amassed fortunes by means of their 'capitalistic' enterprise. Once rich, such groups seldom persist in these enterprises. They prefer to switch to more traditional and more esteemed forms of wealth, like landowning, so that capitalistic notions seldom succeed in dominating the values of their society. The situation was very different for nineteenth-century capitalists, whose drive to make profits and economic gain was not simply a means in order to achieve other goals, but was a major, if not the major, goal in life. Success in business – measured precisely and rationally by the level of profits shown in the balance-sheet – dominated other goals and values in life. Moreover, the life-long pursuit of economic success as an end in itself was not a goal confined to the industrial capitalists. Gradually, the value which they placed on rationality, calculability and efficiency pervaded the attitudes of much wider sections of the society. As we have indicated, these values were related and systematized into a powerful ideology known as *laissez-faire*. Here, achievement, the twin value to success, was sanctified. And achievement essentially meant the success of an individual in carving out and creating a career, ideally by his own efforts, unaided by the traditional advantages of birth, favour or patronage.

Laissez-faire was as much a political as an economic doctrine. It focused on the individual, rather than on groups like families, local communities and even the state as the basic unit of society. This focus, reflecting changes in thinking, was brought about not only by industrialization, but also by the great political revolutions of the late eighteenth and early nineteenth centuries. Of these, by far the most significant was the French Revolution of 1789.

The French Revolution highlighted and confirmed several major shifts in the range and variety of considerations out of which the basic values and attitudes of individuals and groups in society can be created. By attacking and, for a time dismantling hitherto 'unshake-able' and 'unchallengeable' social institutions, the revolutionaries clearly demonstrated the novel idea that men *could* remodel society; and, even more radical, they *should* remodel society. Thus time-honoured and venerable institutions, such as property, the church and religion, the monarchy and its divine right to rule, the family, and even the names and basis for the days, months and years of the calendar, were attacked, reshaped and even replaced in the perceived interests of the 'people', the masses. The needs and rights, note *rights*, of the individuals who together made up 'the people' repre-sented new criteria for social action. To achieve these 'self-evident' rights to justice, to freedom and to equality of opportunity required the development and application of the reason and intelligence seen to be vested in everyone. Such development could occur once the shackles of superstition and ignorance maliciously and self-interestedly imposed by the religious and political leaders of the state were cast off. Hence not only did new values like individualism, the rights to count for something and to be heard politically and socially, emerged, but so also did notions for implementing and securing these rights. For example, the use of reason was to be encouraged through the provision of educational opportunities; social and political justice was to be ensured through democratic political institutions like freely elected parliaments answerable and responsible to the people.

Needless to say, these new values were not institutionalized,

built into, the normal social practices and culture of French society
or any society in Europe for some considerable time. The practical
institutional changes made by the revolutionaries were short-lived.
Their importance derives from helping to motivate and inspire
individuals and groups in the many social and political struggles
which characterized the rapidly changing social structures of all
societies in Europe throughout the nineteenth century. Indeed,
these values provide a fulcrum for conflict throughout the world
today. Never again could tradition serve as a sole and sufficient
reason to halt change; never again could the rights of individuals,
the demands of the masses, be anything other than a major
consideration in the working of societies.

Marx's analysis of nineteenth-century capitalism

Methodological assumptions

Marx would broadly agree with the preceding sociological description of early capitalism. His concerns, however, go beyond
description: his basic aims are to develop a sound scientific explanation of the 'mechanism' of stability and change of society as an
indispensable prelude to revolutionizing the capitalist system. In
order to arrive at his distinctive concepts, theories and explanations, Marx, like all thinkers in all disciplines and fields, had to
make a number of assumptions about the nature of man and of the
world. We can distinguish the following six important and overlapping assumptions which underpinned his conflict perspective in
the social world.

(1) The world, including the social world, is better characterized
    by flux and change rather than by stability and the permanence
    of phenomena.
(2) In the social world, as in the world of nature, change is not
    random, but orderly in that uniformities and regularities can be
    observed and, therefore, scientific findings can be made about
    them.
(3) In the social world, the key to this pattern of change can be
    found in men's relationships in the economic order, the world
    of work. Subsistence, the need to make a living, must be

achieved in all societies. How subsistence is achieved crucially affects the whole structure of any society.

(4) Society can be viewed as an interrelated system of parts with the economy very much shaping the other parts.

(5) Those within a society are shaped, in both attitudes and behaviour, by its social institutions. Marx believed that underlying all the various and different kinds of 'social men' produced by different types of the society – primitive, ancient, feudal, oriental and capitalist – is a basic and essential human nature. For Marx people are essentially rational, intelligent and sensitive, but these qualities can be warped and diverted into their opposites if the social arrangements of a society are so badly designed as to allow some to pursue their own interests to the detriment of others. Very few can escape their historical and social circumstances and study their own society with the detachment and dispassion required of science. Marx, however, considered himself to be such a one.

(6) Finally, Marx's basic philosophical view of the nature of humankind and its relationship with the natural world is generally called *historical materialism*. Historical materialism incorporates most of the preceding points, but will be restated here in view of its crucial importance to Marx's sociological work.

With historical materialism, Marx tries to create a philosophical viewpoint which can produce a compromise between two opposite philosophical views on the nature of reality: idealism and materialism. An extreme view of idealism is to suggest that the world exists in the mind; the world can be changed by changed thinking. Materialism, again pushed to an extreme, suggests that the world 'out there', the world of material or physical objects, shapes thoughts and ideas. Marx decries both of these approaches. Clearly, ideas do not work in a vacuum; nor are they produced in a vacuum. For ideas to have any influence, they must have some bearing and relevance to the historical context in which they are generated. Thus da Vinci might have been 'ahead of his time' in the sixteenth century with his drawings of flying machines; in the sixteenth century, however, such ideas were socially and historically irrelevant. The time was not 'ripe' for such ideas to have any chance of acceptance, development and fulfilment; they were 'ivory tower doodlings'. Ideas are important to social life and behaviour; but not *any* ideas.

No one can think the existence of current social practices into extinction. Neither can sheer thinking power bring new social institutions into being. Ideas must have a sufficient bearing on existing social reality *in that particular historical context* if they are to inspire and move people to take *action*. Only by taking action can ideas serve to transform social practices. In this way, Marx attacks idealism. As for materialism, he argues that the material world is not simply 'out there' in a timeless and unchanging fashion. It has been, is, and will be, continually shaped and reshaped by people *acting* on their ideas and perceptions and thereby changing it. The material world of today is very difficult from that of the Ancient Briton, for example.

Thus it is Marx's view, as a historical materialist, that, of course, ideas and consciousness shape the social and material world if: (*a*) people act on those ideas; and (*b*) they realize that the material features of a particular society in a particular historical period must set limits on the extent to which ideas, even when backed by social action, can significantly reshape the nature of society.

Marx's analysis of early capitalist society draws heavily on these methodological assumptions.

Marx's analysis

In broad terms, Marx viewed capitalism as a social system with the following basic characteristics:

(1) The naked exploitation of many people by a few people.
(2) Contradictions, strains and tensions within the system. These contradictions are, in fact, created by the system.
(3) Given (1) and (2) above, the certainty of drastic and violent change of the system.

In expanding and illustrating these points, we will in effect be giving Marx's distinctive explanatory description of capitalism. We will then proceed to isolate and examine the key concepts used in the Marxian analysis of capitalism.

NAKED EXPLOITATION

With the development of industrialism, institutions which helped to bind individuals into their society – extended families, local communities, the church and, above all, traditional ways of life (culture) and traditional values – were weakened. For Marx, their inadequate substitute was the 'cash nexus'. Under capitalism the major link between people was an impersonal cash tie. Social worth was replaced by economic standing and performance; and one's relationship to the market became the predominant relationship in social life.

Most people had only one marketable asset, their labour power. In sheer scale, they constituted a new category of people in the emergent industrial society, the free labourers. Owning no other assets, they were free to find work on the labour market, or they were free to starve. A much smaller group in society was made up of industrial capitalists. They owned the means of production, the factories, machinery, land and raw materials, which provided increasingly the main means of employment for the bulk of the population, the free labourers. The capitalists had their freedoms: to employ or not to employ. If they exercised their right not to employ and therefore to lose profits, then the free labourers *had to* exercise their 'right, not to work but to starve'. Clearly, then, the industrial capitalists had economic power over their employees. Economic power was supplemented and reinforced by political power; the industrial capitalists successfully used their economic wealth and standing to ensure that their interests were looked after by Parliament and the courts. Attempts by employees to defend themselves by means of collective organization were greatly improved by hostile Acts of Parliament and court decisions.

A situation where one group, the capitalists, had great social and economic advantages, which derived largely from the toil of another much larger group, the free labourers, which received low wages and was ever threatened by the dire prospect of unemployment, could reasonably be described as exploitative. And even nakedly exploitative in that the only relationship between the two groups was a cash one, and the vast difference between the cash return, the profits, to the capitalists and the cash return, wages, to the free labourers was obvious to all concerned. But the capitalists did not regard themselves as exploiters. They regarded themselves as benefactors in supplying work. Naturally, they could not possibly employ all those who wanted work; the workforce must be limited by the total production which in turn was determined, in the last resort, by the demand for goods, the market. And, again naturally, they were in business to make profits; and to make profits they each had to try to beat their many competitors by reducing prices. With existing machinery, the only way to cut prices was to reduce costs: payments for land, equipment and raw materials, and labour. As their biggest single recurring cost was for labour, they had little option other than to try to reduce wages, to reduce the size of the labour force. They wanted as much work from as few workers for as little pay as possible. That was the system and no matter how developed their charitable and humanitarian impulses, they had to work in this manner in order to survive.

Thus, Marx argues, exploitation was not due to the 'evil nature' of some. Rather, it was a structural requirement of the whole social system. In a capitalist economy comprising many small, highly competitive businesses, capitalists had to screw down wages and depress working conditions in order to make the profits that ensured the maintenance of their social and economic position. Likewise, in their economic calculations, capitalists had to regard their fellow human beings, their workers, as 'labour', as one of the three factors of production, as a commodity to be brought or not bought according to price (wage). Hence, the capitalist social system 'structured' a new major bond between people: a depersonalized, calculating cash relationship, unmitigated by welfare or other more humane considerations. Moreover, this relationship reflected and characterized a social system which generated the grossest large-scale inequalities yet seen in the course of human development. Capitalism was a society rooted in naked exploitation of the many by the few.

THE CONTRADICTIONS OF CAPITALISM

Marx argued that the structure of the capitalist system generated conflicts, troubles and tensions, what he called 'contradictions', which could only be resolved by dismantling the system and reconstructing a new one.

For example, the capitalists were 'structured' by the system into 'cutting their own throats'. Their very existence as successful capitalists demanded that they made profits. In a highly competitive business world, they were perpetually trying to cut costs and thereby lower prices in an attempt to undercut their competitors. Now, clearly, if a single capitalist, or a few capitalists, could lower costs by cutting wages while the majority of capitalists had to continue the old, higher, uncut wage, then the wage-cutting capitalist minority would successfully capture the market because they could now sell cheaper goods. But no minority of capitalists could for long get away with this manoeuvre. Very shortly, all capitalists would have to reduce wages or be bankrupted. In this sense, their social actions are determined by the system. Yet the process does not stop at this point. For by cutting the *general level of wages*, that is, the total amount of money paid out in wages, the capitalists are producing the unintended consequence of cutting total purchasing power in the economy. As their market, the demand for their goods, is made up of the spending of the bulk of people in society, the free labourers, whose wage comes from working in the capitalists' factories, then clearly, sales and profits must drop. In order to try to regain higher sales and profits, capitalists would then introduce a further round of price-cutting by way of wage reductions. The result of such actions was recurrent economic crises in the form of a constant succession of booms and slumps which came to be called the 'trade cycle'.

The capitalist system, therefore, itself produced the tensions and conflicts which threatened to tear it apart; conflict with wage-workers over pay and conditions; violent competition between capitalists; and the alternation of euphoria and despair brought about by the trade cycle. Further, Marx argues, these tensions would intensify, given four major trends which he observed in capitalist society. These trends were:

(1) *Polarization.* Increasingly, industrialization was undermining and even eradicating traditional skills, occupations and distinctions. Independent and self-employed people of all kinds – crofters, small landholders, master craftsmen and skilled artisans – were left stranded without land, usable skills, or marketable cheap goods as industrialization transformed the economy. There was, therefore, a tendency for the working population to be 'polarized' into two 'armed camps': the capitalists and the free labourers.

(2) *Homogenization.* As part and parcel of polarization, individuals within each of the two main industrial categories, capitalists and free labourers, were becoming more alike or 'homogeneous', in several crucial respects. Within the category of capitalists, cut-throat competition tended to eliminate with time the 'small-fry', whereas the successful capitalists tended to

expand their businesses. Thus the typical capitalist tended to become the owner of a growing and more complex business firm. He became wealthier. The free labourers, on the other hand, became more homogeneous in terms of their increasing dependence on the need to acquire the new skills dictated by the rapidly changing machinery in factories, rather than on their old reliance on traditional crafts and skills. The workers were also, of course, homogeneous in respect of their dependence on the capitalists' factories for work and subsistence.

(3) *Pauperization.* In their incessant drive for greater and greater profits, the capitalists tended to drive wages down to a minimal level – the bare level required for the workers' subsistence. This tendency was especially apparent in time of slump, but even in boom times the still large number of unemployed checked the rise in the level of wages even though the capitalists' demand for labour increased. Thus, over time, slumps became more protracted, booms shorter, as the capitalists discovered that, despite cutting wage costs, the rate of profits tended to fall. Thereupon they tried to cut wages even further, effectively cutting total purchasing power, and therefore sales in their own market and the profit rate dropped again. The 'floor' to this process of wage-cutting must be the level of wages required to keep the free labourers minimally fit enough to turn up for work and to rear children. A subsistence level of wages was required to ensure the existence of the future supply of workers. In this manner, the wage-workers are made into 'paupers', that is, they are 'pauperized'.

(4) *Monopolization.* An aspect of the homogenization of the capitalist business was the process of 'monopolization'. As the smaller, independent concerns disappeared, forced out by the fierce competition, those remaining became larger units of production. The larger they grew the more they benefited from economies of scale, for example, buying materials in larger quantities and thereby getting them cheaper. Their resultant cheaper products enabled them to corner increased proportions of the market. In extreme cases, the sole producer of a particular commodity could exercise complete control over the supply of that product and over the employment of the relevant section of the labour force. The monopolist no longer had to compete. Thus competition, a driving force for efficiency in a capitalist economy, was no longer relevant to him.

These four trends are clearly interconnected and complementary. Many of their constituent features, for example, the obsolescence of traditional skills, the growth of machine-dictated work and skills, are inescapable features of any industrializing society as we can see from the experiences of modern 'underdeveloped' countries. But the misery and exploitation caused by low wages (or even no wages for unemployed workers), are, for Marx, characteristics of capitalist society and are not inevitable conditions of industrialism. These characteristics are generated by the way capitalism is organized as a social system.

Another major contradiction Marx saw in the capitalist social system was that between 'objective reality' and 'social consciousness'. For Marx, 'objective reality', the 'facts' about capitalism, would include: the technological potential to meet basic human needs: the uneven distribution of goods with the relatively few capitalists receiving a hugely disproportionate share: the way this share-out is justified on the grounds that each person's income reflects his effort and his value to the economy, so that the 'enterprise' of the capitalist is and should be better rewarded than the labour of the worker because 'enterprise' is a scarcer commodity than labour in the economy; and, finally, the fact that the capitalists have effective political control of society.

Marx saw this contradiction between 'objective reality' and 'social consciousness' stemming from the way those in capitalist society, capitalist *and* worker alike, regard these facts about the social system and, indeed, the system itself as 'natural'. They are seen as 'natural', 'God-given' and hence inviolable 'facts of life' and are therefore taken as inevitable conditions of existence. Although workers may despair about low wages and terrible conditions and although some capitalists may genuinely wish to be more humane, neither social category can escape the thinking of the times. They can perceive their social world only through the distorting prism of the monetary system: goods can be distributed if there is money to pay for them; workers can only be employed if there is a market for the goods they produce; businesses can be organized and run only if there are profits to be gained; slumps are caused by the impersonal and 'natural' and 'inevitable' mechanism of market forces (demand and supply) and are therefore outside human control. Instead of using ideas and social inventions like money as tools or means to control their world, they themselves become the tools which serve to operate an impersonal system of their own invention! Such impersonal forces as the price mechanism, the market mechanism, demand and supply, the rate of profits, the general level of wages, are 'out there', above and beyond control. Yet these 'impersonal forces' are nothing more than a codification or systematic summary of the ideas and actions of men in society. In this way, humanity can be seen to be controlled by outside, impersonal forces, that is, to be 'alienated' from its own social world.

VIOLENT CHANGE OF THE SYSTEM – THE REVOLUTION

Marx argued that the capitalist system of society was doomed. The contradictions within the social system would itensify, bringing about ever-worsening crises in home and foreign markets and, hence, in most people's domestic and economic situations. This disintegration of capitalism, as polarization, homogenization, pauperization and monopolization intensified, would effectively open the way for the establishment of a new and alternative type of social system. A new system, however, would not *automatically* be generated out of the chaos of the old system. In stating that 'man makes his own history', Marx was clear that just as humans created the capitalist system, so they would have to create a new order of society.

Firstly, someone had to understand clearly and scientifically how the capitalist social system worked. Only on such a basis of understanding could a new system be constructed; a new system which would avoid building in the errors of the old system. Marx claimed to have achieved this understanding and to have diagnosed the fundamental basis for change, not only for capitalism but for other types of social system: *the private ownership of the means of production*. Marx argued that, throughout history, the basic character of a society was shaped by its economic institutions. The most important of these institutions was private property.

By private property Marx meant, of course property or ownership of the means of production in a society; property which was crucial and directly related to the production and exchange of goods and services in a society. Regardless of whether this property was in the form of the slaves of antiquity (early Greek and Roman societies), or in the form of the serf-plus-land package of feudal society, or, as in the case of his major interest, capitalism, in the form of industrial capital (machinery, factories, and so on), the very ownership of such property necessarily created potentially far-reaching divisions within the social structure. By means of painstaking and voluminous studies, Marx claimed to show how the private ownership of the means of production vitally influenced the entire structure of a society.

He argued, however, that it was not enough merely to provide people with this analysis. What they also needed if they were to bring about an alternative society was the conviction that the alternative would be a *better* society. Part of this conviction would derive from the intellectual understanding of how society worked and how men produced unintended evils like the trade cycle, which was universally deplored, but widely accepted as 'unavoidable'. Part, however, would also derive from developing new ideas, new values, which would underpin the sometimes new, sometimes restyled institutions of an alternative type of society. In fact, a new *ideology*, a 'counter-ideology', would have to be developed. For Marx, an ideology is simply a set of related ideas and values which reflect the interests of a group. The contents of a *counter*-ideology, therefore, would be ideas and values reflecting the interest of the workers; it would provide them with a blueprint for change. It would provide a set of standards for evaluating current social, political and economic events and for assessing whether or not these events assist or impede the development of the new society.

Even so, an analysis of the working of existing society and a blueprint for changing it are still not enough to bring about revolutionary social change. Not only must people know what to fight and what to fight for, they must also fight. By this, Marx emphasized that people must act if they are to determine their own future society. Marx argued that the exploited non-owners of the means of production can only develop consciousness of the counter-ideology suggested by his writings and supported by their bad experiences in capitalist society if they actively oppose the system. They should do so by organizing themselves industrially into trade unions and politically by developing a political party which will further their interests. Only through struggle will the new consciousness develop and the old, false consciousness be eradicated. The old consciousness is false because it reflects the interests of the privileged groups and not the interests of the bulk of the people. 'True' consciousness for the bulk of the people can only come about when they develop an ideology (a *counter*-ideology in contrast to the owners' ideology) which actually reflects *their* interests. The capitalist owners, who try to make out that their way of seeing the social world is the one, the only, true way of seeing it, can only be overthrown if 'true' consciousness develops among the bulk of the non-owning people.

Marx's basic concepts and theories

In the previous section, we have drawn on a number of Marx's major assumptions, concepts and theories to give a descriptive account of how he viewed and analysed nineteenth-century capitalist society. We are now in a position to be able to isolate and to analyse these concepts and theories in a more rigorous and systematic manner.

Surplus value

Strictly speaking, Marx did not talk about 'profits', but about 'surplus value'. To use the concept of profit is to slip into the way of thinking of bourgeois economists who see profits as a proper return on capital, just as wages are the proper return on labour and rent the return on land. By referring to surplus value, Marx intends to highlight his major point about the essentially *exploitative* nature of class-ridden society.

For Marx, value derives from labour power. The value of a commodity is simply the amount of labour power – work – it takes to produce it. In a class society, the workers do not receive the value of their labour power; the return to them in the form of wages is less than the resale value of what they produce. The difference is the surplus value and it is creamed off by the owners of capital. The amount of surplus value is a crucial measure of the degree of exploitation in a society.

In an agricultural feudal society, where payments are made in kind, surplus value is easy to see. The landowner simply carts off a proportion of the peasants' corn, takes away some of their animals and requires them to work so many days per annum on his land. That the peasant is doing unpaid work for the landowner is clearly visible. In a capitalist society, where payments are made in cash, the fact that the worker is actually handing over some of his working time unpaid is less obvious, although the extreme contrasts between rich and poor in the nineteenth century were blatant.

In his major work, *Capital*, Marx greatly elaborated on the concept of surplus value. He tried to calculate it exactly, to make predictions about it and to relate it to his associated theory that there was a tendency for the general rate of wages to fall to subsistence level, that is, the capitalists had this minimum wage to pay if there was to be any labour force at all, otherwise the people would starve to death. The whole argument is most difficult and has exercised economists and Marxists ever since. For our purposes, however, we need to note the basic concept of surplus value and its use as a direct measure of the degree of exploitation in a society.

Social class

Marx wanted to discover the principles of change for society. He was not interested merely in describing the stratification system of a society in order, for example, to show exactly how many layers or strata there were in society, to show which of them had high or low prestige, and to show what kinds of prestige they enjoyed. Thus he never produced a theory of stratification. Instead, he examined society for those key groups which either appeared to have a strong interest in maintaining the existing social system or which had a strong interest in trying to change it. Such groups are the social classes.

Members of a social class may be distinguished by two sets of criteria:

'OBJECTIVE' CRITERIA

People may be seen to comprise a social class if they have one attribute in common: namely, if they share the same relationship to the means of production. Marx claimed that feudal serfs, for example, can be seen to form a social class in that all serfs share the same relationship to property. The rights and obligations they have in relation to the owners of the land and to the land itself are common to all serfs as holders of that position or role in the division of labour of society. Similarly, the owners of industrial capital may form a social class in that they are similar, as owners of industrial capital, in their basic social, legal and economic relationship to the non-owners of capital. In short, Marx suggests that the basis for social classes might be located in the different relationships of people to the means of production. Such relationships are crucial in determining the life-chances and the life-style of the individuals concerned.

'SUBJECTIVE' CRITERIA

Marx suggested, however, that having a relationship in common, even this kind of relationship, is not of itself sufficient to be able to call a number of people a social class. To classify a number of people merely in terms of having some common attribute is to do no more than to create a *category*. There is an infinite number of such categories, for example, all red-headed people, all people over six feet tall, and so on. Such attributes as red hair may be significant for the individuals concerned, but may be of no significance for the social structure. However, relationships to the means of production *do* have great social significance. And this significance becomes even greater if members of a category based on the relationship to the means of production become so *conscious* of this membership that they use it as a basis for organizing social action. Thus, for Marx, a category may only be a 'latent' or potential class until it is transformed into an active social class by men's consciousness of the importance of that category, of that way of seeing or identifying themselves.

Marx summed up these distinctions by remarking that it was not enough for a class to be class *in* itself; it had also to be a class *for* itself. For example, Marx suggested that in history, serfs and peasants were usually not a social class, but only latently or potentially a social class. In terms of social action, they were no more than a 'category' of people. Occasionally, however, when times were especially bad, when the harvest failed or when rents suddenly soared, the widely scattered peasants would unite and form a short-lived avenging army, seeking to put right the injustices they felt. For a short time, such common action transformed a latent social class (in itself) into a viable social class (for itself). Men became conscious of the similarities of their *common* plight, became conscious of the *shared* identity, that is, 'peasant', and, in this way, transformed a statistical category into a meaningful and active social force, a 'social class'.

Social change

The concept 'social class' plays a vital part in Marx's theory of social change. He sees social class as the crucial mechanism for changing social systems. Although he is fully aware that, in any society, there is a large number of categories and groups, he suggests that for the purpose of understanding how the social structure changes in major ways, only two groups are of significance: a group having a strong interest in maintaining the existing system; and a group having a strong interest in changing it. Social change comes about through the struggle – political, legal, economic, possibly even military – between these two groups.

For example, Marx explains in fine detail how the downfall of feudal society came about through the struggle between the new rising group of industrial and mercantile town-dwellers and the traditionally powerful group of landed aristocrats. For their survival and devlopment, the town-dwellers had to wrest power from the feudal lords in order to create better conditions for mercantile and industrial enterprise. Laws which tied men to the land and laws which made land unavailable for buying and selling had to be changed. Such laws had been created in the past by the feudal lords to suit their own particular interests. They were now an obstacle to the development of the new forms of wealth in the towns.

Marx develops this analysis with the aid of some additional interrelated concepts: the 'forces of production', the 'relations of production', the 'economic base' and the 'superstructure'. By 'forces of production', Marx is referring to the way the production of goods is done in a society; to the sorts of technological 'know-how' in operation, the types of equipment in use and the type of goods being produced. The forces of production shape the nature of the 'relations of production'. Here Marx is referring to the social relationships found in production, that is, the nature of the economic roles permitted by the state of development of the forces of production and, further, relationships that exist between these roles.

Together, the 'forces of production' and the 'relations of production' make up what Marx terms the 'economic base', sometimes called the 'substructure' or infrastructure of society. His theory is that changes in society stem from the economic base/substructure. The other parts of society, such as religious, familial and political institutions, are in effect shaped by the nature of the economic base. These other parts he calls the 'superstructure' of society. Figure 3.1 demonstrates in diagrammatic form how these concepts are related. Social change can be represented as starting at the bottom of the triangle and working upwards to the top of it. We will illustrate

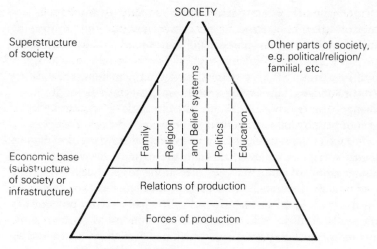

Figure 3.1 Marx's model of society

these concepts by continuing with our example about the downfall of feudal society.

In feudal society, the prevailing and major forces of production were concerned with agricultural production. Most people worked on the land, using primitive tools. The farmer-worker himself was the main instrument of production. In a situation where land was relatively plentiful and workers scarce, the main problem for landowners was to secure and to maintain a sufficient supply of workers on their land. The relations of production in feudal society reflected the need of landowners for a secure supply of workers. These workers, known as serfs or villeins, were effectively tied to the land by a complex set of relationships with the landowners, the feudal lords. In a sense, the serfs were owned by the feudal lords in that they were not free to work elsewhere, even having to pay a forfeit or fine if a daughter married and moved to another lord's territory or manor. There was a 'fit' or congruence between the forces of production and the relations of production in feudal times. The sorts of problems created by the state of technological know-how, the available tools and equipment and the way agricultural production was carried out generated a set of social relations which solved these problems, namely, the serf–lord relationships.

With the development of new forces of production in the towns, such as the growing industrial production by artisans and the growing monetary and exchange facilities, the old feudal relations of production limited the freedom to hire labour, the freedom for labour to be geographically mobile and the freedom for town-dwellers to buy and sell land. Thus there was a contradiction between the new forces of production and the old relations of production.

Changes in the social structure were not, however, automatically brought about by this contradiction. The town-dwellers had to perceive what and who were blocking the pursuit of their interests and they had to act concertedly and vigorously to do something about it.

Critics of Marx often accuse him of being an economic determinist, that is, of arguing that changes in social structure are basically brought about or determined by changes in the economic base. This accusation is true in as much as Marx is convinced that major changes in society must concern people's vital interests. Economic relations are paramount in that a person's relationship to the means of production can shape not only their consumption pattern, but also their life-style and the life-chances of both them and their children. Nevertheless, as Marx is only too fully aware, *people must take action* if changes in the relations of production are to occur.

This awareness of the need for action is further demonstrated in Marx's application of his theory of social change to capitalism. Although the inherent contradictions of the capitalist system created ever-worsening crises and although the relationships sanctified by capitalistic deals concerning the individual's right to private property and their right to compete with others became increasingly irrelevant to the newly developing forces of production, Marx argued that these factors alone could not bring about social change. In order to bring about a new type of society, the bulk of the population, the free labourers, had to become aware of what was happening in their society. They had to see the common bonds, the common plight, which linked them in their common identity of 'free labourer'; they had to become an acting social group, a social class. The workers, organized as a class in and for itself, Marx called 'the proletariat'. By taking common, concerted action in the factories, in the streets and in the courts, by forming organizations like trade unions and political parties, members of the proletariat could begin to develop their own ideology and begin to work for a society which could serve their interests. With capitalism, then, as with previous historical types of societies and epochs, there was no inevitability of social change for Marx.

As we can see, Marx's theory of social change is complex and incorporates a number of further theories. We now turn to a brief outline of the most important of them. Marx did not fully spell out or explicate any of them himself because his major concern was to describe and explain the workings of the capitalist system and to show how it might be changed, rather than to tidy up all aspects of his thinking for the future use of academic sociologists.

Power and the state

Marx argued that power, the ability of some people to exert their will over other people, derived from the economic base of society. Thus in capitalist society, the owners of the means of production (whom Marx called the bourgeoisie) clearly had industrial power; they could determine what to produce, how much to produce, whom to employ, how many to employ and where to employ them. Equally clearly, their incomes could shape a distinctive life-style for themselves and their families; they could purchase opportunities for their children in business, in careers and in education. Furthermore, Marx points out that an examination of laws passed, court decisions made, arrests made, and so on, showed that the influence of the bourgeoisie in the defence and extension of their interests was far-reaching. He felt that if decisions in Parliament and the courts were scrutinized in terms of the key question, 'In whose interests are these decisions made?' the answer almost invariably would be, 'In the interests of the bourgeoisie'. In this way, he argued that the state could be seen as 'the executive committee of the bourgeoisie'. Time after time, laws and their enforcement tended always to penalize the proletariat in the interests of the bourgeoisie. Only after massive struggles could the proletariat achieve any favourable decisions which improved their lives under capitalism. Without constant vigilance, concessions and improvements tended to be quietly removed over time. The treatment of the proletariat in this manner was not due to any massive conspiracy on the part of the bourgeoisie. Rather, in pursuing their own interests and ideals, and in ensuring that people in key and official positions would do likewise, the bourgeoisie were genuinely convinced that their way of thinking about the world was right. To their minds, it was 'the only true way' of thinking about the world. Thus industrialists genuinely believed that industrial production was threatened and the country was in danger when the workers succeeded in reducing the working day to fourteen hours, and when eventually women and children were forbidden to go down the mines.

Knowledge

Marx believed that knowledge was historically and culturally relative. In every society, people believed that their knowledge, their perceptions of the world, their values, their standards of behaviour, their way of going on – all of which we can loosely term 'their culture' – represented 'the best' in some absolute sense. They failed to see how their culture was in fact shaped by their historical circumstances. For Marx, the culture was decisively shaped by the type of economy and the sort of prevailing relationships to the means of production, that is, by the economic base. The leading ideas in a society are those which the dominant group finds congenial and acceptable in terms of its basic economic interests. The dominant group, the owners of the means of production, are thus not only the rulers of the state, they also are the rulers or arbiters of approved and acceptable ideas and knowledge.

Here, Marx might be seen to be posing a dilemma for his own work. If ideas are relative, there being no absolute standard of truth, why should anyone listen to what he has to say? For how can anyone criticize with any conviction one ideology in terms of another? To these objections he might answer as follows. Firstly, the ideas and standards of the bourgeoisie did not 'fit' reality in that the bourgeoisie could neither explain nor control the recurrent crises of capitalism. Secondly, Marx did believe that the truth could be discovered by means of scientific work. He believed that because his own work was scientific, he produced 'true' findings. This point will come up again, especially in the chapter on critical theory.

Alienation

In treating alienation, Marx's key concept is 'fetishism'. By fetishism, he means to suggest that individuals somehow come to dissociate themselves from their own products, whether these be material things or ideas. Somehow these man-made things and ideas obtain a life of their own, become more important than their inventor, humanity and end up by dominating it. These products of humanity's own creativity are treated as 'fetishes': they are treated as objects of mystery, objects outside people's control. Such objects are thus set apart, they are *alien* and come to dominate people. Example of such objects in the realm of ideas are the 'laws' of supply and demand, which impersonally determine what should be produced, how many should be employed, and so on. Humanity fails to see that such laws are the products of its own thinking, thinking which is historically and culturally relative. Instead, they are regarded as 'the truth' – which is 'out there', permanent and inviolable. Similarly humanity sets apart from itself the machinery that it operates, the products that it makes.

In short, Marx argues that people are alienated from one another; they are alienated from their products, material and ideal; and they are also alienated from their society. The root cause of these forms of alienation is to be found in the way social relations are structured by a social system which is organized around the sanctity of the private ownership of the means of production. In capitalist society, such a system dehumanizes people into a mere commodity, labour, which can impersonally be bought and sold on the labour market. In such a system, the alienating effect of the cash nexus extends beyond economic institutions to shape attitudes and behaviour in all of social relationships. Though alienation exists in all societies which have private property of the means of production, Marx argued that only in capitalist society had it reached its fullest, most crippling development.

Religion

Marx's theory of religion is simply an illustration of his more general theory of alienation. He argues that in primitive societies humans resorted to magical-cum-religious explanations to deal with phenomena which were beyond their understanding. With the development of the institution of private property of the means of production, these explanations gradually took the shape of justifications and legitimations of the rights of the dominant groups of privileged property-owners in a society. Religion as a way of thinking about the world was itself one of the alienating products of the social system. It was alienating in that both God and the scriptures were the products of creative imagination. These products became not only independent of humanity's control, but also to exert control over it. Thus humankind looked for solace and guidance from an external source and, in this way, failed to realize that it and it alone could shape its future and society.

In Marx's view, religion served to siphon off potentially revolutionary thoughts and actions by focusing attention on to the next world and by exhorting people to put up with the world for the sake of their immortal soul. Thus religious leaders promised a redress of this world's ills in the next world with such doctrines as 'the last shall come first' or 'it is easier for a rich man to get through the eye of a needle than to get into the Kingdom of Heaven'. In effect, these promises for the next world reversed the social order in this world. In this way religion presented a mirror-image of society.

For Marx, religion was 'the opiate of the people'. It distracted attention from the possibility of taking action to improve the social world by making false promises about a next world and by attempting to offer comfort and solace for the troubles in this world. He believed that scientific knowledge would dispel the mysteries of religion and expose it as the useful ideological tool of the dominant group or groups in society. Humanity had no need of religion and should realize it has only itself to rely upon.

Marx: conclusion

It is Marx's great achievement to have synthesized all of these theories in his analysis of the capitalist social system. Though we may find the intellectual origins of most of his concepts and theories in the work of earlier thinkers, none of these thinkers was able to produce such a penetrating and wide-ranging body of work which could serve to sustain and stimulate later workers in the study of society.

You should note carefully, however, that what we have produced above in this chapter is no more than a 'version' of Marx. It is an interpretation of a very large corpus of work. There are many other ways of interpreting Marx and many claims and counter-claims concerning 'what Marx really said'. Sidney Hook, a well-known Marxist scholar, even wrote a book of that title! These various interpretations derive in part from the sheer volume of his work, generated over a period of forty years, its complexity and its range. They also derive from what the various interpreters want from Marx; most are not neutral readers, but rather are active in the desire for radical social change, finding in their interpretation of Marx a practical way forward for bringing about a better society.

Hence there are arguments about what Marx 'really said'. The fact that Marx was largely unpublished in his own lifetime and that some of his work has come to light only quite recently does much to keep going such arguments as the relation of base and super-structure, the nature of economic determinism and the part human-ity's own actions can play in bringing about social change. There are arguments about whether or not there were really two Marxes, the old and the young, in that some thinkers feel that there is a massive discontinuity in thinking between the young Marx, with his direct focus on such concerns as Hegel, philosophy and the dialectic, and the older Marx, with his quest to establish a science which will expose the 'iron laws of capitalism'. Others can see a clear continuity of thought running througout his writings so that the later work is an obvious development from the earlier. Some regard Marx as a great humanist, others as a scientist *par excellence*; some see exploitation, others alienation, at the heart of his work. Some see his work to be nullified because his predictions about capitalism have not been fulfilled; others feel that when due attention is paid to changing circumstances it can be seen that his predictions are largely coming about; still others argue that the predictions are of little consequence in relation to the key questions Marx posed.

We shall now examine in more depth some of the work of later theorists which have relevance for sociological theory and, in so doing, will also illustrate the controversies generated by interpreta-tions of Marx. In this chapter, we begin with Max Weber's critique of economic determinism and then go on to outline work by a number of largely British sociologists who are largely preoccupied with Marx's predictions, particularly polarization, in the context of modern society. We conclude by showing how Marx's work can inspire virtually opposed conclusions in that G. E. M. de St Croix, (1981), applies class analysis to ancient Greek and Roman societies and argues for its enormous utility; whereas Barry Hindess, dissecting the work of both Marxist and non-Marxist analysts of modern society, concludes that the concept of class is thoroughly misleading and obscures sound investigation. In the next chapter, on critical theory, we greatly widen our horizons by considering some contemporary continental developments of Marx's thinking. As we shall see, these continental thinkers do not allow themselves to be confined by rather narrow, but eminently researchable concerns; rather, like Marx, they ask and pursue questions which seek to expose the innermost workings of modern industrial society.

Weber: basic concepts and theories

Max Weber (1864–1920) is in his own right a giant in the formation of sociological thinking. More than most great thinkers, his work straddles a number of sociological approaches. Here we focus simply on those aspects which seem to be particularly relevant to our discussion of conflict as a perspective:

(1) His attack on economic determinism, that is, an attack on the idea that major social change necessarily derives from the economic base.
(2) His refinements of the concepts of power and class.

Economic determinism and the protestant ethic

It has been said that Weber spent his life having a posthumous dialogue with the ghost of Karl Marx. Certainly in *The Protestant Ethic and the Spirit of Capitalism*, the first of a number of major works on the world religions, he attacks what many believe to be a major tenet of Marx's thinking: economic determinism. As we have seen, Marx's stress on the need for social action in order to produce change in society means that his position is more complex than that of a crude economic determinist. Nevertheless, many of his followers, the Marxists, adopted the straightforward position that only changes in the economic base can change society and Weber can thus be seen to be attacking this position of the Marxists, rather than Marx.

Weber's basic methodological position is that many factors must come together to produce social change. In *The Protestant Ethic* he declares that although he is investigating only 'one side of the causal chain' in the formation of capitalist society, other causes, including economic causes, are also very important.

Weber's basic problem is to explain why capitalism first developed in the West. His basic hypothesis is that a major cause of Western capitalism was the kind of religious ideas which developed in the West, but not elsewhere in the world.

In *The Protestant Ethic* he notes that capitalism developed first in Protestant countries. More specifically, it developed in countries where a particular variety of Protestantism, namely Calvinism, was strong. He argues that the sort of attitude to the world which was shaped by Calvinistic ideals provided individuals with the right sort of attitudes and motivations for bringing about a very major social change, the development of capitalist society. The sorts of attitudes individuals required to bring about a capitalist society were the very attitudes inculcated by Calvinistic religion.

Whereas most religions promote an other-worldly approach to life, stressing the importance of life in the next world, Calvinism, as a set of religious doctrines, made individuals focus their attention on life here-and-now. The basic reason was the doctrine of predestination. Calvinists agreed that God was all-powerful and all-knowing. He knew therefore who were the Elect, that is, those people who would be saved. Thus everyone's ultimate fate was predestined in the light of God's absolute knowledge. As this knowledge was in existence even before someone was born, there was nothing anyone could do in their lifetime to achieve salvation or to avert damnation; their fate was predestined. Unlike other forms of Christian religion, the individual could not achieve salvation by faith alone as in Lutheranism, or by doing good works and truly repenting his sins as in Roman Catholicism. Moreoever, the individual was isolated, on their own; neither their family nor the organization of a church could help them to achieve salvation. All a church could do was to bring like-minded people together. It could not forgive sins, wash the slate clean, or intercede on behalf of an individual.

In the seventeenth century, when the expectation of life was low, when death was an ever-present reality and when religion played a much larger part in people's awareness of the world, salvation was a very important concern. For the Calvinists, the doctrine of predestination might seem to make salvation a hopeless matter. They had no certain way of knowing if they were among the number of the Elect, because the Calvinists did not accept the authority or special powers of priests to know God's will. The Calvinists avoided the despair of hopelessness, however, by arguing that anyone whom God had elected would lead a pure and fruitful life. Thus they looked at individuals for signs of God's grace. If an individual prospered in his work, if he had a virtuous life, if he avoided temptations such as lavish expenditure, selfish adornment and aggrandisement, and if he practised his religion conscientiously, then it was very likely that he was one of the Elect. For why should God allow the unworthy to prosper? In this way, individuals could overcome the psychological uncertainty and insecurity, the spiritual isolation of the individual, induced by the doctrine of predestination.

Weber is arguing that a new set of religious ideals can transform people's daily behaviour, including their behaviour in the economic sphere. The religious ideals of Calvinism motivated individuals to apply to daily life and work a religious intensity. In effect, they became 'God's tool on earth' by working as hard as they possibly could at their work, instead of unproductively (in the economic sense) detaching themselves from the everyday world to pursue their religious interests. By trying to work harder, to produce more, to prove that they were favoured by God, they began to think in terms of the best means of doing their work and of ways of maximizing their efficiency.

For them, traditional ways of doing things were less important than efficient ways. Thus, they began to think rationally rather than traditionally – all with a view to being efficient servants of God's will on earth. As they wished to avoid lavish 'irreligious' expenditure, they devoted more and more time to work, less and less to leisure. Their profits were ploughed back into their work, as it would be a sign of spiritual unworthiness to spend them on pleasures of the flesh. In these ways, they applied to daily work the fanaticism and asceticism which in other religions are usually focused on non-worldly affairs. Moreover, they made of their whole lives a sort of economic calculus: good, fruitful work must be done every day. Given the doctrine of predestination, they could not cease these efforts, for in such a case they could find themselves to be spiritually weak and hence, in all likelihood, damned by God.

The description of the religious view of the world produced by the doctrines of Calvinism is what Weber means by the 'Protestant ethic'. He compares it with a description of what he considers to be the essential features of the way capitalists think about the world, which he calls 'the spirit of capitalism'. He shows that both descriptions have much in common, especially the calculating, rational way of viewing the world in terms of maximizing output by the best possible means. He suggests that there is an 'elective affinity', that is, a causal link, between them. He gives two basic sets of reasons for this link.

Firstly, Weber suggests that a major social change, such as the rise of capitalism, requires a number of people who are tough enough to reject and to replace existing ways of thinking and behaving. The emergence of new technological know-how is not sufficient to ensure that it will be put into operation. Some groups of people must be motivated sufficiently to oppose existing vested interests in order to develop these new technological ideas. The Calvinists, with their fanatical attitude to work, with their disregard of anyone or anything which might distract them from their life's purpose – proving themselves to be members of God's chosen Elect – seem to Weber to be such a group.

Secondly, Weber seeks further support for his hypothesis by exploring the relationship between religious ideas and economic ideas and behaviour not only in the West, but in a number of historical cultures: India, China, Israel and Islam. In these cultures, he shows that in some major world civilizations, many of the 'ingredients' for the development of capitalism were present, for example, technological know-how, free labour and monetary institutions. Nowhere, however, was there also present a this-worldly religious ethic which also stressed that the way to individual salvation was by ceaseless work in everyday life.

Thus, in his work on the world religions, Weber attempts to show how religious ideas – the superstructure for Marx – can affect economic behaviour, Marx's economic base. This work has stimulated much controversy and argument not only among sociologists, but also historians, and provides a good example of how Marx's work has stimulated further thinking on these very complex issues.

Power and class

Like Marx, Weber saw the social world in terms of groups and group interests. In the clash of competing groups, he too drew attention to the importance of power in determining which social groups would dominate over other groups. He did not agree, however, that power solely derived from economic relations, the relationship to private property of the means of production. For him, there were three dimensions to any analysis of power: class, status and party.

By class, Weber is referring to the economic order of society where 'market relationships' were of the utmost importance. By market relationships, he means no more than the relationship of individuals to property. Do they own property? If so what kinds? If not what is their bargaining position on the market for the goods and services they can offer? Clearly, this conception of class is very close to the 'objective' part of Marx's concept of class.

Weber also distinguishes two other dimensions of power: status and party. By 'status', he is talking about the way the organization of society produces different amounts of prestige or social honour for different groups of individuals. Social honour is not achieved simply by the ownership of property or of a skill or attribute. Rather, it derives from a style of life practised by a group in a society. Status groups can be distinguished by their attempt to develop exclusive practices, for example, their own rituals, their attempt to control the marriages of their children to the right kind of people. For Weber, the caste system of India provides a good, extreme example of status groups. Status groups endeavour to maintain and to extend the privileges which distinguish them from other groups.

By 'party', Weber is referring to the way groups may organize themselves to achieve a goal or an objective. Parties may be trying to achieve positions, honours, or outright control of the social order. Clearly, parties may be formed on the basis of classes or status groups or some sort of mixture of both. Parties are found only in societies complex enough to have a clearly discernible 'staff' of power-holders who can be influenced or replaced.

Weber argues that these distinctions allow us to analyse the acquisition and retention of power in society in a sensitive manner. For example, we can see that classes organized in market terms are in some sense opposed to status groups, which, in trying to preserve and extend their privileges, may act against the market principles of supply and demand.

For him, then, the struggle for power and the retention of power in a society are not simply a reflection of the 'economic base'. Although the class or material position of status groups greatly influences how they can operate in the world, perhaps as a party for the extension of their privileges, there is some independence of class, status and party actions. For example, in classical China the highly educated scholars, the literati, were the dominant status group. Other groups, such as rich merchants, endeavoured to associate with the literati by encouraging their relatives to pass the necessary examinations, by selling up their trading interests in favour of the more respectable ownership of land and by trying to adopt the general life-style of the literati. Wealth alone did not guarantee the merchants either high social honour or the power to run the society. Care should be taken, however, not to separate out too sharply these aspects or dimensions of power, for we should note that most of the literati were recruited from wealthy landown-ing families. And, of course, the literati could and did use their power positions to secure more wealth for themselves and to increase opportunities for their children and families.

Control of the society, then, is likely to be wielded in the interests of class and status groups which are organized as a party for the purpose of influencing or running the machinery of the state. The aim of controlling groups is not merely to secure power, but also to establish their *right* to wield such power in the eyes of subordinate groups. In Weber's term they want to *legitimate* their power. If they can do so, if they 'legitimate' their 'power', then they achieve *authority* over subordinate groups. That is to say, they achieve the right to dominate them, where the right to dominate, and thus to have authority, is freely given to them by the subordinate groups. For Weber, there are three basic sources for legitimating power, that is, securing authority to dominate or govern. Authority can come from tradition, where ruling groups may rule because they have 'always done so'; from charisma, where leaders of ruling groups have the personal magnetism or charisma to induce people to follow them; or from rational means, where ruling groups secure power by using the legal and judicial machin-ery of the state. Once in power, ruling groups have to ensure that their legitimacy is maintained in the eyes of subordinate groups. They can do so partly through the control and dissemination of leading ideas (ideology); partly through the more open use of power by way of the state machinery of laws, courts, police, and so on.

In these ways, Weber has attempted to develop and refine Marx's basic concepts of class and power and also his conception of the relationship between 'base' and 'superstructure' in the explanation of social change. Clearly the core ideas and concepts of Marx continue to frame these modifications and refinements.

We can now turn to examples of the work of current sociologists who make a great deal of use of the intellectual apparatus provided by Marx.

Some applications of Marx to modern industrial society

As we have said, Marx's work has provided an enormously rich source for further research. In particular, sociologists and Marxists alike have been concerned to take up issues in terms of his predictions about the future of capitalist society. Should Marx's theories be retained, modified or scrapped in the light of what has happened to modern industrial society in the hundred years since his death?

Ralf Dahrendorf (1959) argues that Marx was largely correct for nineteenth-century capitalism, but since then there have been such massive changes that modern society should be relabelled as 'modern industrial' or 'post-capitalist' because it is, in fact, a new type of society. Thus both capital and labour have 'decomposed' in that capitalists have given way to a new class of salaried managers and the proletariat has itself become more differentiated with the growth of white collar occupations and the decline of unskilled manual labour. Over the last hundred years, both social mobility and equality have increased, and, with the growth of collective bargaining and socialist parties, class conflict has become institutionalized, that is, has become an accepted part of political life and subject to the 'rules of the parliamentary game'. Instead, therefore, of analysing society in terms of class and class conflict based on relations to property, Dahrendorf advocates modifying Marx to incorporate these changes. In particular, he would focus on authority relationships.

John Westergaard (1965), however, continues to see modern society as basically similar to nineteenth-century capitalism. Of course, changes have occurred, but they should not be allowed to obscure the wide range of inequalities in modern society and the utility of explaining what is happening in terms of Marx's classic analysis.

David Lockwood and John Goldthorpe and others have produced much empirical work on social mobility and attitudes in the changing occupational structure. Thus Lockwood (1966) asks whether 'black-coated workers' see themselves as members of the working class, and, with Goldthorpe and others (1969), asks whether affluent workers are becoming 'bourgeois'. Clearly, such questions are generated from the use of Marx's distinction of the objective and subjective aspects of class and his predictions about polarization and homogenization of the class structure. In fact, the authors confirm some 'convergence' of these groups in terms of incomes, political and trade union action and domestic life-styles rather than their 'embourgeoisification'. In noting that a class conscious proletariat is not emerging, the authors are once again following Marx in viewing social class as the vehicle for social change. More recently, they argue that although there has been more mobility in the postwar period in Britain, it is due to changes in society, particularly the expansion of the economic structure. Consequently, society is not becoming more open, there is no greater mixing between classes or easier movement between them apart from that created by the expansion of white-collar employment.

In a lively polemic, Barry Hindess (1987) fiercely attacks both Marxist and non-Marxist users of class analysis. His basic argument is that class as a category is totally confused with class as an actor. Because persons may be placed in the same category as, for example, non-owners of the means of production, it does not mean that they will *act* on this basis or that they share any collective purpose. By going on assuming the importance of Marx's analysis and categories, we blinker ourselves from what is actually going on in the social world. Thus Goldthorpe and his friends appear to be studying what is really going on when they collect data about manual workers – their pay, attitudes, relationships and so on – yet in seeking to relate this work to a model of society in which the 'working class' is seen as a social actor on whose actions is dependent the future of society (will social mobility increase, thereby bringing about a more open society, desired by Goldthorpe?), they fail to see what is actually going on. Instead of examining political associations, trade unions and the like in order to trace how people actually translate their intentions into some sort of social action, they prefer to continue correlating the variables suggested by the categories and assumptions inherited from Marx. Thus Goldthorpe assumes that class is a social reality, albeit somewhat altered since Marx's time, and that changes in the occupational structure will ultimately come out as class interests.

In effect, Goldthorpe – and others – follows Marx in assuming that underlying everyday appearances there is a fundamental reality, the class structure. Such thinkers are led to ask foolish questions like 'why don't the working class pursue their real interests?' The question is foolish because it assumes (*a*) that the working class is a social actor and (*b*) that someone, such as the 'objective' social scientist, can see more clearly than the workers themselves what are their 'real' interests. For Hindess, such an approach is not so much wrong as it is singularly vague and uninformative.

G. E. M. de St Croix provides a complete contrast. For him, class is not an idealized concept, but a 'real element'. No matter whether or not members of a class are conscious of their membership, class is a real force in history and provides a means *par excellence* of explaining social change. St Croix produces an enormous, scholarly analysis of the workings and disintegration of the 'Ancient Greek World', that is, the Graeco-Roman empire from about the fourth century BC to the seventh century AD. He directly and explicitly uses Marx's concept of social class, agreeing with him that history consists of class struggle. Through his massively knowledgeable and detailed researches, he seeks to explain what happened in terms of class struggles, and, in so doing, to demonstrate the enormous utility of Marx's work for historical analysis. For him, the key is exploitation; it is not simply how production is carried out, but rather the size of the surplus value and, vitally important, the way it is extracted by the dominant class. In a nutshell, the more the Roman ruling classes sought to increase their wealth by extracting more and more surplus value from the exploited classes, and the more they devised increasingly efficient methods for so doing, the more attenuated the relations became between the classes. In the end, the struggling peasants might see marauding, invading foreigners as less threatening than their ostensible countrymen and compatriots, their own rulers.

In the course of his book, St Croix takes explicit issue with other theorists who have sought to criticize or modify Marx, including Dahrendorf and Weber, as well as a number of well-known Marxist historians. His heaviest onslaught, however, is reserved for his fellow historians whose work he sees as lacking explanatory force because it fails to make use of Marx's work as a key for the explanation of social change.

Conclusion

We have briefly outlined a wide variety of responses to Marx's work, ranging from its direct application at one extreme, to its virtual rejection on the other. In between these extremes, we have noted some attempts at making changes and modifications. We shall shortly turn to other work stimulated by Marx's thinking. This work is sufficiently different to merit a separate chapter – Chapter 3 on critical theory. Before doing so, however, we need to review how conflict theorists see the social world and how this view relates to the consensus approach discussed in the last chapter.

Clearly, in the approaches described in this chapter, social life is viewed in terms of divisiveness, conflict, hostility and coercion which are inevitably generated by the fact that social organization creates different involvement and interests for people. These interests provide a basis for the formation of groups which seek to preserve, to extend, or to realize them by taking action against other groups. Social changes come about as a result of groups acting in these ways. This approach to understanding the world may be contrasted to the 'consensus approach' of the previous chapter where we saw that consensus theorists tended to emphasize the cohesive and 'solidary' aspects of social life. Society is seen to be based on the reciprocity and co-operation between people and to be generated by their adherence to an integrating system of norms and values. Thus for consensus theorists, social life is strikingly characterized by the persistence rather than by the change of the system.

As we have already suggested, however, these approaches may not be so radically different as they might, at first, appear. For in both approaches, sociologists are interested in finding out how the whole society works, what are its key parts, how they are related and how the social structure might be seen to shape and to delimit individual action. Above all, they both endeavour to study social structures as wholes and, in so doing, must inevitably make assumptions about social structures being systems of some kind, with parts of some kind that are related in some way, and where a sufficient change in the nature of these parts will constitute a change of the social structure as a whole. The differences between the conflict and the consensus theorists, and hence between their approaches to understanding the social world, revolve around their respective views as to the nature of the system, the nature of the parts, the kind of relationships between the parts and the importance, therefore, of certain parts. In their common stress on viewing the social world as a system, both consensus and conflict theorists might reasonably be described as '*structuralists*'. In the following chapter we go on further to develop structuralist considerations – considerations which in many ways go beyond conflict and consensus, bringing in many other concerns.

Further reading

Carver, T., *Marxist Social Theory* (Oxford University Press, 1980). Useful short introduction to Marx's thinking.

Carver, T., *Engels* (Oxford University Press, 1981). Short introduction to Engels's contribution.

Cohen, G., *Karl Marx's Theory of History* (Oxford University Press, 1978). More advanced reading.

St Croix, G. E. M. de, 'Class in Marx's conception of history, ancient and modern', *New Left Review*, no. 146, 1984, pp. 94–111. For those who don't want to tackle his enormous, but magnificent book.

Elster, J., *Making Sense of Marx* (Cambridge University Press, 1985). A big, controversial book usefully read in conjuction with Cohen above.

Giddens, A., and Held, D., *Classes, Power and Conflict: Classical and Contemporary Debates* (Macmillan, 1982). A good selection of short readings.

Hindess, B., *Politics and Class Analysis* (Blackwell, 1987). Valuable for a very lively critique of users of the concept of class for studying modern society.

Marx, K., and Engels, F., *Manifesto of the Communist Party* (Foreign Languages Publishing, Moscow, n.d., or Bobbs Merrill Reprint S455). A lively and polemical expression of many of Marx's key ideas.

Singer, P., *Marx* (Oxford University Press, 19). Another useful short introduction.

Sowell, T., *Marxism: Philosophy and Economics* (Unwin, 1985). Locates Marx's thinking in the wider Marxist movement.

Westergaard, J. H., 'The withering away of class: a contemporary myth' in P. Anderson *et al.*, *Towards Socialism* (Fontana, 1965).

Questions

1 What are Marx's basic methodological assumptions? How do they influence his basic sociological concepts?
2 What do you understand by 'historical materialism'?
3 What, for Marx, were the main characteristics of capitalist society?

4   What do you understand by 'contradictions' in the capitalist system? Give examples. Are these 'contradictions' the same as the 'tensions' of the social system discussed in Chapter 2?

5   Outline Marx's concept of class. What is the importance of his emphasis on the subjective aspect of class for his theory of social change and revolution?

6   Contrast the views of Marx and Weber on (*a*) power, (*b*) the influence of ideas in society.

7   Does Weber refute Marx's notion that religion is the 'opiate of the people'?

8   Do you agree with Dahrendorf that capitalist has been succeeded by a new type of society, namely 'post-capitalist' society? Detail your reasons.

9   With reference to work by Lockwood and Goldthorpe show your understanding of the following concepts: false class consciousness; proletariat; 'bourgeoisification'.

10 What are the similarities and differences between conflict and consensus models of society?

11 'Ideology in the conflict model fulfils the same function as the common value system in consensus model.' Discuss.

12 'Britain is now a classless society.' 'Britain is the most class-ridden society in the world.' Both of these statements are frequently made about modern Britain. So, in your view, what would count as decisive evidence for choosing between them? How would you go about obtaining such evidence?

13 If Hindess is correct in his criticisms of the use of the concept of class, what alternatives are available for use in the study of society? Are we obliged to revert to the concepts we find in the consensus approach?

4 Structuralism as a perspective: III, critical theory

The atmosphere of suspicion

Thomas McCarthy neatly summarizes the content of this section. He writes:

> Since the beginning of the modern era the prospect of a limitless advance of science and technology, accompanied at each step by moral and political improvement, has exercised a considerable hold over Western thought. Against this the radicalized consciousness of modernity of the nineteenth century voiced fundamental and lasting doubts about the relation of 'progress' to freedom and justice, happiness and self-realization. When Nietzsche traced the advent of nihilism back to the basic values of Western culture – 'because nihilism represents the ultimate logical conclusion of our great values and ideas' – he gave classic expression to a stream of cultural pessimism that flows powerfully again in contemporary consciousness. Antimodernism is rampant today, and in a variety of forms: what they share is an opposition to completing 'the project of modernity' insofar as this is taken to be a matter of rationalization. (translator's introduction to Habermas, 1984, p.v)

The belief that through the development of science and technology we can improve human life in general, can set it on a more rational and satisfactory basis, is what McCarthy means by 'the project of modernity', though it is more commonly called the Enlightenment after the historical period (the seventeenth and eighteenth centuries) in which this belief was promoted as an ideal. Almost all of those theorists we will be considering are, to a greater or lesser extent, critics of the Enlightenment ideal.

Some necessary background to the twentieth-century discussion must be provided with a brief mention of the seventeenth-century philosopher René Descartes (1596–1650), who was effectively the founder of the modern era in philosophy. Descartes thought that knowledge came through the working of the mind, particularly through the power of reason. He further thought that the mind was transparent to itself, that just by reflecting upon the workings of our mind we could be aware of what it was doing, of how it was working. Thus, if the philosopher observed carefully how his own mind was working, he would be able to understand how we come by knowledge and to provide rules as to how we can acquire more of it.

These assumptions are ones which, toward the end of the nineteenth century and through the twentieth, come under severe attack. There are three main lines of objection.

(1) Philosophical tradition after Descartes overestimates the power of reason in human affairs. The idea that people are guided in their actions by reason is questioned. It may be that people should be guided by reason, and that they can eventually be, but that as things are they are not and perhaps cannot be. Things would have to be changed to make reason play the decisive regulating role in human life. Others, though, think that reason can at best only play a limited role in human conduct, for there are 'non-rational' forces which do and must play a decisive, and perhaps the major, part.

(2) This links to the idea that the mind is transparent to itself, that we can learn how it works just by reflecting on our own thoughts. Here, the objection is that the mind may have workings of which we are not and cannot be directly aware, that although there are some aspects of our thinking of which we are aware, there are others of which we are not, of which we are 'unconscious'.

(3) Here the objection is that Descartes's conception is altogether too individualistic. Descartes thinks that the philosopher can understand how knowledge is acquired solely by reflecting upon his own, individual mind and its workings, without any reference whatsoever to anything outside the consciousness. Against this view, it can be insisted that some reference to the social and historical environment in which the thinker is situated is essential. Without reference to these environments, one cannot understand why people think what they do.

The further discussion of these matters will involve repeated mention of the ubiquitous Karl Marx. It will do so for a variety of reasons. To begin with, there are two related topics that need further discussion. The first of these is precisely connected with the issues that Descartes raised, the question do people really know what they are doing? The second is about the analysis of modern society – does Marx's analysis apply to modern society? They are not entirely unrelated.

Marx can be read as suggesting that there is an important sense in which people do not understand their own actions, that they are bordering on being the puppets of great social and historical forces which work 'behind their backs' and dictate the course of their lives, unbeknownst to them. This is one way of reading Marx, and as you should already be aware, no single way of taking his arguments is uncontroversial. A great deal of twentieth-century social thought, especially in the periods before the Second World War, and after the 1960s, is occupied by arguing whether it is right to take Marx as saying that people do not know what they are doing, and whether he would be right to say this.

Marx did not have a simple faith in the power of reason to improve the human condition. Indeed, his analysis was concerned to show that under the social conditions of capitalist society it could not do so, for reason, like everything else, was subordinated to the need to accumulate capital. Neither did he think that the unaided work of pure reason could overcome this situation. He did think, however, that scientific thought (in the form of his own theories) *supported by* the political action of the massed working class could achieve not just an improvement in the human condition, but the complete emancipation of all mankind, setting people free from all kinds of oppression.

The second issue, the relevance of Marx to the analysis of modern society, is not unrelated to the first. If Marx predicted, as some say he did (and others, of course, deny) that a working-class revolution would take place in the capitalist societies then he was badly wrong. There has been no such revolution. If he predicted (here again there is disagreement) that the revolution would be brought about because the inexorable logic of capitalist society would reduce the working class to the lowest levels of economic impoverishment and thus virtually force them into uprising, then again he has been refuted by events. If anything, the opposite has happened, with the working class being made ever more prosperous and more comfortably at home within capitalism. Does history then show that Marx's theories are irrelevant to modern society?

As we have seen, there is a tradition of concern with the potential militancy of the working class in Britain which is obsessed with this question. For more ambitious and inspired attempts to consider the relevance of Marx to modern society we need, rather, to look to continental thought, notably that in Germany and France. There, the conviction that the working class shows no signs of being revolutionary does not automatically obviate Marx's theory, for the idea that we may be subject to forces regulating our conduct of which we are not conscious – and hence do not understand – is seen to offer a vital basis for analysing social life in general.

From this continental point of view, Marx is one of a trio of thinkers who are nowadays counted together as 'the masters of suspicion'. One, Friedrich Nietzsche (1844–1900), has already been mentioned. The other is Sigmund Freud (1856–1939). Though Freud and Nietzsche gave less significance than Marx to the extent to which people are unaware of the social forces operating on them, they did stress the extent to which people could be 'unconscious' of their own psychological life, unaware of the drives and motives which prompt their actions. These three thinkers taken together can be seen as teaching us to be thoroughly sceptical of the high ideals that people profess and the motives they openly proclaim.

Consequently, we should not take the reasons people give us for their actions entirely at face value, but should expect to find that these are often the cover for much more discreditable aims and impulses that people cannot openly acknowledge. We should not, though, suppose that a suspicious attitude toward these things is necessary because people are out to deceive us and that conscious lying is involved. If anyone is being deceived it is very often those who are making the claims, for they are deceiving themselves as much as anyone else. They are perfectly sincere in what they tell us, they believe what they say because they are not aware of the true motives that lie behind their actions. In short, the idea that people are not fully conscious of themselves plays an important role in twentieth-century social analysis, and Marx can be seen to have made an invaluable contribution to the formation of this idea, even if the working class have proven to be an historical irrelevance.

One more bit of stage-setting is necessary. McCarthy, in our introductory quotation, speaks of the 'project of modernity' being taken as 'a matter of rationalization'. To explain what 'rationalization' is we need to reintroduce the name of Max Weber. Marx and Weber have long been thought of as intellectual opponents, but more up-to-date opinion recognizes much common ground between them on the importance of economic organization in social life and of economic forces in the formation of social institutions. None the less, there are important divergences between them. For a long time, too, it was thought that Weber's thought lacked a central theme, but here again recent opinion says otherwise, arguing that 'rationalization' is the very theme that unites his work.

Rationalization is simply the business of making things calculable and predictable. If one thinks, as Weber did, of social action as a matter of connecting ends to means, of finding and implementing ways of doing what you want, then optimal effectiveness is obtained if you can calculate just what is necessary to bring about a given end. Within Western society the desire to optimize the connection of ends to means has had a powerful role and therefore the tendency has been to introduce calculation into all spheres of life.

Marx himself had given great importance to the tendency of capitalism to render things calculable in monetary terms and to introduce these terms into all kinds of human transactions. Weber concurs that, in the sphere of economic life, calculability has extended a very long way. It has gone a long way, too, in our dealings with nature, for modern science is permeated by mathematics, which enables calculation and prediction of the behaviour of natural phenomena and therefore their control. In the social and organizational spheres, too, rationalization is well under way, though it is more difficult to detect since it does not involve the introduction of monetary or numerical values, being achieved, rather, through the creation of a particular social form, the bureaucratic administrative structure. It is for spelling out the idea of 'bureaucracy' that Weber has perhaps been most famous. His notion of bureaucracy is of a stable administrative hierarchy composed of a set of positions which will be occupied by specialists in administration, whose activities and mutual relations will be regulated by rules which are written down and are extensively defined. The behaviour of people in organizations is made 'calculable', that is, predictable, if what they are doing is closely regulated by a system of rules, for if we know the rules then we know exactly what they should be doing, when they should be doing it, and so on.

In Weber's view, these tendencies had flowered most fully under modern capitalism in the West, but they did not originate with it. He sees them as having roots in the remote past of Western civilization, in the worlds of ancient Greece and ancient Judaism, so they have been developing for a very long time. The combined and cumulative effect of introducing calculability into the natural, economic and social worlds was to further and greatly advance another process Weber called 'the disenchantment of the world', that is, the removal of all sense of meaning or mystery from life, reducing it to a matter of mundane routine. Though capitalism might make people economically much more comfortable than they had been, it would be a society of discontent, for it would be bureaucratically oppressive and people would find their lives empty and spiritually bleak.

Reading and re-reading Marx

The model of society as made up of 'base' and 'superstructure' which Marx contrived has been discussed earlier. It provides a focal element for this particular part of the discussion. One way of taking this model is as indicating 'one way determinism', that is, the economic base simply drives and determines the shape of the institutions and ideas in the rest of society. Engels, however, claimed that no such simple, unilateral relation was intended and that the development of institutions and ideas was *to some extent* independent of the base. Further, parts of the superstructure could react back upon and influence the development of the base. The issue is, then, how far and in what ways is the superstructure independent of the base?

Marx's own late writings, as found in his *Capital*, were relentlessly economic in character, concerned to show how the capitalist system of production exploited workers through the extraction of 'surplus value'. Much contemporary work in sociology, work which would say it owes much to Marx, is not directly concerned with these economic analyses, but examines cultural phenomena, such as television soap operas, popular music, novels and the like. In Marxian terms, their analysis is of 'superstructural phenomena'. The formation of this interest owes much to the re-reading of Marx which took place in the 1920s and 1930s, involving three main sources: Georg Lukács (1885–1971), a Hungarian, but much connected with German sociology, and with Max Weber personally, Antonio Gramsci (1891–1937), an Italian, and the 'Frankfurt School', a group whose name indicates their origins in Germany.

Lukács and reification

Lukács had not lost faith in the revolutionary potential of the working class, but took Lenin's view that the working class would only achieve revolution if led by a 'vanguard party'. The working class could neither achieve a true consciousness of their position within capitalism, nor of the need for and means toward revolution, without the leadership of a party in possession of the very theory which provided all these things. That theory, of course, was Marxism, but Marxism understood in the right way.

Lukács insisted that Marxism did not offer dogmatic statements about the relation of base and superstructure. In his *History and Class Consciousness* (first published in 1923) he argued that what made Marxism distinctive was *a method*, the dialectical method, and its essence was the idea of 'the totality', the socio-historical whole. One can understand things at a certain level by breaking them into their constituent parts, isolating these from one another, that is, analysing them. This is the idea which guides much science, that we get to know things by breaking them into their parts. Real, comprehensive understanding, however, requires that we recognize that parts are parts of wholes; we understand the parts by seeing them relative to the whole, the totality, as Lukács calls it. However, the very nature of capitalist society denies this kind of understanding to most people. It certainly denies it to science, which, concerned with fragmenting reality into easily intelligible bits, does not see – *cannot* see – the need for the whole picture. It denies it too to the working class, whose individual members cannot be aware of the way in which their own experiences fit together and fit into the whole degrading logic of capitalism.

They are prevented from understanding their position by a process of 'reification'. This is an aspect (or 'moment' in the jargon) of the more general process of alienation. Alienation is found in all types of society but reaches its most developed and intense condition in capitalism. Alienation is the separation of things from the people who have created them, and such a separation is the very essence of the productive process of capitalist manufacture. Industrial workers actually create economic goods through their physical labour, but though they make these things they do not themselves possess them for the goods belong to the employers. This actual separation even means that the workers' capacity to identify things they have created as their own creations is also attenuated. For example, within the highly specialized division of labour involved in assembly line production the individual worker's contribution to the finished product is such a small part of the process that the workers cannot really have any sense that the object – the car, washing machine or whatever – that results is in fact their own individual creation. Where people's sense of their relation to their creations is attenuated there is the possibility that people will not only lose sight of the connection between their actions and the things that result from them but that they will start to misrepresent connections. They may come to imagine that things they have created are in fact quite independent with lives of their own and beyond human control. This is reification, the tendency to treat creations of human thought and action as independent and unalterable realities. For example, if we do not believe that there is a God then 'God' must be the creation of human minds, a figment of their imagination. People who believe in God do not, of course, see it that way for they think that God exists independently of them, and rather than conceive themselves as the creators of God they believe that God is their creator. They get the actual relationship the wrong way round and suppose that they are at the mercy of God, that what happens to them is ruled by his will, thus underestimating the extent to which their own fates are in their own hands, not those of an imaginary being.

Following the logic of this idea, Marx treats the process of economic production as one essentially organized through alienation and engendering reification. The capitalist system is the creation of its workers, for they are the ones who physically create and circulate the goods – 'commodities' Marx calls them, meaning 'goods produced for sale on the market' – which are the be all and end all of the system, and yet the organization of industrial employment is such that the workers are made unaware of the extent to which capitalism is their creation and ought to be within their control. On the contrary, they think of themselves as dependent upon capitalism and at its mercy: they need it to provide them with jobs that give them their living, but may find themselves deprived of these through movements of the business cycle. They therefore reify the capitalist economic system as something independent, subject to laws of its own and regulating the lives of workers when the reality is that the system is created by their actions and depends upon their efforts.

At the heart of the capitalist system, its industrial system, there is reification. Lukács argues that this is not confined to industrial production but is spread throughout the whole society, affecting all its parts, including the life of the mind, its intellectual and scientific aspects. Working-class consciousness is prevented from obtaining the comprehensive overview of capitalist society essential to the recognition of its own role as the creator and therefore loses its potential to reshape it all. The structure of capitalist society is such as to prevent almost anyone else becoming aware of these realities either, so that *bourgeois* science is limited by the lack of the dialectical method, its whole approach to knowledge being severely restricted (a point which will apply to any *social* science conducted outside the Marxist framework). It is therefore necessary to examine critically the intellectual apparatus of the society to understand the part it plays in reifying the system.

Gramsci and hegemony

Antonio Gramsci, imprisoned by the fascist government during the late 1920s for his political views, considered class domination in capitalist society. There is a tendency to think that according to Marx the ruling class rules by the use of power. It has economic power and by virtue of that can exercise influence over the politically powerful, if indeed those with political power are not actually the same ones as those who hold economic power. Force is available to enable the state to gain its ends. The state controls the police and the military, and if the working class get politically out of hand they can be arrested or the troops can be called to ensure compliance. This conception, Gramsci thought, was not adequate for a proper understanding of the dominance of the *bourgeois* class under capitalism. This class was dominant not only in the sense that it held economic and political power, but in the sense that it also provided the moral and intellectual leadership of the society. The *ideas* of the bourgeoisie were as important to its ascendancy over other classes as the possession of physical force.

This ascendancy was characterized with the catchword 'hegemony'. The idea is of course an extension of a passing comment of

Marx's to the effect that the capitalist class controls not only the means of production of material goods in society but the means of intellectual production and communication, that is, mainly newspapers and book publishing in Marx's time, with film, television, video, and so on coming after. Gramsci's idea also represents explicit convergence with the functionalist/consensus view, that social cohesion is advanced by sharing of ideas and values. The capitalist class rules so effectively because it has given rise to ideas and values which promote its interests and strengthen its position; it has been able to permeate the whole of society with them, to spread them around and inculcate them into the other classes.

Gramsci rejected the idea that the economic base could determine the course of social development. To suppose that the working out of the economic laws of capitalism would inevitably bring socialism was to adopt a fatalistic attitude. It was clear to him that it was up to people to bring about socialism. It is the activities of people which make things happen, not 'iron laws of history', and so people need to be encouraged to see the necessity for change as requiring a challenge to the hegemony of *bourgeois* ideas (for these, of course, would never encourage the thought that revolution was either desirable or possible). Accordingly, criticism of the whole dominant culture becomes a vital part of the promotion of the Marxist cause.

The Frankfurt School and instrumental reason

Lukács and Gramsci are united in the view that a central part of what they are doing is criticizing the ideas of capitalist culture, and they are joined, at least in this respect, by the 'Frankfurt School'. This name derives from its connection with the Institute for Social Research based in Frankfurt during the 1920s and much of the 1930s. Hitler's rise to power compelled it to remove to America from where it returned to Germany in the 1950s. The School involved many different people and the homogeneity of its views must not be presupposed on the basis of the thumbnail sketch given here. Amongst the best-known names are those of Max Horkeheimer (1895–1973) and Theodor Adorno (1903–69), dominant figures of its heyday, and Herbert Marcuse (1898–1979), whose importance was more recent, being highly influential in the days of 'student revolt' in the 1960s. The members of the 'School' disagreed amongst themselves, and revised their own views over time, so it is easy to exaggerate their consistency. Still, the School did initiate 'critical theory', a title we have appropriated for the whole of this chapter although it particularly applies to their own distinctive standpoint. This standpoint derived from Marx and was influenced by his thinking but eventually drifted away from strong Marxist attachments.

Like Lukács and Gramsci, the Frankfurt School had reasons for giving priority of place to the criticism of *bourgeois* culture. Its practitioners would, for example, engage in the examination of modern classical music, popular songs or jazz to show that these expressed, circulated and communicated a debased consciousness, one which would, at the least, mislead people about the realities they lived under, and would sentimentalize and falsify them. Like Lukács and Gramsci, they were critical of the way in which reason and thought were subordinated to the requirements of capitalism and, to express their own objection to this, they adopted the expression 'instrumental reason'. This concept meant that reason had been domesticated by capitalism, that thought was directed into investigating those problems which were effectively capitalism's problems and which were therefore substantially problems of an 'instrumental' kind, that is, problems of controlling things and turning them to the purposes of capitalist exploitation. For example, standard social science was not concerned to investigate the oppressive nature of capitalism as such, but rather to study, say, the immediate reasons for workers' dissatisfaction and to make suggestions for minor improvements in order to reconcile the workers to continuing exploitation. In contrast, the role of 'critical theory' was not to adapt people to, or enhance the workings of, the *status quo*, but to expose its oppressive character, to show the false nature of the consciousness encouraged in the arts and mass media and to indicate the possibility that things could be fundamentally different.

The Frankfurt School, however, did not share the faith of Lukács and Gramsci in the working class's revolutionary potential and their 'critical theory' eventually came to be conceived as simply denouncing the shallowness and emptiness of modern culture without any hope that it could be otherwise. In effect, Marx had been right in arguing that nothing less than the power of the massed working class would be sufficient to totally transform society in a new direction, so the realization that the working class had effectively been absorbed into capitalism meant that the dominance of that form of society was complete. There was no real internal challenge to it, *except for the critical complaints of a few intellectuals*, expressed in 'critical theory' itself or in the works of art which had not been neutered in the way in which the products of mass culture are.

By filling their bellies with food and their heads with 'mass culture', capitalism had made the workers irremediably contented, but this did not mean that the *bourgeois* class had therefore triumphed. Ironically, the process of rationalization had triumphed over *all* classes, and the process of extending scientific and technical control to all spheres of life had now acquired virtually a life of its own. Earlier the Frankfurt School had talked about the dominance of 'instrumental reason', but now they spoke of the dominance of the instrumental processes themselves, of the unstoppable movement of science and technology, resulting in the ever greater and more refined control of people. Control was now becoming an end in itself, rather than a means of providing one group with control over another.

In an important move, which certainly shapes much contemporary thinking, the Frankfurt School portrayed the development of control under capitalism as being a matter of the iron hand donning ever thicker velvet gloves. Control and oppression should be thought of not as an invariably direct and coercive means of making people do things they do not want to do, but rather as indirect and subtly persuasive ways of making people think that they want to do things that they would not otherwise do. Increasingly, the dominance of the system is gentle and seemingly friendly, moving Marcuse in the end to talk of 'repressive tolerance'. He claimed that the system controlled people by letting them do what they wanted to, by tolerating even attacks upon itself, and turning those into saleable and commercially profitable business, for example, his own book! The very title of Marcuse's book *One Dimensional Man* epitomizes his key idea, namely, the dominance of the *status quo* comes about through the creation both of a culture and also a people without depth: they are 'one-dimensional'. The book condenses the sense of utter hopelessness that the Frankfurt School felt in viewing the progress of technology and science as leading to the almost infinite development of Weber's process of rationalization. In the absence of a militant working class, there was no possibility of effective opposition to it.

Althusser against humanism

During the 1960s there came a reaction against this whole tendency in thinking about Marx, with Louis Althusser, the French theorectician, playing the centrol role. He condemned theorists like Lukács, Gramsci and the Frankfurt School for 'humanism'. For their part, they would concur they are rightly called 'humanist' but would deny that this is a charge one can be 'guilty' of. They sought to counterbalance accounts of Marx which made history seem like the product of the inexorable working of the influence of the economic base on the superstructure by emphasizing Marx's real understanding that human beings themselves make history and that what happens is ultimately up to people themselves. They tried to awaken people to the need to change history by making them conscious of the true nature of capitalism and sought to encourage them, where it looked realistic, to take charge of their own destiny and reshape the world they lived in.

Once again, the argument turns on the reading of Marx. Althusser makes much of the difference between the 'young' and the 'old' Marx. We have described the late work, *Capital*, as a volume of unrelenting economic analysis, very different from the much more philosophical early writings, explicitly avowing arguments akin to those of, for example, Lukács. Lukács argues for a continuity in Marx's thought, saying that no matter how different *Capital* may look from the early philosophical scripts, there is an essential continuity of theme. Althusser denies this argument.

There is, he says, a decisive break between the early and late works. The former are contaminated by an ideology – humanism – which the later Marx decisively rejects. The difference between the early and late work is that between ideology and science. In *Capital* Marx is developing a science (one fit to stand comparison with those created by Galileo or Charles Darwin) which is a science of 'the social formation', that is *the socio-economic whole*. It is not a science of 'the subject'. 'The subject', which Lukács, Gramsci and their like have put at the centre of their attention, is itself an ideological creation. The purpose of Marx's later theory, according to Althusser, is to expose the ideological nature of the concept 'subject', not to put it at the centre of his science.

It is vital to differentiate between 'the individual' and 'the subject' in order to understand Althusser. That they seem to be one and the same thing results from our being under the influence of ideology.

No one is going to suggest that the individual, in the sense of the individual physical being, is an ideological invention, but Althusser is saying that the way we think of a human being as 'a subject' *is* such an invention. For Althusser, the invention of ourselves as 'concrete, individual, distinguishable and (naturally) irreplaceable' (1971, p. 162) beings, of ourselves as people who form our own ideas and who act on the basis of these ideas is to think of human beings in *the ideological category of 'subjects'*. This idea that people have of themselves as 'subjects' is instilled in them by the ideological apparatus of society. To interpret Marx as if he were saying that society is the creation of subjects turns his arguments upside down, for what he saw was that 'the subject' is the creation of society.

Althusser's argument on ideology differs from one usually attributed to Marx. It is thought that ideology consists of false ideas, and that these false ideas are made necessary by the class-divided, exploitative nature of society, so that ideology would disappear with the abolition of societies organized in this way. Althusser does not think that this will occur. He does not think that the category of 'the subject', though ideological, is one which will be or can be abolished. If readers are struggling to see how they could dispense with thinking about themselves as subjects and finding it impossible, they can give up trying, for Althusser does not suggest that it is possible to do so.

We give this particular argument from Althusser considerable attention because it combines with others from quite different origins to provide one of the most distinctive features of recent French theorizing, namely an almost concerted 'attack on the subject'. We shall have much to say about it in the section on structuralism and post-structuralism. Because of this convergence, Althusser has often been counted as a 'structuralist' although he clearly dissociates himself from this movement.

Althusser's own account of Marx is meant to retain the 'base/ superstructure' idea, which he treats as a useful metaphor. However, he does not intend that we should revert to the simple, mechanical conception of the economic order as directly dictating the shape of the other institutions of society, the sort of conception that Lukács, Gramsci and the Frankfurt School had also tried to get away from. We need to recognize that the social whole is a complex structure made up of parts to some substantial extent independent of one another. Engels had explicitly made this point, acknowledging that only 'in the last analysis' does the economic base exercise a determining influence on other features of society. This idea Althusser intends to retain, and therefore also speaks of the economic structure as determinant in the last instance.

The economic structure is no longer seen by him as a straightforward determinant of the organization of society. Because economic organization dominates everything else in society, all social organization no longer has to be examined simply in terms of its relation to economic organization and activities. For Althusser suggests another part of the social structure may be dominant. He draws a distinction between that structure (the economy) which is *determinant* (in the last instance) of features of the organization of the socioeconomic whole, and that structure which is, in any given historical context, the one which actually dominates the society, which he calls 'the structure-in-dominance'.

In nineteenth-century capitalism, where the class of industrial property owners were very powerful in society and could dominate even those with political power, the economic base might well be seen as dominant. In modern capitalism, though, it seems that the political sector is dominant over the economy, for the state controls and intervenes in economic activity. In medieval society, by contrast, religion, or at least the church, had a dominant position *vis-à-vis* both economic and political organization. Thus the structure 'in dominance' varies from society to society, but the role of the economy as 'determinant in the last instance' is preserved since the form of economic activity determines the possibilities for which particular other structures can be dominant. For example, it is the advanced state of capitalist economic organization which allows the state to assume its currently dominant role.

The role of the state, Althusser goes on, is to secure the reproduction of the conditions of capitalist production, to ensure those circumstances in which there will be no disruption of capitalist activity. This role has two elements, much the same as those identified by Gramsci. Firstly, the role of the state as we would ordinarily think of it (that is, government, the law, the police, prisons and military) is seen by 'classic Marxism', as Althusser dubs it, to be essentially a repressive organization, designed to contain and subdue any opposition to capitalism. Consent, however, has to be gained: people are not just made into 'subjects', but into *willing* 'subjects' of capitalism. Such people do not oppose it; their consent is ensured through what he calls 'the ideological state apparatus'. This apparatus includes a whole range of institutions, such as religious and educational organizations, trade unions, political parties, the media and culture. Though we would think of these institutions as private, for Althusser they are counted as part of the *state* apparatus. He can do so because he views the distinction between 'private' and 'public' (for we would normally count the state as 'public') as created by capitalist ideology, not meriting respect from Marxist analysis. As the state itself (that is, the government, civil service, military) is a unified, centrally directed entity, it is easy to see why the whole repressive apparatus works together. The range of organizations making up 'the ideological apparatus', on the other hand, is heterogeneous, comprised of organizations which are formally independent of each other. Nevertheless, they work together because they are unified at the ideological level, they are all under the sway of the one ruling ideology.

He takes the argument a step further. Just as we expect the identity of the 'structure in dominance' to vary from society to society, so we may expect to find that there is, in any society, a dominant sector of the ideological apparatus, and that its identity will vary from society to society. In our society, it is the educational sector which plays the dominant ideological role (not, as we might think, the ideology of democratic government). This sector essentially prepares the young for a compliant role in productive activity, equipping them with the knowledge to do the relevant work and with attitudes making them accept authority.

Habermas and the legacy of the Frankfurt School

Jurgen Habermas has been working (also since the 1960s) on an elaborate re-examination and synthesis of social thought which was framed within the conception of critical theory developed by the Frankfurt School. He attempts, however, to escape from the pessimistic conclusions they had reached about the inexorable dominance of instrumental reason. Remember, the essential problem for the Frankfurt School was that, far from being the revolutionary vehicle of emancipation, Marx's working class had become irremediably co-opted into modern society. Further, there was no alternative source from which general emancipation might be sought. Habermas is more optimistic. He seeks at the very least to emancipate reason from the domination of instrumental concerns and suggests that possibilities for the further development of human freedom are built into the organization of social life. To arrive at these conclusions, however, requires him to revise Marx's arguments. These revisions go beyond arguments about the nature and role of the working class and concern the general understanding of social life and historical development, to the extent that many commentators think he has essentially moved away from Marxism altogether.

Habermas's theories are essentially a composite of ideas drawn from a vast mutiplicity of other sources, in the fields of social theory, linguistics, philosophy and psychology. In his case, more than most of those theorists we have been discussing, we must therefore reduce and simplify an elaborate and enormously eclectic argument. Again we draw on Thomas McCarthy, who clearly and concisely indicates some of the key elements in Habermas work:

> [the] program represents an attempt to integrate basic categories and assumptions of action theory (meaning and intentionality, roles and norms, rules and standards) with elements of functionalist systems theory (structure and function, system and process, differentiation and adaptation, and so forth). The framework in which this is accomplished has the form of a theory of social evolution inspired by Marx's materialism. (McCarthy, 1978, p. 223)

To these elements McCarthy further adds 'structuralism' (which we discuss on pp. 128–131) and Jean Piaget's developmental psychology. Habermas wants to follow Marx in giving an account of the history of society as a process of development, that is, one in which things get better in the sense that societies become more complex and better adapted. Marx certainly sees society as developing in this sense; for him, capitalism is altogether more effective in organizing economic production than its predecessors. However, Marx puts the growth of economic production at the centre of his conception of social development, whereas Habermas has moved it from this key position, seeing the growth of society's adaptability as a matter of learning and thus of the accumulation of knowledge. Here he draws on Jean Piaget, who has conceived the growth in the mental processes of the individual child as a sequence of stages of increasing complexity and adaptability. Piaget's version of individual development can therefore be used as a model for the growth of society's knowledge. This knowledge is therefore also seen to develop through a series of increasingly complex stages which enhance the adaptability of the system. (Parallels with Parsons's conception of social change may also be noted.)

Habermas argues that the pessimism of the Frankfurt School is a result of their limited conception of the way that knowledge is connected with human interests. Following Marx, they have seen two main kinds of interest. Firstly, instrumental interest, the concern with the domination of nature for the purpose of satisfying material needs. This interest also involves the domination of people in order to organize them into the required economic activity. Secondly, the emancipatory interest, the desire to be freed of all oppression, which was expressed in critical thinking. The Frankfurt School thought that the emancipatory interest was effectively neutralized by the triumph of instrumental reason. There is, however, a third interest, the interest human beings have in understanding one another, in intelligibly communicating with one another. Habermas argues that this interest has not been effectively recognized and puts it at the centre of his own analysis. By so doing he gives his critics a major reason for seeing him to have abandoned Marx altogether. For Marx had made economic production the core of social organization; to give 'communication' this role calls for a major shift in thinking about the social world.

By making this shift, however, Habermas is able to argue that there is hope for a greater role for rationality (i.e. reason) in society. Instead of examining the problem relative to the co-option of the working class by capitalism, he explains it in terms of the decline of the sphere of 'public life' in capitalist society, in other words the restriction of democracy.

The triumph of instrumental reason and technological organization has meant that decision-making has increasingly fallen into the hands of experts. Thus the public at large cannot have an effective say, even though they are ostensibly in control through parliaments and elections. These are side-shows. Yet, he feels, there is built into the very process of communication a demand for greater freedom and democracy.

Habermas gives communication the central place by construing rationality and truth as phenomena of communication. He argues that truth is really a matter of agreement. We arrive at the truth by discussion, by argument amongst ourselves. We agree that something is the truth because we are convinced by argument, by what we all accept as the best argument. Of course, this process can only apply when argument proceeds with complete freedom, thereby allowing all the necessary intellectual exploration, letting all contribute as equal participants. Habermas maintains that this process does not operate in societies like ours where communication is 'sytematically distorted', where there are all kinds of constraints not only upon what we can say but even on what we can possibly *think* (because of ideological influences). Discourse does not proceed without interference and control and people are by no means counted as equal participants in debate in a society permeated by inequalities. Consequently, in societies like ours, communication has built into it a discrepancy between those conditions required for the full excercise of reason and the reaching of truth, and those which govern how we actually talk to one another. The obvious implication is that we will want to move from the actual to the ideal conditions. In many ways, it calls for further realization of the ideal of democracy by creating an effective public whose free discussion is neither institutionally constrained nor subverted by the handing over of power to administrators and technocrats.

Unlike the Marxists, Habermas does not propose the working class as the force that will produce social change. Indeed, the Marxists challenge him to nominate which groups in society will provide the energy necessary to transform society in these emancipatory ways. He does not have a direct answer, not being able to single out a specific agency which might realistically look as though it could produce some change. Instead he attempts to provide a partial counter to the criticism by analysing advanced capitalism to show that it is still subject to profound crisis, that it has chronic problems in legitimating its order and existence.

Ironically, the very process of rationalization itself is creating these problems for capitalism. The extensive intervention of the state and the administrative regulation of more and more areas of social life may extend control, but at the same time the traditional bases upon which the legitimacy of the *status quo* has rested are also disturbed and even destroyed. There are, then, possibilities for 'legitimation crises' which might well focus upon the fact that the advanced capitalist system generates inequality but has only rather tenuous legitimations for it. Further, there may also be 'rationality crises', resulting from the fact that the state, required to regulate the economy in order to sustain economic growth, will intervene more and more extensively in economic and social organization, thereby becoming overburdened and incapable of satisfying all the different demands people make on it. Consequently, there will be dissatisfaction because the state is not providing what people want from it. In short, the state may be extending control in some ways, but at the same time it is creating questions about its own legitimacy.

Structuralism and post-structuralism

So far our use of the concept of 'structuralism' has referred to how the organization of the whole society shapes or structures individual behaviour. Now we turn to a different though associated meaning deriving from the work of Claude Lévi-Strauss, who sees individual behaviour as shaped, albeit unconsciously, by underlying structures of language and meaning. This approach too has come to be called 'structuralism'.

By putting 'communication' at the centre of his scheme, Habermas reflects a strong tendency in modern social thought, which is to give a prominent place to the role of language – a point which will come over strongly in the next chapter on interactionism. In order to see something of the origins of this tendency in European theorizing it is necessary to step back in time to the period around the First World War and sideways in terms of disciplines to linguistics.

Ferdinand de Saussure (1857–1913) made a key move toward this different sense of structuralism with his distinction between *parole* (or speech) and *langue* (or the language system). He declared that *langue*, not *parole*, is the object of scientific linguistic study. The language system is a system of signs. The key question is one of meaning. How do signs get their meaning? A common answer is that signs get their meaning through what they stand for, therefore encouraging us to try to see how a given sign (word) means what it does by seeing how it relates to what it stands for. Saussure takes two steps away from this position:

(1) The sign gets its meaning from and within the system, so we seek to understand how it does so by looking at its relation to the rest of the system.
(2) The sign gets its meaning within the system from the ways it *contrasts* with other signs in the system.

The important consideration in the language system is difference, so much so that we can think of a language as a system of differences. For a simple example, consider the level of sound, and the words 'bat', 'pat', 'cat', 'hat'. These words mean different things and are only different words because of the different initial sound, the *b*, *p*, *c* and *h*.

The success of this idea in linguistics led to its adaptation into social anthropology.

Lévi-Strauss and myth

The French anthropologist Claude Lévi-Strauss argued that the method of thinking of things as systems of differences could be applied generally to social phenomena. He applied it particularly to the study of myths, arguing that stories which appeared quite unintelligible to us could be shown to make sense and to have a rigorous order. Myths feature human beings, supernatural beings and talking animals as characters and involve such events as people being taken to the equivalent of heaven or hell and them being cursed, and so on. Superficially, the sequence of events in these stories look quite arbitrary, but Lévi-Strauss claimed that if we think of the characters and events in terms of contrasts, of opposites, then there appears much greater order, one which is almost mathematical. For example, the characters in the myth may be classified as, amongst other things, natural and supernatural, human and animal, male and female, living and dead, old and young. Thinking of them in terms of such pairings reveals that these pairs are comprised of contrasting, 'opposed' elements. Similarly, the events in the stories should also be examined in terms of the more abstract categories they exemplify. For example, journeys involve movements and movement too is conceived in contrastive ways: North and South, up and down, to heaven/to hell, away from home/back to home, into the sky/under the ground. The analysis of the characters and events of myth stories into often intricate patterns of contrasting pairs shows an order through which all kinds of intellectual problems are being worked out. The myths are vehicles of systematic thinking.

Underlying an immense amount of Lévi-Strauss's work on myth is the assumption that the contrast natural/cultural is fundamental and problematic. Although human beings are natural creatures like other animals, in other respects they are not natural, but cultural creatures. Being both natural and not natural (cultural) creates a kind of perennial puzzle which human thought tries to resolve, apparently because we want to be either natural or cultural. Clearly, these are *opposed* categories – that which is natural is not cultural, the cultural is not natural. The display and attempted resolution of this puzzle can be found to play a fundamental role in the organization of myths.

In a way, myths are only a stalking horse for Lévi-Strauss's real topic, the nature of the human mind. The myths he examines are taken from societies which are supposedly 'simpler' than our own, from among people who are often thought incapable of thinking with our intelligence and sophistication. Lévi-Strauss says that the difference between us and 'primitives' is entirely superficial. The human mind is everywhere the same because the human brain (like a computer) operates through 'binary oppositions', that is, contrasts. 'Primitive thought', like myth, is every bit as sophisticated, complex and *intellectual* as our own, though it expresses itself in different ways.

Two big possibilities arise. Firstly, social phenomena in general can be regarded as phenomena of communication, involving the organization of systems of signs, that is, the *structure* of language and meanings, that, as we shall see, 'shape up' the actions of individuals – hence the label 'structuralism'. Lévi-Strauss himself argues that 'primitive' kinship systems, a perennial puzzle for anthropologists, could be better understood if they were taken as ways of sending 'messages' between social groups. For example, the incest taboo, the prohibition on sexual relations with close kin. He says, 'The prohibition of incest is less a rule prohibiting marriage with the mother, sister or daughter, than a rule obliging the mother, sister or daughter to be given to others. It is the supreme rule of the gift' (Lévi-Strauss, 1969, p. 481).

In other words, the fact that women cannot marry inside their kinship group means they must marry into another one, and are therefore circulated between groups of men. They are effectively gifts passing between such groups. Readers will readily appreciate that gifts are means by which we express ourselves to others, send messages to them about how we feel towards them. Thus, Lévi-Strauss is proposing that the organization of kinship can be understood in terms of communication. This possibility of looking at social relations in terms of the sending of messages was further elaborated by Roland Barthes, Lévi-Strauss's compatriot, who tried to show that all kinds of socio-cultural phenomena, from magazine photographs to wrestling, could be analysed as systems of signs, transmitting myth-like statements about our own society.

The second possibility arising from Lévi-Strauss's analysis of myths is the further erosion of the importance of 'the subject'. Descartes had pictured the formation of knowledge as the production of the isolated, individual mind, and assumptions of the same sort have underpinned theories of meaning. We think of ourselves, as individuals, as the ones who give meanings to our own words. Yet we are not, if conceptions like those of Lévi-Strauss are right, the source of meaning, for the meaning comes from the language system. Thus the linguistic system works through us in ways of which we are not conscious rather than it being something over which we have conscious control. Lévi-Strauss explicitly made the point that he saw the workings of the human mind as proceeding unbeknown to us individuals. The generalization of these structuralist ideas of social life as a collection of 'languages' opens up the idea that all systems of meanings may be 'working behind our backs' and we therefore do not realize what the things we are saying truly mean. Our individual consciousness is virtually irrelevant to an understanding of socially and culturally organized phenomena; it is perhaps little more than a by-product of the working of these systems of signs.

Although structuralist ideas enjoyed an immense vogue, quite quickly dissatisfactions arose amongst those who thought they did not go far enough and soon there was talk of 'post-structuralism'.

Nietzsche's scepticism

The post-structuralists, though they do not entirely eschew Marx, for he is one of the three masters of suspicion, owe much more to another member of this trio, Friedrich Nietzsche. Nietzsche was utterly sceptical of all our pretensions to knowledge. He says that we cannot know reality through concepts and theories. To formulate his ideas he used a contrast between two figures from Greek mythology, Apollo and Dionysius. Dionysius, the god of wine, represents the powers of nature and is associated with those things which stir the emotional and undisciplined side of humans. Apollo stands for civilization, the essence of which, of course, is law and order, containing and disciplining the spontaneity of human nature. Human life thus involves tension between its Dionysian and Apollonian aspects. In connection with the life of the mind, concepts and theories play the role of law and order, attempting to impose shape and discipline on things. We think that our concepts and theories enable us to know reality because they bring out the organization inherent in it. But, argues Nietzsche, it may not be so much a matter of bringing out what is in reality as of projecting on to it our own needs for things to have form and be controlled. In other words, our theoretical schemes may be impositions upon reality; they attempt to discipline and control its unruly ways just as laws are imposed upon individuals in order to control their disruptive dispositions. This imposition, then, does not originate in an idealistic desire to know reality, but in something rather more disreputable, the drive to dominate and control nature and one another, a 'will to power'.

Such inspirations lead to the deepest scepticism about our systems of knowledge, including 'structuralism' as just one more of these in so far as it claims to gain knowledge of reality. The natural sciences, and more especially the humanities and social sciences, are not to be taken at face value in so far as they present themselves as the product of a disinterested search for knowledge, but should be examined for their connection with social power, the part they play in promoting domination. The post-structuralists, then, cannot be expected to be suitably respectful of the conventions of scholarly and scientific work, at least in so far as these are supposed to further the acquisition of knowledge, nor on their own behalf can they hope to add to our knowledge. They must, instead, intend to undermine and disrupt the whole quest for knowledge, to expose the way it is so thoroughly entangled with the business of domination, so pervaded by 'will to power', that knowledge and power are inextricable.

Foucault and knowledge

Michel Foucault (1926–84), one of the two most prominent post-structuralists came to talk of 'knowledge/power', to emphasize this intimate conjunction.

The structuralists were concerned to understand human conduct as a system primarily of communication, as a product of the working of the rules of that system. In consequence, they were not interested in the historical aspect of social life, treating the system as effectively timeless and unchanging. Out of their concern to map out the organization of the *system* of signs, the great emphasis was upon finding order and unity in the system. Further, by conceiving of social organization as a system of signs, the extent to which the organization of communication was set within a social organization was neglected, and the role of communication in the system was not examined. Foucault sought to reintroduce an historical emphasis into studies of language and idea systems and to do this at the expense of the idea of system. Structuralists were assuming systematic organization to the underlying structures which shape conduct, but were in fact overestimating the extent to which there is such basic coherence, as the historical investigation of the origins of modern arrangements makes plain, bringing out the discontinuities and incoherences which are present in them. In short, he saw the need to locate the communicational practices of people within specific institutional arrangements. These various moves, though deviating from structuralist assumptions, none the less pursued relentlessly the attack upon 'the subject'.

Foucault was dedicated to identifying the historical origins of the modern conception of the idea of the individual (particularly the individual mind) and he therefore analysed the formation of the various 'discourses' (ways of talking and thinking in, for example, medicine, psychiatry and linguistics) in which we express that conception. Given his presuppositions, this approach led him quite naturally into the study of the appearance, at the beginnings of our 'modern age', of various organisational forms, such as the clinic, the asylum and the prison. Any 'structuralist' suggestion that social organization originates in the system of meanings is here countered by the claim that the discourse, the organization of meaning, originates in historically quite specific social and organizational contexts. It is the clinic that makes medical ways of talking possible, not the other way round.

Foucault's work followed a varying line and we can only note one or two points from its course. An early study sought to show that reason, far from being intrinsically liberating, was itself rooted in oppression. The creation of our modern ideas of reason and of madness go hand in hand, for the identity of reason can only be achieved through contrast, by setting itself from unreason, that is, madness. In *Madness and Civilization* Foucault aims to show how the 'great incarceration', the locking up of the insane, effectively arose from the availability of the 'lazar houses' in Europe, places where lepers had been confined but which were now in disuse. This practice of physical exclusion broke the more humane relations that had hitherto obtained between the insane and the rest of the community. Reason originates in domination, for its development in Europe demanded the repression of its opposite, unreason.

The production of places of incarceration is a general characteristic of the development of our society, also illustrated by Foucault in *Discipline and Punish* on the emergence of the prison. He points out that the brutalization of the body, a traditional method of punishment, is being replaced by a general emphasis upon discipline exercised through the control of the mind. He highlights the ways in which the creation of the prison involves the production of settings in which constant surveillance is possible and argues that although physical control is important, even more important in our society is a concern to develop surveillance of what cannot physically be restrained, our thoughts. The prison is in many ways a metaphor for modern society itself, a place in which we are all surveyed and controlled (by police, psychiatrists, teachers, doctors and social workers). Later work, especially *The History of Sexuality*, further specifies this theme. Though he himself had tended to characterize power as repressive, we must not go on doing so, says Foucault. We have to recognize that power is 'productive'. By contrast, we normally think of power as working through repression. We think of the Victorians as trying to control sex by refusing even to mention it, suppressing it into total silence. By comparison, we think of ourselves as free and without repression because we can speak about sex, but this freedom does not mean we are not, in this connection, subject to power. For Foucault suggests that our talking about sex is not a sign of our freedom but rather a result of the fact that we are compelled to talk about it. Our civilization *demands* of us that we talk ceaselessly about sex. Thus power has 'produced' a vast discourse on sexuality and thereby extended its hold over us even further for, as indicated, thorough going control requires access to our thoughts. If we do not voice them, if we keep them to ourselves, if we keep sex private, we escape the reach of power. If, however, we are compelled to talk about sex, then we make it public and so amenable to surveillance and regulation.

Note that we say that 'power extends its hold' for Foucault wants to impress upon us that power is virtually an autonomous force. It is certainly wrong to think of power as the means by which one social group controls others in its own interests, for we are all of us effectively in the control of power itself. Actions of ours which may be intended to be helpful and liberating, like the creation of social workers, for example, unwittingly extend the hold of power to the farthest corners of social life, for we are licensing social workers to investigate and supervise the lives of those they supposedly help.

Though Foucault is not necessarily consistent on the point, his work does strongly imply that the apparatus of science and scholarship is pointless and inevitably ineffective, for we cannot know reality through our concepts and the theories they make up. The search for truth has been self-deluding; far from making us more capable of controlling our destiny it has only changed the nature of our imprisonment, binding us more tightly within an ever more elaborate and subtle system of control. Yet, though Foucault may not believe in them, he still retains the trappings of scholarly investigation, whereas his fellow post-structuralist, Jacques Derrida, makes mock of them and is willing to play havoc with academic convention. Derrida goes even further than Foucault in unravelling our usual ideas of meaning and truth.

Derrida and writing

Jacques Derrida's ideas are far more problematic than any of the others we have dealt with in trying to produce a simple and clear summary, not least because they are designed to resist such treatment! Indeed, Derrida's aim is to avoid producing any concepts or theories, and those that he does spawn have no more than 'throw away' status. If our concepts do not help us know reality, then there is no point in producing them and building them into systems. Derrida, therefore, tries to provide us with a method, known as 'deconstruction', which will make us aware of the delusory nature of our attempts to come to any unified understanding of things.

Derrida attacks the whole Western tradition of philosophy. Structuralism is not excused, being seen as a late manifestation of this tradition, breaking with it to some extent, but incapable of giving up entirely some of its key assumptions. Centrally, his argument is with the view this tradition of philosophy has taken of language. This tradition looked upon language as potentially a servant of thought and as an instrument in the acquisition of knowledge. Yet language is not unqualifiedly suitable for these tasks, being usually conceived as insufficiently controlled and needing to be disciplined before it can be of proper use in the quest for knowledge. For example, philosophers usually make a contrast between the philosophical and the literary (though Nietzsche did not). Literary writing is treated as a collection of misleading tricks and philosophers are therefore required to purge their writing of literary devices and effects. Derrida completely rejects this approach, showing that the distinction between literary and philosophical writing will not hold up, that philosophy itself is thoroughly literary.

The philosophical tradition has, therefore, been concerned with working out how the subject can master language. To some extent the structuralists have undermined this project, by showing that the language system, rather than the subject, produces meaning. However, the structuralists have themselves tried to treat meaning as something that they can master by means of their theory of language as oppositions; they themselves have been concerned to use language as an instrument of knowledge. Derrida wants to take the view that the language produces meaning to the end of the line, so to speak. He argues that language always has the capacity to produce meaning in ways that writers and speakers cannot control. The role of his 'deconstructive' procedures is to show how attempts to impose coherence on our discourse are destined to be self-defeating. An application of them can be found, for example, in his treatment of the 'logic of the supplement'. Writers frequently make distinctions between the authentic thing and something else, which is its pale shadow, a mere supplement to the real thing. Saussure does this with speech, which is the real thing, and writing, which is the supplement, and in Jean-Jacques Rousseau's work Derrida finds masturbation being treated as the substitute for, the supplement to, sexuality. Derrida argues that the writing of Saussure and Rousseau shows that these distinctions and relations cannot be sustained. In the case of sexuality and masturbation the separation between them breaks down, and the relation of dominance between them also shifts, so that sexuality is virtually a form of masturbation. By simultaneously reversing and collapsing the seeming distinction between sex and masturbation Derrida is alluding to the inherent instability of all oppositions, whereas structuralism had, of course, assumed their fundamental, fixed and stable nature.

One of Derrida's targets is the attempt of literary criticism to look for a unified organization within writings, to look for a coherence of theme and design which co-ordinates all the apsects of the work. Derrida's method highlights the way in which literary texts defy this kind of treatment. He brings out the extent to which their organization is discontinuous and fragmented, with different aspects working against one another rather than contributing to some single theme. The critics' attempts to impose unity upon a text can themselves be treated in a deconstructive fashion, for they too will contain possibilities of internal disunity and self-contradiction. By attempting to overcome this problem, the critics simply reproduce the very difficulties they are trying to eliminate. Hence the dismantling of the pretensions to rigorous coherence of any text or system of thought can go on for ever, so that the main ambition of our Western tradition of thought, to know reality through language, is shown to be quite futile. The only lesson to emerge is that language is too versatile and elusive ever to be brought within the confines of our schemes. If taken seriously, the upshot of Derrida's argument is in marking out a major change in the use of language: not to speak about reality, but rather to use it for its own sake, revelling in the multifarious possibilities of meaning it provides. One very visible expression of this viewpoint is in rejecting the attempt to make a distinction between literary writing on the one hand and philosophical or sociological writing on the other, thereby freeing the academic writer to use all the devices available to the novellist. Indeed, the extensive first part of Derrida's own *The Post Card from Socrates to Freud* consists of what might well be an epistolary novel. Whereas the Western tradition sought to arrive at truth through the eradication of uncertainty and equivocality, the post-structuralist movement multiplies and re-lishes these. Consequently, we only say that the first part of *The Post Card might* be a novel!

A note on post-modernism

Arguments like Foucault's, and even more so Derrida's, are taken by some as signalling a major social change, and certainly their arguments do involve the wholesale rejection of the 'project of modernity' as we identified it at the beginning of the chapter. If we are leaving the epoch dominated by the idea of modernity behind, we are entering a post-modern one. The Enlightenment idea promoted the idea that a coherent overall view of society, its history and its future prospects was possible, that a 'grand narrative' encompassing all could eventually be composed. Over the greater part of this century, however, that expectation has disintegrated and scepticism about the possibility of any single tale giving the whole story has mounted. Derrida's deconstructionist line takes this scepticism perhaps as far as it can go.

The question is, what kind of change is this? Naturally there is disagreement. Frederic Jameson (1984), for example, sees more continuity than change here, whereas Jaques Lyotard (1984) thinks we are entering into an unprecedented social condition which is affecting the whole nature of our knowledge. The way in which Derrida's techniques serve to collapse accepted distinctions reflects the way in which the boundaries between academic disciplines are imploding, for example, between philosophy, sociology and literary criticism, and between these and literature itself. In its turn, this feature is part of a more general pattern of social change in which the boundaries between different areas of life are being liquidated. These changes, for Lyotard at least, are the product of the information society, of computers and other new technology and their use in re-organizing social relations. Jameson, who has Marxist leanings, sees what is happening as 'the cultural logic of late capitalism', the latest stage of the continuing process – now more than two centuries old – through which capitalism transforms all relations into relations of commercial exchange, even those of information and knowledge.

Conclusion

A main aim of this chapter has been to explain the change in the nature of much criticism of modern (or capitalist) society, which, though often having Marxist roots, is no longer so prominently concerned with economic exploitation and injustice. The criticism is more frequently concerned with the role of (in Marxist terms) superstructural elements and particularly cultural ones (such as music, literature and television) in creating ideological illusions and contributing to the maintenance of an oppressive system. In the course of the discussion 'language' and 'meaning' have been introduced as central considerations and they assumed an increasingly larger role as the chapter went on. In this respect the work described in this chapter shares one characteristic with the approaches considered in the next chapter, and, more generally, with most social sciences and humanities in the second half of the twentieth century, the discovery of the importance of language.

Further reading

Althusser, L., *For Marx* (Allen Lane, 1969). Includes the essay 'Marxism and humanism'.

———, *Lenin and Philosophy* (New Left Books, 1971). Includes the essay 'Ideology and ideological state apparatuses'.

Bottomore, T., *The Frankfurt School* (Horwood, 1984). A concise account of the school.

Callinicos, A., *Althusser's Marxism* (Pluto, 1976).

Connerton, P., *The Tragedy of Enlightenment* (Cambridge University Press, 1982). Essay on the Frankfurt School.

Dreyfus, H., and Rainbow, P., *Michel Foucault* (Harvester, 1982). A clear discussion of his main ideas.

Femia, J., *Gramsci's Political Thought* (Oxford University Press, 1981).

Foucault, M., *Madness and Civilization* (Tavistock, 1971).

———, *History of Sexuality*, vol. 1 (Allen Lane, 1979).

Geuss, R., *The Idea of a Critical Theory* (Cambridge University Press, 1982). Short but exceptionally clear discussion and evaluation of the Frankfurt School and Habermas.

Habermas, J., *Communication and the Evolution of Society* (Heinemann, 1979.) Contains 'Legitimation problems in the modern state'.

———, *Toward a Rational Society* (Heinemann, 1971). Contains 'The scientization of politics and public opinion' and 'Technology and science as "ideology"'.

Lévi-Strauss, C., *Meaning and Myth* (Routledge, 1978). Very short account of his key ideas.

McCarthy, T., *The Critical Theory of Jurgen Habermas* (Hutchinson, 1978). A lengthy but clear account of the development of Habermas's thought up to the late 1970s.

Marcuse, H., *One Dimensional Man* (Routledge, 1964).

Norris, C., *Deconstruction* (Methuen, 1982). Concise introduction.

Sturrock, J., *Structuralism and Since* (Oxford University Press, 1979). Contains brief accounts of Lévi-Strauss, Barthes, Foucault and Derrida.

White, S., *The Recent Work of Jurgen Habermas* (Cambridge University Press, 1988). Updates the dicussion.

The Fontana Modern Masters Series has published short volumes on Derrida, Engels, Foucault, Gramsci, Lévi-Strauss, Marx, Marcuse, Nietzsche, Saussure and Weber.

Questions

1 What do you understand by 'anti-modernism'?
2 Why should the recognition of the unconscious mind be significant for thinking about society?
3 What does the thinking of Nietzsche, Freud and Marx appear to have in common?
4 Show your understanding of the following concepts: alienation, hegemony, instrumental reason. How are they linked?
5 How can tolerance be seen as 'repressive'?
6 Discuss the view that society produces the subject, not the subject society. Is this also Durkheim's view?
7 Does the notion of a 'structure in dominance' overcome the difficulties of economic determinism?
8 To what extent can it be argued that rationalization is the ultimate contradiction of capitalism.
9 'Humanism is not an ideal but a means of ideological control.' Explain and discuss.
10 'Better communication has replaced the working class as the major vehicle for social change.' Discuss with especial reference to the work of Habermas.
11 Outline Lévi-Strauss's basic structuralist ideas about the relation of language and society.
12 Evaluate Foucault's notion that 'reason is rooted in oppression' *or* his notion that 'power is productive'.
13 Does Derrida's deconstructionism mean the beginning or the end of illuminating thinking about society?
14 Of all the thinkers touched on in this chapter, which ones, in your opinion, have most significance? Why?
15 'Structuralism' has been used in two senses in this book. Can you trace any links between them?

5 Meaning and action: I, symbolic interactionism

Introduction

Over the past twenty years or so theoretical approaches in sociology have been roughly divisible into two types. These are referred to sometimes as 'macro' versus 'micro' approaches and sometimes, more accurately, as 'structural' versus 'action' approaches. As we have seen in the previous chapters, structural conceptions of social life, whether consensus or conflict in orientation, begin from the assumption that social behaviour is conditioned or shaped by forces which reside at the level of society as a whole. This concern with the whole society as the basic unit of analysis most clearly distinguishes structural approaches from action ones. Action theories do not view society as an entity which can be analysed independently of the actions which make it up. They do not regard these actions as things which can be explained sociologically in terms of 'needs', 'constraints' or 'contradictions' generated in and by the structure of society viewed as a whole. Instead, they point to the intimate connection between actions and meanings. 'Society' does not act, persons do. Actions have the essential property of meaning. What is being done, by whom and with what purpose are all matters which persons, 'social actors', make sense of in producing their own actions and in responding to the actions of others. From this point of view, then, meaning and understanding are not incidental to social life; they create or constitute it.

The concept of meaning marks a fundamental difference between structural and action approaches. Structural sociologies do not deny that the understandings actors possess can be important for explaining their response to their social circumstances. But for structuralists the key issue tends to' be how these 'subjective' understandings relate to and are shaped by the 'objective' meaning of those circumstances when viewed from a holistic standpoint.

Action theories, on the other hand, reject the notion that meanings and understandings can be treated as a set of dependent factors. Any adequate sociological analysis of social life must begin from 'the point of view of the actor', that is, the understandings that the participants in a social situation have of what the situation is and what their place is within it.

Weber: the action frame of reference

The basic ideas of 'the action frame of reference' originate from Max Weber. Weber argued that sociology could have no legitimate methodological foundation unless it grounded its methods in a clear conception of the relationship between meaning and action. He argued that every sociological description was 'interpretive' in character. If the interpretive dimension was not adequately recognized, sociological generalizations and causal explanations would be arbitrary and empty. The aim of Weber's methodological writings was to show how a sociology based on *verstehen* (understanding) could none the less meet the accepted canons (rules) of scientific explanation and objectivity. He believed that such a *'verstehende* sociology' involved the construction and use of 'ideal types'. These would form the bridge between subjective understanding and objective explanation.

An example of an ideal type is Weber's complex concept, the Protestant ethic (see Chapter 3). By 'ideal', Weber means a description which explicitly is constructed as an idealized, exaggerated picture of a phenomenon. This 'type' can then be used to make comparisons with what actually can be found in the real world. In this way, he hoped to be able to show causal connections, for example, between the Protestant ethic and the 'spirit of capitalism' (another ideal type), and hence to be able to propose general laws. These laws, identifying invariable causal connections, would be scientific *and* would build in the meanings social actors attribute to the phenomena being studied.

In this aim, Weber must be deemed to have failed. Sociologists who take seriously his emphasis on the centrality of meaning and understanding find major difficulties (some would say insurmountable difficulties) with the notion that sociological explanations should take the form of general laws. Conversely, those who accept the need for sociology to try to formulate such laws, based on 'objective' data, can only incorporate 'the actor's point of view' into their research in the most marginal ways.

As Weber's work indicates, many of the central concerns of action sociologies are methodological. They revolve around questions of how to conceive social life and social behaviour as interpretive phenomena and the methods appropriate to their study. As we shall see, it is hard to draw a line between 'theory' and 'method' in action approaches. The close ties between theoretical concepts and assumptions and the form of empirical investigations is a consistent theme. Thus Weber thought that the development of interpretive sociology involved beginning from a definition of the basic forms of action, working out what forms of relationships could be created out of such basic modes of action and, moving 'upwards', specifying all the forms of group association, organization and institution which could be compounded out of these relationships. In his view, even the most complex forms of social organization – the massive world civilizations – should be looked on by the sociologist only as a complex made up of relationships among its members. In these ways, Weber's theoretical conception of social life and his deductive, typologizing methodology – both focused upon individuals and meaning – were strongly connected.

Other action approaches: philosophical background

In sociology, Weber was a major pioneer of the action frame of reference as an approach to the study of social life. Many of the most influential ideas about the connections between meaning, understanding and action, however, have stemmed from philosophical critiques of the assumptions and methods of mainstream sociology. These critiques have influenced the formation and development of action approaches. The three most significant philosophical sources for such critiques are (*a*) the social behaviourism of G. H. Mead, (*b*) the phenomenology of Edmund Husserl, and (*c*) the analytic philosophy of Ludwig Wittgenstein. While the philosophical orientations of these writers is markedly different, the implications for sociological theories and methods that can be drawn from their works have certain common dimensions. The most important of these is the emphasis they place upon the role of *language* in social life. In so far as language is conceptualized at all in structuralist approaches, it is treated as just another 'factor' making up society. For action sociologies, language cannot adequately be conceived in this way. It is 'special', in that the very *social nature* of social life is constituted in and through language. Each of the philosophies referred to has stressed this view of language. Therefore, each has inspired attempts to rethink the foundations of sociological knowledge along lines very different from those of conventional 'scientific' sociology. In the course of these rethinkings, ncw methods and topics of investigation have emerged along with new concepts and theories.

Philosophical critiques of 'scientism' in sociology often centre around attacks upon behaviourism and causal explanation. In its extreme form, behaviourism holds that scientists must *only* study things which are movements of material bodies. They cannot deal with unobservable and intangible things like ideas and states of mind. Critics argue that in order to describe 'what people do', it is not adequate to describe them as though they were simply material bodies; adequate description *must* make reference to ideas and intentions. The difference between a 'twitch of the arm' and a 'friendly wave' does not reside in some difference in the movement of the arm but in the fact that in the case of the wave the movement is *meant* to signify recognition of another person. Without reference to thought and intention the wave is only a twitch.

Similarly, causal explanation is attacked for its inappropriateness as a way of conceiving human action. A commonly used example of causation is to explain the movement of one billiard ball as 'caused' by the impact of another. This model of causation may be perfectly adequate for the movement of billiard balls but is completely inadequate for human action. Pursuing ends, selecting means, shaping intentions, finding rules – none of these typical kinds of human actions is in the slightest like being propelled by an external force in the way in which the ball is moved.

Although they by no means encompass the whole range of action sociologies, there are two approaches that must be regarded as central to any account of the contemporary sociology of action. These are symbolic interactionism and ethnomethodology. We discuss symbolic interactionism in this chapter and ethnomethodology in the next.

Both symbolic interactionism and ethnomethodology are best understood as research traditions rather than as tightly bounded theories. Each encompaasses a range of empirical studies of various kinds. There are undoubted similarities between some kinds of work in both approaches. Also, there are some studies that are not easily classifiable as either 'symbolic interactionist' or 'ethnomethodological'. Partly for these reasons, new (and sometimes not so new) students to sociology can find it hard to see what differentiates them. Especially when viewed from the standpoint of structuralist sociology, they can appear to be saying and doing very similar things. Yet there are genuine differences which, while they might seem small from the 'outside', are actually very significant when viewed in relation to the aims of each approach. Therefore, we will postpone discussion of these differences until the conclusion of Chapter 6, after we have examined the two approaches.

Symbolic interactionism: introduction

In some ways it is strange to refer to symbolic interactionism as a theoretical perspective. To many sociologists, 'theory' means a systematic body of abstract concepts and propositions from which precise and testable predictions can be made (see Chapter 6). In these terms, symbolic interactionism is notable for its lack of integrated theory and its emphasis on the particular rather than the abstract and general. Indeed, many of those most often described as 'symbolic interactionists' eschew the label and prefer to define themselves simply as 'qualitative researchers'. Nevertheless, it is possible to identify a number of characteristics of the approach that make it distinctive. Chief among these are: (*a*) a commitment to a 'naturalistic' strategy of inquiry; (*b*) a view of social life as process rather than as structure or system; and, most centrally, (*c*) a concern with the construction and transmission of social meanings in and through individual and group interaction.

All these elements have their origin in ideas which emanated from the University of Chicago in the 1930s and 1940s. The principal source for these ideas was George Herbert Mead (1863–1931), who lectured in philosophy and social psychology at Chicago between 1894 and 1931. But others were important also. Herbert Blumer, who studied with Mead at Chicago, sought to show the relevance of Mead's teachings for sociology in a series of papers written over many years. Everett Hughes and his associates, again over a long period since the 1930s, and most frequently from Chicago, developed a style of empirical research which gave significance to these ideas.

Mead: the bases of symbolic interactionism

Mead's 'social behaviourism' was an attempt to rethink the nature of human behaviour in a way which avoided the 'dualism' which permeated conventional philosophical views. The dualist maintains that reality is composed of two realms of phenomena, the 'material' and the 'mental'. Mead rejected the notion that a sharp separation could be made between mind and nature. Instead of conceiving human nature as composed of body and mind, essentially different but *somehow* connected, Mead sought to explain mind as a natural phenomenon, produced by the same general processes as any other part of nature. Mead's approach to these questions was influenced by two very powerful sets of ideas. The first was evolutionary theory, stemming from Charles Darwin. The second was a philosophical theory of knowledge called pragmatism. From Darwin, Mead took the idea that more complex phenomena develop out of more simple ones, and that this evolutionary process of development can involve qualitative change of *type*. Pragmatism emphasized the ways in which knowledge is the product of human inquiry and therefore is conditioned by the problems that human beings address and the reasons they have for addressing them.

In rethinking mind as *part* of nature, Mead sought to show how mind emerged out of the development of behaviour. It is for this reason that he called his ideas 'social behaviourism'. Mead's use of this term should not be confused with the behaviourism of John B. Watson and B. F. Skinner. These psychologists argue that the requirements of scientific objectivity can only be met by expunging all reference to mental states from psychology, replacing these with terms which refer only to 'observable behaviour'. Far from regarding the mind as unobservable and intangible, Mead believed that the proper way to study mind was through behaviour. But what sorts of behaviour display mind? Here he made a distinction between animal *reaction* and human *conduct*. In his view, the life of most animal species is dominated by the stimulus–response relationship. This relationship involves an automatic association between the circumstances of behaviour and behaviour itself. When something happens, the animal automatically and invariably responds in a fixed way. The 'meaning' of a piece of animal behaviour thus is fixed by the stimulus which evokes it. In contrast, human conduct has a much greater degree of flexibility. Human beings can plan their conduct and reflect upon past situations in deciding the course of action they wish to take.

This reflective dimension of human conduct requires and displays the possession of mind. Further, Mead argues that mind is intimately tied to the possession of a *self*. If human beings are to anticipate the future, plan their actions and reflect upon past conduct, they must also be able to reflect upon themselves, to look at themselves in the same way as they look at any other object. It is this capacity for self-consciousness, for reflection upon themselves, which is the most distinctive characteristic of the human animal in Mead's account. Self-consciousness depends upon the ability of a human being to take the same attitude towards himself or herself as others take towards him or her. To be aware of oneself, in Mead's view, is to see oneself from the point of view of others.

Mead argues that the qualitative differences between human conduct and animal reaction do not mean that human social life is less amenable to scientific study than animal life. It can be studied like any other natural phenomenon, provided that we recognize its distinctive properties in the ways such studies are conducted. Mead was very firmly of the opinion that thought, consciousness and experience *must* be studied by any serious science of social life. It is a mistake to identify science with the material phenomena it usually studies; similarly, it is a mistake to identify it with specific methods or techniques devised to account for certain types of phenomena. For Mead, the hallmark of science is the public nature of its observations. Thus his account of human social life is built upon the observation of ordinary activities of daily life, upon publicly available and commonly observable facts that any of us might notice about our lives together. He uses such observations to construct an analysis of the development of mind and self.

Mead's approach is best illustrated by his analysis of the development of the child. In play, the young child engages in imitation of the behaviour he or she sees around him or her. He or she acts now like a postman, now a parent, now a policeman. This imitative play gradually develops into participation in games with others, where competent involvement demands more than just copying of behaviour. It requires that players appreciate the viewpoints of one another. Effective participation in the game requires each player to assess their circumstances, not only in terms of their own interests but relative to those of other players. In competitive games, for example, one can only hope to win if one attends to what others are doing and attempts to anticipate their moves. In doing so, one also attends to how one appears to them, since they too are trying to plan their moves in relation to their opponent, oneself.

For Mead, the transformation of the child, from a creature capable of engaging only in imitation to one manifesting the self-consciousness required by games, displays in microcosm the general process of human development. It is not only in games that human beings possess and display self-consciousness; they do so in all social activities. Of course, the individual cannot work out how he or she looks to each and every person in their social environment; the task is too complicated. Instead, the individual responds to the 'generalized other', that is, they respond to their sense of the general, typical and predominant views of themselves shown by others. This grasp upon the attitudes of others is made possible via the 'significant symbols' that persons share. Human language is made up of such symbols, and through them meaningful communication is achieved. Through communication with others, the individual comes to learn their views and attitudes and the ways of acting that are expected in a situation. Mead's account thus places language at the centre of any analysis of the development and organization of social life. This emphasis on language, as we shall see, runs through symbolic interactionism and ethnomethodology, as well as other contemporary sociologies of meaning and action.

Blumer: the methodology of symbolic interactionism

In following Mead, Herbert Blumer attacked 'scientism', that is, the modelling of sociological inquiry upon the specific procedures followed in the natural sciences. Blumer's arguments are fairly represented by his criticism of 'variable analysis' in his paper 'Sociological analysis and the variable' (Manis and Meltzer, 1967). Much research in the natural sciences is aimed at discovering how specific properties of phenomena are related. This involves treating the properties as variables and, using techniques of measurement, showing whether and how their respective magnitudes are associated. On the basis of such findings, the natural scientist tries to formulate laws describing the behaviour of the properties under study. For example, physicists propose laws about the relationship of pressure, temperature and volume of a gas; pressure, temperature and volume are all variables and all can be measured. Variable analysis in sociology adopts the same kinds of procedures with the aim of formulating the laws which govern the behaviour of 'social variables'.

Blumer calls this strategy, as it is used in sociology, 'so-called variable analysis'. In his view, the things it identifies are not clear and discrete 'objects' with the clearly and precisely defined properties that genuine variables should have. Instead, they are typically nothing more than 'abbreviated terms of reference' for complex patterns of social organization which the researcher has not described and, usually, cannot describe. They may be *called* 'variables' but, except in the barest manner, they do not express quantifiable relations between known dimensions of phenomena. Sociologists cannot say *exactly* what sorts of activities will, in any empirical case, be instances of such abstract categories as, for example, 'social cohesion', 'authority' or 'group morale'. Such expressions, according to Blumer, typically lack any fixed or uniform indicators across different occasions of their use. Consequently, any claim to be able to measure them is spurious.

Blumer's critique goes deeper than merely saying that measurement techniques in sociology are unreliable and frequently invalid. The basic problem comes from conceiving social life as an object for study appropriate for these techniques. Variable analysis seeks regular connections between variables, which it expresses in this way: change in one variable leads to change in another. The kind of understanding of the organization of social activity which this strategy involves essentially is a 'stimulus–response' one: stimulus leads to response. For Blumer, as for Mead, it is this conception of human conduct which is at fault. It may produce 'findings', but such findings give us no picture of the people to whom they refer *as human beings* in the world they inhabit. Because the self-conscious character of human beings is left out, variable analysis tells us nothing about how human beings *work* as interpretive social actors. The stimulus–response model emphasizes the primacy of external events; human actions are seen as relatively automatic responses to external stimuli. Blumer emphasizes that human beings can *initiate* lines of actions. Action can be both deliberative and creative. Not only can human beings *think* about what they are doing, making plans and revising them in the light of events, but also they are often engaged in 'putting together' their actions with those of others in order to attain desired ends.

As well as rejecting the idea that action may be treated as mere reaction, Blumer also attacks the treatment of social circumstances as stimuli. For human beings, circumstances do not exist 'in themselves' as stimuli to which we must react in the manner of a mindless, instinct-dominated organism. What 'the circumstances' are for an actor depends upon the plans, purposes and knowledge he possesses. For example, how one responds to rainfall differs according to whether one is a horticulturalist concerned for the welfare of one's crops or a holidaymaker in search of sunshine. The 'same' stimulus is different – blessing or curse – relative to one's purposes or preoccupations. In Blumer's view, both terms implied in the stimulus–response relationship are misleadingly invoked if they are extended to the systematic description of human action: circumstances are not mechanical stimuli, actions are not mere reactions.

In place of variable analysis, Blumer advocates a more 'naturalistic' approach to research. Social life is enormously complex, made up of elaborate and multifarious processes about which sociology has only the sketchiest knowledge. In these circumstances little is to be gained by pursuing the examples set by other, more developed sciences. A better strategy is to seek to learn about the complexities of social life through careful and detailed studies of particular situations and settings. Instead of beginning with abstractly defined concepts, research should start by learning at first hand about the ways such situations are experienced by those involved in them. In so far as technical concepts arc used at all, they should be regarded as 'sensitizing concepts', that is, general ideas which suggest aspects of a situation that may be of sociological interest. Sociology's methods should recognize and take account of the vague state of its theoretical knowledge. Precise knowledge, Blumer emphasizes, is the *goal* of empirical inquiry, not a precondition for it.

Blumer's writings provide a methodological framework for symbolic interactionist studies, but they provide the researcher with no specific guidance as to the manner, aims and techniques of work in the field. They offer no 'blueprint' for how to do studies. This 'lack' is a deliberate one. For Blumer, such matters cannot be settled in advance of actual empirical investigations. The development of empirical methods, and the advancement of theory, both are best achieved through the conduct of studies.

Symbolic interactionism as research

The fieldwork tradition

In the view of many, including some critics, the major contribution that symbolic interactionism has made to sociology is found in the great quantity and variety of studies it has produced of particular activities and ways of life in modern society. These 'ethnographic' studies are based on first-hand involvement of the researcher with the people he is studying and form a distinctive research tradition in sociology. The principal, though by no means the only, technique which is used in such studies is participant observation. However, it is not the use of this (or any other) technique *in itself* which gives such studies their symbolic interactionist character. Participant observation, after all, has long been the predominant research technique in social anthropology, yet the theoretical perspective with which it was most closely associated there was structural–functionalism. The pioneer and first champion of the fieldwork method was the arch–functionalist, Bronislaw Malinowski. What is it, then, that gives interactionist ethnographies their distinctive character? The symbolic interactionist orientation of ethnographic studies is manifested in a number of common themes that can be distinguished in them. The main ones are: (*a*) a concern with 'the actor's point of view'; (*b*) an emphasis upon process rather than structure or system; and (*c*) a preference for formal generalizations.

The actor's point of view

At the heart of symbolic interactionist inquiry is the assumption that social life is characterized by a multiplicity of points of view. How any aspect of social life is perceived and understood depends upon the standpoint from which it is viewed. Therefore there is no one 'ultimately correct' description to be given of any social situation. Most often sociology tends to take a holistic point of view, describing situations from the standpoint of the society conceived as a whole. By contrast, symbolic interactionists adopt a 'ground level' perspective, seeking to view situations as they appear to those directly involved in them. In so doing they are less interested in asking whether actors' understandings are 'correct' or 'justified' and much more interested in trying to appreciate *how and why* actors perceive things in the ways they do. The researcher tries to avoid making 'external' judgements about the people he or she studies. Instead, he or she tries to describe their circumstances and actions as *they* see them.

The rationale for this strategy is expressed in W. I. Thomas's frequently cited slogan: 'If men define situations as real, they are real in their consequences.' In other words, it is the meanings actors give to their circumstances which are central to any explanation of why they act as they do. These meanings may seem puzzling, arbitrary or biased if viewed from the 'outside'. But symbolic interactionists propose that such meanings, if looked at in relation to the particular circumstances in which actors find themselves, can often be seen to fit with those circumstances in previously unsuspected ways.

One consequence of this approach is that symbolic interactionist studies often demonstrate 'rationality' in what appear to be irrational beliefs and activities. A good example is John Lofland's study of a small religious sect in California in the 1960s, *Doomsday Cult* (Prentice Hall, 1977). The beliefs of 'The Divine Precepts' centred around the idea that at a given date in the near future the entire world order, and most of the world's population, would be destroyed, to make way for a 'new order'. The only survivors of this transformation would be a specified number of persons in each country who had accepted the Divine Precepts – the principles upon which the new order would be based. The group Lofland studied was the American branch of this (would be) world-wide movement. It was charged with the task of producing 144,000 converts. Since during the two years Lofland spent with them the group never numbered more than about twenty persons, it can be seen that their task was formidable.

The group had a sacred duty to carry knowledge of the Divine Precepts to as many persons as possible. Yet, from the standpoint of most of those they came into contact with in the course of their proselytizing activities, they were defined as 'cranks' and 'crazies'. Somehow this 'resistance' to their ideas had to be overcome. Lofland describes the activities of the group and the relationships of the members within it in terms of the ways in which this problem was handled. Far from being 'irrational' and 'crazy', the group tackled the problem by means of courses of action that, *given their beliefs*, had a rational character. For example, the group operated with a 'means–ends' principle of organization. They tried a large number of different proselytizing methods, evaluating each one in terms of its effectiveness in gaining recruits. Strategies that were deemed 'unsuccessful' (as most were) were abandoned and new ones sought. This means–ends rationality meant that some of the ways the group went about publicizing their ideas only contributed to judgements of 'nuttiness' by non-believers. For example, one tactic the group tried, in order to reach as many people as possible with their message, was to tour the streets in a loudspeaker van broadcasting extracts from the Divine Precepts and announcing their meetings. This method was abandoned when it was found that the one or two persons it attracted were more interested in the 'eccentricity' of the group than in its religious message.

Lofland shows, therefore, that there is an unrecognized rationality in the activities of those who hold 'bizarre' religious beliefs. Edwin Lemert and Erving Goffman have both made similar kinds of observations about the activities of persons deemed to be mentally ill. The very behaviour perceived by 'normals' (including psychiatric professionals) as displaying an abnormal mental condition can be seen to comprise rational responses to the situation the individual has found themselves in, if looked at independently of the assumption of 'illness'.

Such observations have led symbolic interactionists to be accused of bias towards 'underdogs'. Many studies have been sympathetic to the views of those low down in organizational and social hierarchies and critical of those who are better placed. For example, one of the most notable areas of symbolic interactionist inquiry has been the sociology of deviance. By contrast with sociological approaches that (implicitly) accept official conceptions of deviant groups as immoral or irrational, symbolic interactionist studies typically seek to understand the activities of such groups in relation to their social circumstances *as seen by members of the deviant group*. Consequently, the deviant group often emerge in a more favourable light than official definitions would allow, as with Lofland's study.

In line with this tendency, studies which focus upon relationships between professionals and their clients often have a 'debunking' quality. Professional occupations tend to project an image of themselves as dedicated to the service of the public, as putting aside preoccupations with monetary reward in favour of the interests of their clients. Yet professions, like other occupational groups, develop ways of carrying out their tasks which economize effort and time. These 'working practices' can be to the detriment of their

clients. Consequently, symbolic interactionist studies often concern just those matters which professionals themselves would
prefer to underemphasize or conceal.

Thus the accusation of 'underdog bias' may be true, but to
symbolic interactionists there are good intellectual reasons for it. If
we agree that society is characterized by a plurality of viewpoints
and a continuing tussle among diverse groups, then it is likely that
the 'popular image' of less powerful or less well placed groups will
reflect the viewpoints of the better placed and more powerful. The
relative placement of groups in the social hierarchy will inevitably
lead to the ethnographic researcher having more revelations of a
favourable kind about 'underdogs' than he will have about the
privileged. Thus newspapers, television, judges, the police, criminologists, psychiatrists and other officials have their say about
criminals and mental patients; everyone *except* the criminal or
the mental patient is allowed a say in the public formation of his
image. The sociologist may be able to make 'discoveries' simply by
showing that deviants and other underprivileged persons are in
truth only 'normal human beings' acting within particular, peculiar
circumstances.

The importance of process

Social life takes place in time. The sociologist needs to be attuned to
the fact that any social situation is a continuingly unfolding
experience. The events that the researcher observes are occurring at
some point along a course and may not be fully understood unless
they are viewed in relation to events which precede and succeed
them. This point seems obvious, yet sociologists often conceptual-
ize social phenomena in ways which leave their temporal character
out of account. There is a tendency to focus upon the *end product* of
a situation at the expense of the processes by which that end
product is produced. Symbolic interactionists, by contrast, seek, in
the ways they conceive and study social life, to build an emphasis
upon process.

This emphasis on process can be illustrated by reference again to
the study of deviance. The symbolic interactionist approach to
deviance has come to be known as 'labelling theory'. The labelling
theorist argues that in dealing with 'deviants', the sociologist is not
usually studying the whole class of persons who have committed
an act of deviance. Instead, he is merely studying those persons

who have been seen to commit an act of deviance and have been labelled accordingly. This apparently simple point has significant implications for what the sociologist should seek to explain and for how such phenomena should be conceptualized. Standardly, sociologists (and psychologists, criminologists, etc.) have been concerned to discover the 'underlying causes' of deviance in terms of such factors as hereditary traits or social background. Causes are sought by means of relating these factors to the deviant population. The labelling theorist argues that such a strategy ignores the ways in which the identification of persons *as deviants* is itself a social process. The sociologist is not entitled to assume that because someone has been officially designated a deviant he 'really did' the thing he is accused of. For example, the sociologist cannot know whether criminals have committed the offences with which they have been convicted, any more than he can know how many persons walking around free may have actually committed a criminal act and not been caught. After all, even the massive investigative apparatus available to the police and the courts cannot provide certainty. Therefore, the sociologist cannot assume that the population of labelled deviants can be distinguished from the population of 'normals' by virtue of their performance of deviant acts or their possession of deviant tendencies.

What deviants indisputably have in common is the label itself. They have all gone through the social processes by which the label is attached. Criminals have all experienced being apprehended, charged, tried and convicted. Consequently, there are two issues the sociologist can investigate.

Firstly, he can examine the ways in which the process of labelling is socially organized. To understand why some people are in prison, he must understand how the police are organized in their daily work, how they come to make arrests, why some cases go to court and others do not, how courts operate to produce convictions, and so forth. The second investigable topic is to study the effects of the labelling experience on the deviant himself. Rather than supposing that there *must* be something different about the personality of the deviant from that of 'normals', the labelling theorist prefers the view that people who transgress moral rules are often, in the first instance, ordinary people who are motivated in quite conventional ways. One of the effects of the labelling process is to create circumstances in which it can be impossible for individuals to continue to think of themselves as 'like everyone else'. Being publicly labelled as a deviant has profound repercussions for the individual's place in society, their social relationships and their image of themselves. Deviant identities tend to be 'master statuses'; they tend to override the individual's other, normal identities in the eyes of others. The individual comes to be treated as a deviant *first and foremost*. As a result, they may find it impossible to carry on their life as a normal, even though they may wish to do so. Frequently, their 'treatment' (or punishment) involves being thrown together with other deviants who are perceived as being 'the same' as them. Though they may try to resist this definition, the pressures of the situation may eventually lead to the individual coming to see themselves in the way others see them, and accepting the deviant identity as their 'true self'.

The preference for formal generalizations

Although the tradition of fieldwork research emphasizes the study of particular situations and cases, symbolic interactionists are interested in making general statements about social life. In their view, however, such statements cannot be usefully derived from variable analysis and a quantification of human conduct. Nor are they best arrived at by presupposing that one type of group or one pattern of relationships holds the basic key to the workings of society – as, for example, Marxist theory and social classes. For the symbolic interactionist, society is a relatively loose arrangement of quite heterogeneous groupings – occupational, organizational, ethnic, class, status, religious, political, and so on. The working of society shows a continual and fluid interplay of these groupings, usually involving competitive struggles for advantage *vis-à-vis* sources of legitimation, influence and control. Since society is complex and continually changing, the symbolic interactionist is sceptical about sociology's ability to generalize at this level about its workings. Rather, he believes that generalizations are more usually cast at the level of group and individual action.

Further, symbolic interactionists aim to change not only the level, but also the nature of generalizations. They prefer generalizations shaped in terms of 'form' rather than 'content'. The distinction between form and content in social life reflects the influence of the German sociologist Georg Simmel (1858–1918). Simmel thought that a vital part of sociology should be the formal analysis of social relations. He suggested that whereas the 'content' of social phenomena, such as economic organizations, political associations, kinship relations and friendship groupings, is different, the same 'formal' structure of social relationships might be found. For example, the sociologist with an interest in 'social conflict' might find that the formal components of a 'conflict relationship' are displayed in the same ways across a variety of social settings. Such components as 'opposition', 'affiliation' and 'co-operation' might provide the basis for formal generalizations about the general nature of conflict as a type of social relationship.

The distinction between 'form' and 'content' cannot be pressed too far. There is, after all, a sense in which all sociological generalizations could be said to have a formal character. But it does give some idea of the direction taken by symbolic interactionists. In general, they have tended to concentrate on the location of social processes which they take to be descriptive of, and applicable to, a variety of social settings. For example, Anselm Strauss's concept, 'negotiated order' (Strauss, 1979), emphasizes the fact that social organization is fluid and revisable. Social arrangements are rarely fixed and static, being continually 'worked at' by those who live within them; they are modified, rearranged, sustained, defended and undermined. The members of society are, therefore, constantly involved in a process of 'negotiation' with one another as they reaffirm, revise and replace the social arrangements under which they act together.

Strauss's concept of negotiated order has particular relevance for the analysis of organizations. It was originally formulated to describe the nature of the division of labour and hierarchy of authority in large psychiatric hospitals. Strauss and his associates (Strauss *et al* 1964) noted that these hospitals did not display the kind of stable and clearly defined division of labour and hierarchy that sociologists have come to expect in any large organization. Instead, the situation was fluid and constantly changing; lines of responsibility, speciality and control were continually revised and redefined. Strauss found that groups such as doctors, nursing staff, social workers, patients and relatives were continually 'negotiating' over organizational issues, such as the proper forms of patient care, the right to take treatment decisions and the control of information. He found that not only was there no fixed consensus between the major groupings on these issues, there was often little consensus *within* them either.

It is important to recognize that the concept of 'negotiation' must be understood metaphorically. Strauss is not suggesting that people are all the time engaged in explicit negotiation of their relative positions; they are not openly making deals or writing agreements. Sometimes they are, but more usually they are involved in implicit, unspoken, mutual adjustment of action, feelings, attitude and interest. Strauss believes that such implicit jockeying for social position may be interactionally similar across different kinds of social settings. The concept of 'negotiation' is useful as a first description of the formal character of these general features of social interaction. Its value is that of a signpost, pointing the sociologist in the direction of phenomena that should be explored and given a more precise description.

With its emphasis on the qualitative study of a particular social setting based on first-hand involvement of the researcher, the fieldwork tradition is the predominant style of empirical investigation in symbolic interactionism. But it is by no means the only one. A very different approach to empirical analysis is displayed in another body of work, which is associated with one writer in particular, Erving Goffman (1911–82). Goffman's books, while they are recognizably symbolic interactionist in orientation, look quite unlike the studies produced from within the fieldwork tradition.

Goffman: the interaction order

It has been said of Goffman's books that they are straightforward to read but that it is difficult to grasp the point of what he is saying. To many sociologists he seems to be obsessed with the minutiae of social life, writing in considerable detail about face-to-face interaction and lavishing as much analytical energy and conceptual definition on the 'small behaviours' of daily social life as other sociologists do upon the large structures of society. He appears, moreover, to be unconcerned, at least in any conventionally recognizable way, with the construction and testing of theories about the phenomena he describes. Although his books have a common concern with the social character of interaction, they do not offer a cumulative body of findings; the approach taken and the concepts used vary widely from book to book. He uses empirical materials in what strikes many to be an unorthodox, cavalier fashion; sometimes he draws upon his own fieldwork or that of other researchers, but interspersed with these sociological sources are references to unconventional materials, such as novels, biographies and memoirs, books of etiquette, rule books and instruction manuals, newspaper cuttings, and so forth.

These peculiarities have led some sociologists to dismiss Goffman as an eccentric and marginal figure, whose work has little more than curiosity value. Others have an opposite view of him. For them, Goffman's contribution to modern sociology is almost inestimable. He is credited with opening the eyes of sociologists to things that are literally under their noses, staring them in the face, things they had previously been unable to see as having any sociological interest or recognizable order. Specifically, Goffman's work has shown that the organization of social interaction can be studied as a phenomenon in its own right. Goffman (1983) refers to that phenomenon as 'the interaction order'. Much that goes on in face-to-face interaction is relatively independent of the wider social structures within which the interaction can be located. The organization of interaction arises in large measure from the *interactional* circumstances themselves; most fundamentally from the fact of people being physically present together in the same place, within range of one another's observation and communication. Goffman's work can be seen as a persistent and unremitting exploration of the sociological possibilities opened up by this observation. Seen *as* a project of exploration, the 'peculiarities' of his style and methods begin to make better sense.

Take, for example, the frequently stated opinion that Goffman has a 'cynical' view of human nature; that he regards human beings as manipulative performers, always engaged in creating some 'false front' in their relations with others. This charge comes about because Goffman views individuals as *self-conscious* beings. Following Mead, he regards social behaviour as essentially communicative, as involving the ability to project and interpret socially defined attitudes and actions. The self is not to be seen as a kind of 'inner cause' of an individual's behaviour, but as the socially communicated *person* which that behaviour displays. Individuals are continuously communicating (giving and giving off) self-impressions in all they do, for everything they do displays their social character as persons in one way or another.

Goffman's problem here is methodological: how to make the socially organized features of interactional behaviour visible and describable. His favoured solution involves the use of analytic metaphors. Most famously, he uses the metaphor of the theatrical performance to describe aspects of self-presentation in daily life. On stage, the actor has the task of presenting himself to the audience as a particular character in the play. He has to make them aware that he is, say, a policeman or a king through the use of costume, props, scenery and movement, as well as the dialogue that has been written for him. Of course, he does not have to achieve the projection of the character all by himself. He is aided not only by the other actors on the stage but also by those who work behind the scenes – the make-up staff, scene-changers, director, and so on. All these parties are involved in staging the play and projecting the identities of the characters to the audience.

In some respects the individual in everyday situations can be seen as having the same problem as the stage actor. When we enter a setting or occasion, we have the task of communicating to others who and what we are. The only way others can judge what type or kind of person we are is through our conduct and appearance. Therefore, while we may not literally 'put on a performance', we can be seen as using the resources at our disposal to communicate an impression to our 'audience' in a way comparable to the stage performer.

The analogy can be taken further. The presentation of a play involves 'teamwork'; all those involved have a function in maintaining the audience's impression that they are watching a struggle for power in a medieval court or a murder investigation in an English country house. Similarly, Goffman seeks to show us that the presentation of self in everyday settings involves teamwork. Thus in professional settings much can depend upon an impression of professional competence being communicated to the client. The maintenance of such an impression is often the outcome of the behaviour of a number of people. The staff of a hospital, for example, can be looked on as a team seeking to sustain for patients and their relatives the conviction that competent and effective medical work is being done on their behalf. In a court of law, the judge, barristers, courtroom officials and the jury can be viewed as collaborating to establish a solemn and serious legal atmosphere, one that will assure the defendant and others that the case will receive a proper hearing.

Just as in the theatre where much of the work necessary to create a definition goes on behind the scenes, out of sight of the audience, so also social settings like hospitals and courts can be divided into 'front' and 'back' regions. This distinction points up the fact that there are activities restricted from public view, which only professional participants are allowed to witness and participate in. Often the things that get done in these 'backstage happenings' are important for keeping up the image of proper, competent work. If they were witnessed by laymen, such as patients and their families or the relatives of an accused person, they might give rise to disillusionment or protest. For example, the smooth, effective working of the courtroom may require a high degree of co-operation and agreement between prosecuting and defending counsel and the judge over the handling of a case. But such discussions, were they to be conducted in public view, might lead defendants and their relatives to feel that their interests were being compromised. The public image of the defending counsel, as adversarial champion of his client, necessitates that such conversations be conducted in the privacy of the chambers.

The dramaturgical metaphor points up the 'expressive' dimension of social behaviour. The distinction between 'instrumental' and 'expressive' actions is widely used in sociology to distinguish between behaviours engaged in for pursuing a purpose or goal and those which contain their meaning or value *within the act itself*. From the description we have given it might seem that Goffman views interactional conduct in strictly instrumental terms, designed to achieve favourable or desired self-impressions. Some of his other analytic metaphors would appear to confirm this reading. Most obviously, he makes repeated use of the model of the game and game-playing, drawing from this analogy concepts such as 'move', 'strategy' and 'advantage'. We shall not deny that this instrumental theme is strongly present in much of Goffman's work. To see his writings wholly in such terms, however, would be to miss something fundamental.

What this something is can be seen by noticing the central place accorded the notion of 'ritual' in Goffman's writings. Ritual is fundamentally expressive rather than instrumental. For example, in religious rituals the believer *expresses* his reverence by relating himself to the sacred realm through prayer. He may pray for something, but the meaning of his prayers transcends the particular purpose; they are expressions of faith. Goffman makes use of this expressive dimension of ritual to describe the detail of social interaction. He views the relationships between individuals as a set of interactional rituals by which the self is expressed. All aspects of social interaction – posture, clothing, ornamentation, physical distance, the deployment of limbs, the distribution of looks, as well as verbal exchanges – can be viewed as rituals of self-expression. In other words, they can be examined for the part they play in regulating face-to-face encounters. Speaking of them as rituals draws attention both to their expressive and to their standardized character. Goffman's concern was to subject these interactional phenomena to close and detailed study, thereby showing that social order can be found at the level of mundane, everyday behaviour.

Symbolic interactionism: conclusion

There are those who would reject the whole thrust of symbolic interactionist thinking. From this kind of oppositional standpoint, what is offered is not so much a considered evaluation as a simple rebuttal. Thus sociologists committed to the idea of 'scientific sociology' reject symbolic interactionism's critique of this conception and reciprocate with the criticism that it is indifferent to problems of evidence, proof and systematic theory. Similarly, 'structuralist' sociologists reject its charge that their conception of the relationship between the individual and society is overly deterministic, and reply with the claim that symbolic interactionism itself underestimates the importance of 'structural' constraints upon actions. The drawback with this kind of evaluation is that essentially all it does is criticize symbolic interactionism because it differs from another approach, one which the critic favours.

A less doctrinaire way of evaluating symbolic interactionism is to ask about its impact upon the practice of sociology. It can be argued that its influence has been considerable but diffuse. Symbolic interactionism has been around for a long time now. By focusing upon the work of a few key figures we may have given the impression that it is a tightly-knit approach clearly demarcated from the rest of sociology. If this was once the case, back in the 1940s and 1950s, it is not the case now. Many of its ideas have been absorbed into the sociological 'mainstream'. Some would say, though, that in this process of absorption the 'cutting edge' of these ideas has to a large extent been lost. What was originally formulated as a radical critique of sociological orthodoxy has been transformed into an integral part of that orthodoxy. Thus in the view of many present-day sociologists, the 'lessons' of symbolic interactionism have been learned and little more is to be gleaned from its classic texts. They point to the fact that sociologists now pay more attention than they once did to the social meanings that situations have for those within them. They also note that sociologists have more respect nowadays for the value of case studies as a form of sociological research, no longer seeing them merely as 'poor relations' of large-scale survey-type studies.

This 'absorption' of symbolic interactionism into the mainstream of sociology perhaps explains why it has lost much of its distinctiveness as a sociological approach. Rather than viewing it as an alternative to structuralist approaches, some sociologists have argued that symbolic interactionist ideas are *reconcilable with* structuralist ones, at least in principle. Mainly, such arguments have attempted to integrate interactionist ideas with ones drawn from Marxism. It is not hard to see how certain themes in symbolic interactionism, such as the emphasis upon process and the adoption of an 'underdog' standpoint could, at least superficially, be connected with Marxian concerns with inequality and domination. In the study of deviance, for example, it is claimed that such an 'integrated macro-micro' approach can explain not simply how certain categories of deviance are imposed by agencies of control, but also how these categories come to be available and the societal-level interests they serve.

Some present-day interactionists would argue that the price of this absorption into the sociological mainstream has been a watering down, or even an emasculation, of many of symbolic interactionism's key ideas, Whatever the merits of such claims, it is clear that symbolic interactionism has lost much of its impetus as a distinctive sociological approach. The materials we have drawn upon in this chapter are ones which have played a crucial part in shaping the framework of this way of thinking, but they are all now relatively old pieces of work. Though many more people are now influenced by, if not actually working directly within, the interactionist scheme, their work tends to amount to variations rather than real developments on established themes. The sociology of meaning and action has, in theoretical terms, moved on.

But to what? The past fifteen or twenty years have witnessed a proliferation of theoretical approaches and styles of analysis, all of which can (loosely) be gathered together under the heading of 'sociologies of meaning and action'. These include 'ethnosemantics', 'reflexive ethnography', 'ethnogenics', 'social representation theory', 'phenomenological sociology' and 'cognitive sociology'. All these approaches have in common an emphasis upon the place of meaning in social behaviour and a belief that the orthodox assumptions and methods of 'scientific sociology' are inappropriate in face of the interpretive nature of social life. Beyond this minimal agreement, however, they differ from one another in their assumptions and concepts. Although all have had some impact upon sociology, there is one 'meaning' approach which has been more influential than any other. This approach is ethnomethodology to which we turn in the next chapter.

Further reading

Baldwin, J. D., *George Herbert Mead: A Unifying Theory for Sociology* (Sage, 1986).

Becker, H., *Sociological Work: Method and Substance* (Allen Lane, 1971). This work contains his 'Whose side are we on?' which discusses the charge of 'underdog bias'.

Brubacker, R., *The Limits to Rationality* (Allen & Unwin, 1984). An excellent introduction to the thought of Weber.

Drew, P., and Wooton, T. (eds), *Erving Goffman* (Polity Press, 1988). A useful collection of papers on the theme of Goffman's influence upon and importance for contemporary sociology.

Hammersley, M., and Atkinson, P., *Ethnography: Principles in Practice* (Tavistock, 1983). A useful discussion of the interactionist approach to research.

Manis, J. G., and Meltzer, B. N. (eds), *Symbolic Interaction: A Reader in Social Psychology* (Allyn & Bacon, 1967). Contains Blumer's 'Sociological analysis and the variable'.

Rock, P., *The Making of Symbolic Interactionism* (Macmillan, 1979).

Rose, A. M., *Human Behaviour and Social Processes: An Interactionist Approach* (Routledge, 1962). For Blumer's 'Society as symbolic interaction'.

Rubington, E., and Weinberg, M. S., *Deviance: The Interactionist Perspective* (Collier Macmillan, 1968). For Howard Becker's 'On labelling outsiders', Erving Goffman's 'The moral career of the mental patient' and Edwin Lemert's 'Paranoia and the dynamics of exclusion'.

Stone, G., and Faberman, H., *Social Psychology Through Symbolic Interaction* (Xerox College Publishing, 1970). A good source book for symbolic interactionist studies.

Worsley, P. (ed.), *Problems of Modern Society* (Penguin, 1972). For Blumer's 'Sociological theory in industrial relations' which explores some implications of symbolic interactionism for the study of work. For Everett C. Hughes's 'Mistakes at work' showing how persons organize to deal with their own mistakes and the mistakes of others. For Edwin Lemert's 'Primary and secondary deviation' showing the role of society's reaction in creating deviance.

Questions

1 Why did Weber believe that 'understanding' of actions was essential to sociological explanation?
2 Explain how Mead viewed the mind as socially produced and socially displayed.
3 Why is Blumer opposed to 'scientism' in sociology?
4 How does Lofland's study of a religious cult demonstrate the value of taking 'the actor's point of view'?
5 How do symbolic interactionists justify an emphasis upon the 'underdog'?
6 What is distinctive about the interactionist approach to deviance?
7 What is meant by 'formal generalization' and how do symbolic interactionists use such generalizations to illuminate social life?
8 Explain Goffman's notion of 'the interaction order' and discuss the methods by which he seeks to describe it.

6 *Meaning and action: II, ethnomethodology*

Introduction

It is tempting to think of ethnomethodology as the heir of symbolic interactionism. There is some truth in this view in so far as ethnomethodology has inherited the role of a minority, critical voice which stands over against the dominant theoretical and methodological tendencies of mainstream sociology, once occupied by symbolic interactionism. There are also some superficial similarities of approach, though more at the level of what could be called 'investigative attitude' than in terms of phenomena or findings. The notion of ethnomethodology as successor to symbolic interactionism also has some chronological credence. Ethnomethodology came into existence as a publicly identified approach with the publication of Harold Garfinkel's *Studies in Ethnomethodology* in 1967. The radical character of its ideas, and the problem of understanding them, made it the focus of considerable controversy in sociology throughout the 1970s, just as, to a lesser extent perhaps, symbolic interactionism had been in the 1950s and 1960s. But beyond this point the differences become significant. We shall consider these differences in more detail at the end of this chapter.

As we have noted, one major outcome of the debates engendered by symbolic interactionism was to motivate sociologists to look for ways of incorporating interactionist ideas into their researches and integrating its methods with those drawn from other approaches. Despite its distinctive assumptions and its critical stance, symbolic interactionism seemed, in the end, to be containable within an, albeit modified, sociological mainstream. The same cannot be said of ethnomethodology. The heat of controversy has abated in recent years, but not because ethnomethodology has been incorporated into the mainstream. It remains on the whole a minority pursuit, very distinctive from the rest of sociology. In fact, as its conceptions of its phenomena and how to investigate them have developed it has drawn further away from conventional sociological inquiry.

The origins of ethnomethodology

The formulation of ethnomethodology as a distinctive perspective in sociology is very largely the achievement of one man, Harold Garfinkel. It was Garfinkel who outlined its basic approach, in a series of papers written in the 1950s and 1960s. It was Garfinkel who introduced these ideas to students and colleagues and encouraged their own empirical studies. And to this day Garfinkel remains ethnomethodology's leading figure. But the ideas of ethnomethodology did not spring spontaneously from his head. They can be traced to two major sets of influences: the writings of Talcott Parsons on the problem of social order and the phenomenological writings of Alfred Schutz (1899–1959).

Garfinkel studied under Parsons at Harvard University in the late 1940s. At that time, Parsons was fully engaged in a project of grand proportions, which was to occupy him for the rest of his life. In Chapter 2 we outlined Parsons's conception of the 'problem of order' and his theory of society as a social system. As we saw, it was part of an even bigger project, involving nothing less than an attempt to rethink the fundamental categories of sociological knowledge with the 'theory of action'. In Chapter 2, we saw how it attempts to relate culture, personality and social system. At the heart of his theory of action is the problem of 'voluntarism', that is, how to account for the systematic character of social life in terms which recognize the fact that, as social actors, persons *choose* the courses of action they engage in. The key to this problem, as Parsons saw it, was to identify the forces which *socially structured* the choices actors could make. Since these social structural forces had to be rooted in action itself, yet had somehow to transcend it, Parson referred to them as 'emergent properties' of action. The most significant of these emergent properties are *normative value commitments*. These are shared commitments actors have about what sorts of action choices are appropriate in what kinds of situations. Because actors share these commitments they are motivated to comply with the requirements society makes of them.

They do so, fundamentally, because they perceive these requirements as *morally right*. Thus Parsons conceives the 'solution' to
the problem of order as involving 'motivated compliance to the
normative order'.

For Garfinkel, Parsons's achievement lay not so much in his
theoretical solution to the problem of social order as in his
recognition that sociology required some worked-out-analysis
of its fundamental phenomenon, the nature of action, as the basis
of its empirical knowledge. In his view the test of Parsons's
ideas had to be the kind of knowledge they generated. What
descriptions of ordinary social life did they make possible? What
kind of access did they give the sociologist to everyday activities as
socially organized phenomena?

In posing these questions of Parsonian theory, Garfinkel was
influenced by Alfred Schutz's philosophical writings on the foundations of sociology. Schutz's differences with Parsons have their
roots in the wholly different approach he took to the analysis of the
foundations of sociological understanding. For Parsons, the foun-
dational issue was how to conceive action to show how *systems
of action* were built, systems that had the properties of co-
operativeness, predictability, stability and rationality – in other
words, properties of *orderliness*. For Schutz, the foundations of
sociology were to be located not at the level of action as theorized
from the point of view of the 'system', but at the level of action *as
experienced by the actor in the world of daily life*. Schutz argued that the
Parsonian approach aimed at unifying the 'subjective' standpoint of
the actor and the 'objective' standpoint of the sociologist, and did
so by transforming the actor's subjective viewpoint *into* the
sociologist's objective one. Parsons thus avoided analysing the
actor's actual understandings by putting in their place a set of
sociological *idealizations* of what these understandings would have
to be for the system to be maintained. Consequently, the world of
everyday life in which actor's actual understandings are located is
'lost' as a sociological phenomenon.

Schutz first presented his ideas in the early 1930s, in terms of a
critique of Max Weber's conception of 'interpretive sociology'.
Schutz agreed with Weber that human beings experience their
social environment as a socially meaningful reality. When we hear
or see another person saying or doing something we *understand* the
meaning of those movements or words. The everyday social world
is an 'interpretive reality'. Weber defined 'action' as 'all human

behaviour when and in so far as the acting individual attaches a subjective meaning to it' and defined social action as action which 'takes account of the behaviour of others and is thereby oriented in its course'. In any investigation, the sociologist must try to 'grasp' the subjective meanings actors 'attach' to their actions. If he fails to do this correctly or adequately, his investigations will be based on a misunderstanding of the actor's actions and thus be of little scientific value.

Schutz argued that Weber's analysis presupposed the very questions that a sociological analysis of meaning and action should address. To go beyond Weber, it was necessary to 'take one step back' and make problematic the things Weber had assumed. Specifically, Weber's concept of 'subjective meaning' seems to imply that an action has a single meaning, and that this meaning stems entirely from the actor who is performing the action. Since, in Weber's view, the sociologist can never 'really know' what is in the mind of this or that actor, the only description he can give of meaning is idealized and exaggerated (ideal-typical). Also, if each actors understandings are wholly 'subjective' in Weber's sense, the sociologist has to explain how these understandings mesh together sufficiently to produce stable and orderly patterns of social life by invoking some 'external' source of agreement. This line of thinking leads inevitably towards Parsons's solution to the problem of order.

In Schutz's view, Weber crucially fails to bring out the *intersubjective experience* that actors have of their social world. By 'intersubjectivity' he means that though the everyday social world is experienced through each individual's own consciousness, it is not understood as a 'private' world, personal and unique to each individual. Rather, the social world is experienced as a common, shared world in which the individual is personally *involved*. The common, 'objective' nature of everyday life is something taken for granted by all of us as social actors. We expect others to know what we are talking about, to see what we are seeing. But we also take it for granted that the ways we are invovled in this common world are, at least in some respects, particular to us. For Schutz, then, the 'objective' and the 'subjective' are dimensions of *the actors commonsense perspective*. It is this common-sense perspective which is the focus of Schutz's analysis.

The social world, says Schutz, is experienced as a 'given' world, that is, it is organized, orderly, 'out there'; it is independent of, and pre-exists, any particular individual. The 'givenness' of the world is not a hypothesis that individuals seek to 'test'. Rather, it is treated as an unquestioned and unquestionable 'fact'. Here, Schutz was heavily influenced by the phenomenological philosophy of Edmund Husserl, and especially Husserl's concept of the 'natural attitude' of daily life. By this term Husserl drew attention to the assumption of reality with which persons going about their daily lives invest their experience. For Husserl, 'phenomenology' referred to his attempt to describe the nature and foundations of human experience. In order to be able to examine experience *as* experience, the philosopher has to 'suspend the natural attitude', that is, to detach himself from the normal assumption of the realness of things and thereby 'put the world in brackets'. In this way, Husserl suggests that the phenomenologist can examine the character of consciousness itself.

While he rejected Husserl's ultimate philosophical aims, Schutz recognized the value of these ideas for analysis of social experience. In daily life one does not, indeed *could not* treat the 'realness' of things as a matter for systematic doubt. The social world is *there*, for ourselves as much as for others. At the same time, this world has to be made sense of by each of us in terms of our particular experiences. The means by which we do so involves what Schutz called 'common-sense knowledge'. This concept refers to the knowledge of the social world which actors possess by virtue of living in and being part of their ordinary, *everyday* world. The actor's sense of the orderliness and understandability of the things around him derives from the use which he makes of this common-sense knowledge. Thus, common-sense knowledge enables us to categorize and name the things we experience so as to see 'what kinds of things' they are. The concepts which comprise this knowledge are 'typifications'; they refer to what is typical or standard among a collection of objects, events or actions. As members of society, we possess a stock of typifications which enable us to see the everyday world as familiar, ordinary and mundane. These typifications are not our own personal invention. They are embodied in the language we share with others. Through language a store of typifications is handed down to us and we acquire an immense stock of knowledge of things in the world. Only a tiny fraction of this stock derives from our own direct observation of the world.

Central to our common-sense knowledge are typifications of others as social actors. We are able to make sense of the actions of others, quite routinely and without difficulty, by virtue of knowing what *type* of actor they are and what kinds of motives and interests they have, for example, a 'good teacher', an 'angry father'. On the basis of our typifications, we can assume that others will act in certain ways towards us, and will respond in predictable ways to our own actions towards them. We can attribute 'because motives' (reasons) and 'in order to motives' (intentions) to others, and thus know how to plan our own behaviour.

The existence of typifications make it possible for the actor to treat his social environment as 'known in common', that is, as the same for others as for himself. Schutz stresses the fundamental importance of what he terms 'the reciprocity of perspectives'. By this concept, he means that on the basis of their stock of typifications, individuals can assume that events and actions in the social world are understandable to others in the way that they are to themselves. Furthermore, differences in understanding can be treated as *socially organized differences*. For example, we expect a doctor to know more about medicine than we do. That the everyday world is in some definite ways different for others does not undermine its 'accent of reality' for us.

Schutz goes on to introduce the concept of 'multiple realities', by contrasting the structure and organization of knowledge in the 'reality' of everyday life with 'other realities', such as the 'world' of dreams and the 'world' of fantasies. Of particular relevance here is his comparison between the world of everyday life and the world of scientific theorizing.

The common-sense perspective of the everyday actor is essentially a *practical* perspective. The individual's primary focus of attention is his immediate circumstances. He is involved in these circumstances in a practical way; others act towards him and he must in turn act towards them. In the process of practical living, the individual copes with everyday situations *as they occur*, in 'real time'. How he does so will depend in part upon his own 'projects at hand'. What features of his circumstances are most immediately relevant will be determined by his own interests and purposes in the situation. Much that *could* be attended to will be ignored, not because the individual is incapable of responding, but because he has no practical reason, 'here and now', for doing so. That some action could conceivably be understood differently from how it appears is something that can be ignored because it is not relevant to the practical situation at hand.

The perspective of the scientist is not practical in this sense. The scientist's theoretical interests are not determined by the need to cope with the 'here and now'. Instead, they are shaped by his 'scientific project', which is the pursuit of formalized knowledge. The realization of this project involves the adoption of a stance that would be quite out of place in the world of everyday life. Thus the scientist can, and should, operate with attitudes of doubt and scepticism that, were they to be attempted in everyday life, would get the individual labelled as 'crazy'. Also, the scientist treats objects of knowledge as *revisable constructs*, not as unquestionable 'realities'. For Schutz, then, the difference between scientific and everyday knowledge is not simply a matter of degree of precision or generality; it is a qualitative difference in how one looks at, orients to, the world. In this sense, the 'worlds' of the scientist and the everyday actor are fundamentally different.

Schutz believes that the differences between the 'realities' of everyday life and scientific theorizing raise particular problems for sociology. Unlike the natural sciences, where these differences can largely be ignored, sociology has to find ways to *relate* the 'sociologist's world' to the 'everyday world' because human interaction is the subject being studied. Schutz gave a considerable amount of thought to this problem. He suggests that sociology has to employ 'constructs of the second degree', whereas everyday actors operate with 'constructs of the first degree'. Sociology's concepts are produced and used for scientific purposes, but they refer to phenomena – human actions – which already have meaning in common-sense terms, that is, as first-degree constructs. The sociologist must therefore clearly relate these two levels of concepts. Only in this way can sociology attain its scientific goal of formalized knowledge of social life without losing contact with the everyday world.

Perhaps because he was essentially a social philosopher rather than a practising sociologist, Schutz was vague on the specifics of how a 'sociology of everyday life' was to be constructed. It was Garfinkel who set out to establish such a sociology as an empirical programme. At this point, therefore, we need to return to Garfinkel's exploration of the Parsonian theory of action.

The establishment of ethnomethodology as an empirical programme

Parsonian theory had 'solved' the problem of order by simply assuming that actors were (*a*) able to recognize and (*b*) motivated to comply with the normative constraints of society. In his theory, actors were able to interact co-operatively on the basis of common understandings because such understandings were 'built into' their circumstances in the form of shared normative commitments. Garfinkel took the theoretical step of suspending this key assumption of Parsonian theory. Instead of assuming that actors *must* possess shared understandings, Garfinkel proposed to treat this possibility as problematic. If shared understanding is not pre-given by actors' social circumstances (that is, by the 'social system' and the 'common culture' on which it rests), how do actors attain their sense that social life is orderly, rational, predictable, and so forth? From a Parsonian viewpoint, once the assumption of shared understanding is removed the actor is cast adrift in a chaotic and meaningless world, or, what may in effect be the same thing, a unique and solipsistic world. Removing this assumption meant moving outside the whole framework of Parsonian theory, while retaining the analytic aim that inspired it, namely, the exploration of the basis of social order.

The 'local production' of social order

If actors' understandings of their situations are not guaranteed 'from without', by the common culture, how should they be described? Following Schutz, Garfinkel took the radical step of conceiving them as *constructed from within*. This does not mean simply that actors form 'subjective' understandings of events and actions which stand over against the real, 'objective character that these happenings possess. Rather it means that the constituent features of social order, the identity, intelligibility and orderliness that an activity possesses, is conceived as the *product of the activity itself*, done in 'just this' way by 'just these' participants. In other words, Garfinkel conceives of social order as 'participant produced'. Whatever recognizable features an activity or setting displays should be seen as 'locally' produced, that is, produced in and through the ways the activity is being done by those engaged in it. That it is recognizable as 'this' activity or setting in the first place is a local production.

This idea, the 'local production' of social order, is *the* key idea of ethnomethodology. It is not easy to grasp its implications, and many misunderstandings of ethnomethodology have arisen from taking it in ways that Garfinkel does not intend. Most importantly, it does not mean that individuals are 'free to do what they like' in social situations. How much 'room for manoeuvre' persons have in a particular situation depends upon the kind of situation it is, their responsibilities and obligations within it, the involvement of others, and many other possible features. These features make up the *social reality* of the situation as a setting of social action. It is against the background of this practical reality that the individual acts. Garfinkel does not *deny* this reality; ethnomethodology could hardly be regarded as a sociological approach at all were he to do so. The difference between ethnomethodology and other sociological perspectives lies in how it *conceives* the realities of social life.

Garfinkel proposes that the realities of social life be conceived as *consisting in, and only consisting in, members' understandings*. In other words, he assumes – for sociological purposes – that it is the understanding of some feature of a situation as 'fixed', 'required', 'normal', 'proper', 'typical' or whatever that gives that feature its 'objective' character. In acting on the basis of these understandings, persons *produce* their activities as social ones, ones that are fitted to their circumstances.

Two further ideas follow on from the local production of social order. They are captured in two 'recommendations'. The first is 'treat social settings as practically accomplished' and the second 'treat members as practical inquirers'. These recommendations draw attention to the ways in which settings, and the activities that comprise them, are managed and organized in the course of their production. For Garfinkel, social settings are not 'out there' and independent of the actions of members at any given moment. Rather, they are to be seen as ongoing accomplishments of the interactional 'work' in which the members of a setting or event are continuously engaged. By conceiving of interactional activities as 'work', Garfinkel views the orderliness of settings as both the product and process of members' actions. He is proposing that members have to accomplish or achieve their social world. This accomplishment is 'practical'. By this term he emphasizes the fact that members, in an infinite variety of ways, perceive and treat their social world as a *constraining* world. Often members regard themselves as unable to perform an activity in the way they ideally might wish. They may perceive that they have little control over circumstances which can affect the outcomes of an activity. They may believe that they lack sufficient knowledge to decide properly how to act, but that their circumstances necessitate that an action is taken nevertheless. They may find that an action for which they had anticipated one sort of consequence turns out to have a different one, and for reasons beyond their control and which they could not have forseen.

For Garfinkel, the issue is not, and cannot be, whether members are 'right or wrong' in these notions. His concern is not to criticize the understandings members construct but to investigate *how* they are constructed. Therefore, the question is how members *achieve* such perceptions of their circumstances and how these perceptions inform their actions. How do members 'assemble' the sense of an occurrence or setting? How do they 'recognize' unanticipated problems and emergent difficulties? How do they distinguish between features of a situation that are real, relevant and unavoidable and those which are irrelevant, imaginary or can safely be ignored? And how do they do these things *interactionally*, in concert with others in the setting?

Garfinkel recommends that the ethnomethodologist treats the features of social settings as identical with the ways in which members perceive and recognize such features. This recommendation is expressed in his concept of 'reflexivity'. This idea also has been subject to frequent misunderstanding. In *Studies in Ethnomethodology*, Garfinkel speaks of 'the essential reflexivity of accounts'. What he is pointing to by this expression is that the ways members refer to the perceived features of a setting or event are – from a sociological point of view – *part of* the setting or event they describe. Descriptions are not disinterested verbalizations, nor are they detached from the particular circumstances in which they are made. Rather, in describing a feature of a situation in this or that way, we give a certain sense to what is happening, or what has just happened or is about to happen. Addressing, describing, referring and naming are all *ways of giving sense* to things and events. What is more, they are *practical actions*, that is, actions-within-the-setting. As such, they may be treated by others as routine and expectable or as problematic and in need of explanation. It is not just the description someone gives that may indicate how an event is understood, but also the response which giving that description elicits from others.

The basic point that Garfinkel is making here is that there is no sociological value in attempting to make a general distinction between 'actions/events' on the one hand and 'talk about actions/ events' on the other. Talking *is* acting. Members do not have a general problem of describing or explaining 'everything' that happens. They do not typically produce actions and then, separately and independently, try to describe or explain what they have done. Sometimes, of course, when what is happening is 'specifically senseless', members will explicitly offer descriptions or explanations to make sense of something – they will produce what Garfinkel calls 'formulations'. Most of the time, however, such explicit 'repairs' of meaning are unnecessary; activities are produced in such a way as to make it clear to others, *in the course of the activity itself*, what is happening.

Unfortunately, some sociologists have assumed that, appearances notwithstanding, Garfinkel *must* be assuming just such a general distinction between talk and actions. Therefore they have interpreted the notion of reflexivity as claiming that 'actors' explanations' must take priority over 'sociological explanations' of actions. Since actors (sometimes) give explanations, and since these explanations formulate what is being done or give reasons why, it is claimed that the 'essential reflexivity of accounts' commits the ethnomethodologist to the notion that members' explanations are the only valid sort of explanations. Whatever a member says something is, is what it 'really' is; whatever a member gives as the reason why he did something, is why it 'really' was done.

A few moment's reflection on our earlier discussion of Garfinkel's ideas should be enough to see the misunderstanding here. In order to investigate members' understandings as practical accomplishments, ethnomethodology abstains from taking any position on what an action or event 'really is'. Its central interest is in how members decide such matters. Often, of course, members disagree amongst themselves over what something is or how it should be explained. More often still, members give different kinds of formulations of the 'same' thing, simply because they have different kinds of practical interest in it. None of these variations matter for ethnomethodology, except in providing more phenomena for investigation. Ethnomethodology, as a form of sociological inquiry, does not depend upon giving final or definitive descriptions of actions or events, far less upon giving unchallengeable explanations. Indeed, it is little interested in giving 'explanations' at all, at least as these are conventionally understood in sociology.

Membership and the occasioned character of common-sense knowledge

So far in our outline of Garfinkel's ideas, we have made many references to the concept of 'member'. For Garfinkel, this term refers to membership of a collectivity, which implies possession of a shared stock of knowledge about the world. As such, the concept of 'membership' resembles the traditional sociological concept of 'culture' in that it refers to a set of concepts and beliefs which constitute what 'anyone' in a given collectivity should know about their social world. The concept of culture, however, is used to refer to a decontextualized body of knowledge – a set of ideas that are general in character and universally applied – which is attributed to the members of a collectivity by sociologists in order to account for the activities of persons. Garfinkel wishes to examine how persons themselves treat their own and others' knowledge as socially organized. He seeks to study how *they* attribute knowledge to make sense of activities. To refer to 'members', then, is to direct attention to the ways in which persons treat themselves and others as 'members of a socially organized world'.

Garfinkel proposes that in any encounter, persons treat one another *as* members, that is, they allocate collectively memberships to themselves and others and treat some items of knowledge as things they common-sensically 'know' others share. This universal membershiping activity is central to our experience of the world as an objective, factual reality. For in any encounter it is possible for us to treat ourselves and others as 'the same' in some respects, thus constituting the social world as a 'real' world which is 'there for anyone to see'.

It is against the background of this factual, 'known in common' world that members recognize and handle 'out of place' behaviour. If someone appears not to see the world as he 'should', this does not lead us immediately to doubt our own sense of the social world. Rather, we may seek to revise our understanding of the collectivity membership of that person. We may invoke our knowledge of category memberships to account for the person's 'odd' behaviour, and find reasons why he cannot see what should be 'plainly there' for 'anyone' to see. For example, he may be a 'stranger', a 'foreigner' or 'someone distraught'. Such sense-making accounts are constructed *ad hoc*, there and then, to meet the requirements of the particular occasion. Thus common-sense knowledge is used in occasioned ways, in the course of members' *practical reasoning*. As members, we find the social world to be orderly, not because we treat every occasion – or every person – as the same, but because we make sense of the particularities and contingencies of occasions as knowable and accountable.

Members' methods

Garfinkel proposes that the self-production and self-organization of activities is a *methodical* accomplishment on the part of members. In other words, while the *outcomes* of practical reasoning, in terms of the ways members recognize and account for the particulars of this or that occasion, may differ, the *methods* by which such understandings are constructed may have a general character. The distinction Garfinkel is suggesting here is central to ethnomethodology as a programme of inquiry. Crucial as it is, the distinction is not an easy one to grasp. Garfinkel argues that we have to deal with occasions in their local detail, finding whatever order and sense we find *in* that detail. But this does not mean that the methods by which we do this 'sense-making work' will be wholly different each time. Indeed, it is hard to imagine how this could be the case., The task for ethnomethodology is to describe what these members' methods look like. In *Studies in Ethnomethodology*, Garfinkel offers characterizations of a number of them, including the 'documentary method of interpretation', the practice of 'et cetera' and the 'retrospective-prospective sense of occurrence'. We can illustrate the notion of members' methods by examining the documentary method of interpretation.

The documentary method of investigation allows members to make some definite sense of activities in face of the 'indexicality' of particulars. By the concept, indexicality, Garfinkel is drawing attention to the occasionsed nature of everyday social situations. Faced with this or that item of specch or action, which, viewed in isolation might be capable of being understood in a multitude of possible ways, we impose a definite sense upon an item by seeing it in relation to its relevant circumstances. Thus members have to 'repair' the indexicality of talk or actions. To make sense of what is being done, we may produce a 'gloss', or general description of the occasion, such as 'a meeting', 'a family quarrel' or 'an arrest'. In this way, we boil down all the possible ways of describing the many circumstances and details of any social encounter into a description which provides a definite sense of 'what is happening'. The documentary method of interpretation is the name Garfinkel gives to the process of selecting from or boiling down the particulars of a situation to provide it with a definite sense. Members select some items to 'document' what is of significance, as they see it, and describe what is happening in this 'shorthand' manner. Two brief examples may help to illustrate the notion of the documentary method.

Firstly, Garfinkel made observations on the work of suicide investigators, working at a suicide prevention centre. Part of the work of these officials was to investigate cases of sudden death on behalf of the coroner's office and to assist in the legal categorization of such deaths. At the conclusion of their investigation, called a 'psychological autopsy', they were required to produce a recommendation on the legal status of the death. The investigator's central problem is formulated by Garfinkel: presented with the body of the deceased, the physical location of the body, the objects found in the vicinity of the body, the information about the deceased collected from relatives, friends, acquaintances, neighbours and, sometimes, strangers – in other words, presented with all those things which might be 'evidence' – the investigator must try to construct a recognizably rational account of the course of events which produced the body of the deceased as its end result.

Producing such an account could only be done by a process of selection and interpretation. The investigator cannot construct an account that encompasses all the possibilities, including every item that could conceivably be treated as 'evidence'. In constructing his account, the investigator makes reference to 'what anyone can see', to what is 'obvious' as opposed to what is 'questionable', to what he knows 'from past experience', and so on. Of course, any account could be challenged by claiming that further investigation might uncover other materials that would place things in a different light. The only answer that the investigator can provide to the claim that 'more' could possibly be discovered, possibly giving rise to a different judgement, is simply to say that any amount of inquiry would still leave the problem of 'more'. All he can do is to appeal to the practical circumstances of the task. At some point investigation has to stop and a recommendation be made. At this point, whatever has been treated as evidence stands as the grounds upon which a judgement *can and has* been made.

The second example is taken from the work of Garfinkel's associate, D. Lawrence Weider. In his *Language and Social Reality* (Weider, 1974) he describes the workings of the 'convict code' in a hostel for paroled prisoners. The code is a set of unwritten, unofficial rules for proper behaviour, separate from the official regime, which governs the relationships inmates have with one another and with the staff. Weider was not the first sociologist to report the existence of such a code in a penal institution. Much of the literature on prison life focuses upon the ways in which the 'informal' prison code influences the lives of inmates. Thus the 'reality' of the code is recognized by sociologists as well as by inmates themselves.

As an ethnomethodologist, the question Weider poses is: what is the nature of this reality as an interactional accomplishment? Weider is not content with describing, in an idealized, decontextual-ized fashion, the rules that 'make up' the code. Describing what these rules mean involves showing the ways in which they are *treated* as facts in the ongoing activities that comprise daily life in the hostel. Weider found that the code entered into the social life of the hostel in myriad ways. It was referred to, hinted at, complained about, formulated, and joked over, in occcasioned ways – that is, according to the particular circumstances (the contingencies) of this or that occasion. The sense or reference of a particular rule is not absolute but varies according to the particular circumstances in which reference to it is made. For example, an inmate may invoke a rule, or just make generalized reference to 'the code', in order to explain why an action requested of him by a member of staff is, in practical terms, impossible. But this does not mean that every time any such a request is made it will be responded to in the same way. The participants in the hostel, both inmates and staff, use the idea of the code routinely to interpret the patterned and orderly character of activities and, in so doing, help to make these activities patterned and orderly. For all competent participants share a taken-for-granted assumption that events *are* patterned and orderly, and that this pattern and order can be seen through the use of the code. Thus it is not a *discovery* on the part of participants that the code regulates hostel social life. Rather, this assumption serves as an interpretive resource, by means of which events and activities are assigned a definite sense and seen for what they 'really are'.

Conversation analysis: members' methods for accomplishing social activities through talk

We emphasized earlier that Garfinkel conceives ethnomethodology as a programme of empirical inquiry, rather than a theory or explanation of social life. So conceived, the proper test of its power lies in studies which it makes possible. If social life is conceived in the terms Garfinkel proposes, what kinds of phenomena are uncovered and what sorts of observations can be made about these phenomena? For many ethnomethodologists, the most impressive and powerful body of studies produced under the auspices of ethnomethodology are those of conversation analysis (CA). Conversation analysis has built up a large body of empirical studies concerning the sequential and interactional organization of ordinary conversation. These studies demonstrate that the structures of conversational organization operate at the finest levels of detail in talk.

A feature of ethnomethodological analysis is that it seeks to ground its descriptions in the phenomena it investigates in a strong and detailed way. Instead of deriving its analytic categories from a given theory, ethnomethodology is committed to the principle of formulating its categories in the closest possible consultation with the actual conduct to which these categories refer. Therefore it rejects the notion that real worldly social events should be 'simplified', in order to provide idealized phenomena more readily amenable to analysis and explanation. It favours techniques of investigation which as far as possible preserve the naturally occurring content of activities. Thus there is a strong preference for the use of audio- and video-taped data in ethnomethodological studies. These forms of data have the dual advantages that, firstly, they make it possible to examine closely the fine detail of behaviour and, secondly, they can be reproduced for disinterested perusal so that the reader can have available the actual data upon which an analysis is based.

Conversation analysis follows this methodological principle in its use of immensely detailed transcripts of tape recordings of talk. But it is not simply in its extremely close attention to detail that CA displays its ethnomethodological orientations. In analysing these materials, conversation analysts seek to identify the structures in and through which conversationalists accomplish the constitutive features of 'ordinary conversation'. They are concerned to analyse the ways in which the patterned, orderly properties of conversational talk are achieved by speakers *in the course of the talk itself*. Their approach to their materials thus embodies Garfinkel's conception of social activities as self-producing and self-organizing.

The leading figure in the establishment of CA as a research tradition was Harvey Sacks (1936–75). Much of Sacks's work took the form of mimeographed transcriptions of lectures he gave at the University of California (Irvine) between 1964 and 1972. Most of this material remains unpublished. The variety of conversational phenomena Sacks investigates in these lectures is vast, ranging from storytelling and the conversational telling of a joke, through the performance of introductions to the use of pro-terms (words that comprise abbreviated references to things, for example, 'we', 'it', 'here'). However, a few key papers of Sacks' have been published, as have the studies he produced jointly with two colleagues, Emmanuel Schegloff and Gail Jefferson. These jointly authored papers are concerned with the topic that Sacks and his collaborators came to focus upon most consistently, the sequential organization of conversation. We will briefly characterize the nature of their interest in this dimension of conversation and the main findings they present.

Conversation has a number of grossly obvious features. One of these is that it is *sequential* in character. If one looks at any conversation as a string of utterances, one can see that these utterances *follow on* from one another in particular ways; they are 'sequentially tied'. This tying operates utterance by utterance. There is no overall rule or structure which determines the placing of all the utterances in a conversation *vis-à-vis* one another, such that, for example, one could predict at the outset of a conversation what was going to be said in what order. Conversation is a spontaneous activity; it is worked up on the spot, in the course of its production. Yet there is overall structual organization of a kind, at least in the sense that conversations have recognizable beginnings and endings. They neither 'just begin' nor 'just stop'. There are certain kinds of utterances that properly and recognizably occur at the beginning of a conversation and others that properly and recognizably happen at the end.

A second grossly apparent feature is that conversation is an interactional activity, which involves *turn-taking*. Speakers take turns to talk and turns at being recipients or hearers of the talk of others. The basic character of conversation as a turn-taking activity is captured in the principle 'one person speaks at a time'. That this is a normative principle, rather than a statement of empirical fact, can be seen by closely inspecting any actual conversation. One will see that 'overlaps' occur frequently; in any conversation there are many places where more than one person is speaking simultaneously, as well as 'gaps' where no one is speaking. But where overlaps and gaps occur one will also see conversational 'work' by participants which marks these events as problematic, for example, various kinds of 'repair work' designed to restore the 'proper' one-speaker-at-a-time situation.

Sacks, Schegloff and Jefferson conceive the 'problem' of conversational turn-taking as a technical phenomenon. This does not mean that they suppose conversationalists find it difficult to take turns. On the contrary, conversation is an activity that any competent member of society can engage in with any other. It means, instead, that they regard the methods used to accomplish turn-taking are amenable to *technical, sociological description*. They wish to describe how the sequential character of conversation and its interactional 'one at a time' character are *structurally* related. In their analysis, the rules which organize conversational turn-taking operate (*a*) on an utterance by utterance basis and (*b*) serve only to organize a single speaker transition. These rules have three features: (1) to identify possible speaker transition points in talk; (2) to specify a set of alternative transitional possibilities that obtain at such a point; (3) to structure these possibilities in an order of preference. The particularity of the application of these rules to 'one transition at a time' means that overall characteristics of a conversation, such as speaker order or number of utterances, are not systematically organized in themselves, but are the outcomes of the particular ways in which the turn-taking structures have operated over the course of the conversation.

To say that conversation is sequential is to say that utterances are *produced and heard* as tied utterances. This fact provides the key to the connection between the tying rule – 'produce (hear) a current utterance as tied to the immediately preceding one' – and the organization of speaker turn-taking. They are connected by virtue of the fact that conversational utterances can perform *speech actions* of various kinds – for example, a greeting, a complaint, a request, a suggestion and so on. Speech actions are organized into sequential structures, between the parts of which there obtain relationships of 'conditional relevance'. The most powerful form of conditional relevance is that which holds between the two parts of an 'adjacency pair' of speech actions. The adjacency pair relationship is the most common form of sequential action structure and is the material out of which all structures of more than two utterance length are constructed. In addition, adjacency pairs are fundamental to the operation of the turn-taking system for conversation. By producing a first part of such a pair, a speaker both occasions speaker change and projects what should be done in the next utterance (next action). Upon the production of a first pair part speaker change should occur and the next speaker should produce the utterance type, or one of a set of alternative utterance types, that constitutes a proper second part to the pair.

An adjacency pair, therefore, can be defined as (*a*) a sequence of two utterances, which are (*b*) adjacent, (*c*) produced by different speakers, (*d*) ordered as a first part and a second part, and (*e*) tied, so that a first part requires a particular second part (or range of second parts).

This structure is a *normative* framework for actions. In other words, it is treated by members as 'normal and proper' and as the *enforceable* form that certain actions should take. This normative orientation is most apparent in cases where the sequence of actions speakers produce does not conform to the 'base structure' of an adjacency pair. We give three examples of such 'deviant cases':

(1) Atkinson and Drew, 1979, p. 52
    Ch: Have to cut the:se Mummy
        (1.3)
    Ch: Won't we Mummy
        (1.5)
    Ch: Won't we
    M: Yes

(2) Heritage, 1984, p. 250
    J: But the *trai*:n goes. Does th'train go o:n th'boa:t?
    M: .h .h Ooh I've no idea. She ha:sn't sai:d.

(3) Schegloff, 1972, p. 78
    A: Are you coming tonight?
    B: Can I bring a guest?
    A: Sure
    B: I'll be there.

In example (1), an initial question by the child fails to elicit a response from the mother. The child re-initiates the question and then, when no response is forthcoming again, re-initiates it a second time, this time obtaining a response to the question. We say 're-initiates' since it can be noticed that the child does not simply *repeat* the original question. The child's second and third utterance reformulate the question in 'truncated' form, thereby treating the 'absence' of a reply by the mother as a *motivated action* and not a non-hearing of the initial utterance. In this way, the child's second and third utterances *display within themselves* a normative hearing of the 'relevantly absent' second part.

In example (2), the question asked by speaker J is responded to by speaker M, but is not given a 'yes' or 'no' answer. J's question differs from the previous example, in that unlike the child's question to the mother, J asks what could be called an 'information-seeking' question rather than a 'confirmation-seeking' one. Addressing this question to M implies that M possesses the relevant knowledge J lacks. It is this *implication* that M responds to in framing his second part utterance. M's reply accounts for his failure to produce a yes/no answer by formulating his ignorance and explaining this by reference to another who does possess the relevant knowledge ('She hasn't said').

Example (3) illustrates how a question can be responded to with another question which does not hearably 'answer' the first, but yet the conditionally relevant answer is not treated as 'relevantly absent'. A's initial question is also hearable as an invitation. B's rsponse can be heard as raising a matter *conditional to* accepting or declining the invitation. In technical terms, B's question and A's response comprise an 'insertion sequence', which temporarily 'suspends' the conditional relevance of the initial question. Through insertion sequences, which are themselves structured as adjacency pairs, a projected pair sequence can be 'expanded' beyond two utterance length.

The operation of adjacency pairs requires that speakers produce utterances that are *recognizable* to their co-conversationalists as speech actions of particular kinds. In accomplishing this recognizability, conversationalists produce their utterances in ways which attend to the particularities of the social occasion of their talk, that is, they produce talk which recognizably is for 'here and now'. One aspect of this particularity is the interactionally relevant knowledge which a conversationalist can expect his co-participants to possess.

In technical terms, speakers orient to the requirement of 'recipient design'. In other words, they produce their talk in ways which display that they are taking account of *who* they are speaking with and *what* that person can properly and relevantly be assumed to know. In non-technical terms, the principle of recipient design can be stated as 'Do not tell a co-participant what he already relevantly knows, use it' (Schegloff, 1979). In the ways in which they orient to this principle, conversationalists construct their talk so as to make it talk for *this* occasion with *this* co-participant on *this* topic.

CA stands for many people as ethnomethodology's most impressive body of empirical work. Its achievement has been to demonstrate in detailed and elegant ways how conversational organization involves powerful general structures which are highly 'context sensitive'; in and through these structures conversationalists build conversations which are not, *in themselves*, general, but particular and specific to their local social circumstances. The 'machinery' may be general, but its *local uses* and *particular outcomes* are not.

Studies of work: ethnomethodology and the study of 'naturally occurring ordinary activities'

In calling the machinery of conversational sequencing general, we do not mean to imply that it is a machinery for doing anything other than conversation. Of course, many social activities are performed through talk, and often this talk may be similar to 'ordinary conversation' in some respects. Since conversation itself is a very common social activity, it is not really surprising that when members do other kinds of 'talking activities', they employ resources derived from, or similar to, those they use in producing ordinary conversation. A number of studies have shown that this is indeed the case; interactional activities such as classroom lessons (Mehan, 1979), industrial negotiation (Francis, 1986) and doctor-patient consultations (Heath, 1987) involve sequential machineries that are adaptations of those found in ordinary conversation. Referring to these machineries as 'adaptations' draws attention to their similarities with conversational structures and their distinctive properties. For though other activities done through talk may resemble conversation in some ways, the fact remains, of course, that participants in these activities are not 'doing' ordinary conversation; they are 'doing' teaching, or negotiating, or medical consultation. The distinctive character of these activities can be seen, at least in part, in the specific ways in which conversational structures are 'modified' to do the 'work' of the classroom, boardroom or consulting room.

In recent years, Garfinkel has emphasized more and more strongly the need for sociological studies to come to grips with the detailed and distinctive *content* of activities. His favourite way of expressing this requirement is through an anecdote about an exchange between Fred Strodtbeck and Edward Shils in the 1950s. They were discussing Strodtbeck's research on juries, specifically a paper in which Strodtbeck analysed the jury as a small group, using the concepts and methods of 'small group theory'. At one point in the discussion, Shils asked why, instead of asking 'what makes the jury a small group?', Strodtbeck didn't ask instead 'what makes the jury a jury?'. Shils was persuaded that this was a naive question. But Garfinkel disagrees. Sociological studies, in their concern to depict activities in generalizable ways, tend to gloss over the detailed content of the activity in question. Garfinkel therefore refers to the 'missing whatness' in sociological studies. In the sociology of work, for example, one can find many studies of occupations, from working on a factory assembly line to being a jazz musician. But one looks in vain in these studies to find any detailed description and analysis of the actual *work* itself, in its real world, experienced character.

The reason for this absence, he argues, is that in investigating such activities, sociologists act as though they *already know* what an adequate sociological depiction of them will consist in. The detailed and distinctive character of the activity, what makes it *this* activity and not some other, is therefore not treated as of any interest. But Garfinkel refuses to assume that we can know in advance what sociological features an activity might possess. He seeks to focus on the 'this-ness' of the activity, in order to discover how it is accomplished as the recognizable, 'real' activity it is.

The studies Garfinkel and others have carried out along these lines are 'studies of work' in a dual sense. Many of them concern activities common-sensically describable as work, things people do as a job, or as part of their job. But the term 'work' is also being used here in an analytical sense, to refer to the '*in situ* accomplishment' of the activity. In this sense, *any* activity which involves expenditure of effort and time to attain an outcome can be investigated for the 'work' which constitutes it. Thus among the activities ethnomethodologists have studied are fixing multi-piece truck wheels (Baccus, 1986) and playing basketball (MacBeth, 1989) as well as operating an air traffic control panel (Anderson *et al.* 1989), designing computer simulations on a white board (Suchman, 1988) and constructing a mathematical proof (Livingston, 1986).

Garfinkel refers to these activities as 'naturally occurring ordinary activities'. On the surface, this description seems strange. In common-sense terms, basketball may be an 'ordinary' activity, but being an air traffic controller or an artificial intelligence researcher surely is not? What Garfinkel is emphasizing, however, is the fact that, from a practitioner's point of view, these activities are indeed 'ordinary'. If you are an air traffic controller, then using a radar screen to control the movements of aircraft is the routine stuff of your everyday work. This is not to deny for a moment that such work is responsible and important – after all, the lives of hundreds of airline passengers depend on the decisions the controller makes! But making these decisions is, for the controller, a normal, everyday activity. The controller takes for granted the competencies involved, such as knowing how to 'read' a radar screen and judge the positions of aircraft in the sky from the blips it shows. It is these taken for granted practical competencies that the ethnomethodologist seeks to describe.

To illustrate further the kinds of investigations that ethnomethodologists make of 'naturally occurring ordinary activities' we will look at Michael Lynch's (1985) study of research in a psychobiological laboratory engaged in experimental research on animal brain functions. Lynch wished to study how the researchers' scientific activities were conducted as practical activities, that is, how 'discoveries' were made, how experiments were judged as 'successes' or 'failures', how 'results' were achieved and checked against other results, and how the objects that the research was directed towards were recognized and identified. Lynch points out that descriptions of science by sociologists, historians and philosophers typically are reconstructions and idealizations rather than descriptions of what scientists actually *do*. These idealized descriptions usually are aimed at characterizing the *kind* of thing science is as a social activity or form of knowledge; in contrast, Lynch aims to analyse the detailed, practical work of science.

Much of the work of the laboratory consisted in the construction and examination of specimens of brain tissue, usually from rats. Slides of sections of brain tissues were prepared and examined using optical and electron microscopes. In this way, theories of brain structure and processes were developed and tested. In working with these specimens, researchers would quite frequently come across 'artefacts'. An artefact is a visible feature of a specimen, or a representation of a specimen (for example, a micro-photograph from an electron microscope) that 'ought not to be there'. An artefact does not represent the 'actual' phenomenon that the researcher 'should' be able to see. It is not a 'real' feature of the brain tissue, but a product of some error or failure in laboratory technique. For example, an artefact may be identified as a 'staining error', deriving from careless use of staining fluid in the preparation of the slide. Or it may be 'knife marks', streaks on the photograph caused by the microtome scratching the specimen during the cutting process. Therefore, artefacts are 'troubles'. They get in the way of the research and cause much frustration to the researchers.

Lynch found that artefacts figure prominently in the interactional activities of the laboratory. Newcomers are instructed in the 'typical causes' of artefacts and the need for care at all stages of the work to minimize them. When they are found, decisions have to be taken about their implications. For example, do they make a specimen unusable for research purposes? Lynch notes that these decisions were taken in the light of specific practical circumstances. Whether or not an 'imperfect' slide or photograph was used depended not on some universal, absolute criteria, but on the local circumstances of the occasion. Thus researchers might ask if they have time to prepare some more, or whether there were other specimens that were 'okay' so that the flawed ones need only be used for 'corroboration', or whether a 'perfect' example was needed for a research publication.

From an ethnomethodological point of view, the factual character of artefacts as real problems with which the laboratory researchers routinely had to cope are constituted by the practical reasoning involved in 'noticing', 'assessing' and 'explaining' them. Researchers were able to see that something on a slide 'must be an artefact' because they 'knew' what to look for and knew what they 'should' be able to see. Thus researchers 'knew' that 'through no one's fault' laboratory instruments could sometimes 'distort' the very phenomena they made visible in the first place. In exercising this knowledge, researchers did not treat as a logical problem how natural

phenomena could be found to be 'distorted' by means of the very
same technical procedures that made them observable. Their interest was entirely in the *practical implications* of artefacts, not in
their logical or epistemological status. When a possible artefact was
'discovered', members of the research team would consult and
decide what to *do* about it. Opinions would be solicited and interpretations proffered, resulting in a decision about whether the feature should be followed up or ignored. Over the course of further
work, researchers would treat subsequent specimens as indicating
what the previously noticed feature 'must have been'.

Lynch's study, then, shows how the facts of science are socially
constituted in the everyday activities of the research laboratory. His
purpose is not to criticize these activities in terms of some version
of how science ideally should be done. Rather, as an ethnomethodologist, he seeks to show how researchers produce 'scientific
knowledge' as the practical outcome of situated, judgemental work
in the daily round of the laboratory.

Criticisms of ethnomethodology

As we remarked earlier, ethnomethodology has resisted incorpor-
ation into the sociological 'mainstream'. Perhaps for this reason it
has come under more fire from critics than almost any other
approach. We have already mentioned two of the most common
criticisms – that ethnomethodology denies the 'constraining' character of social life upon individuals and that it proposes that
sociology can do no more than reproduce members' versions of
things. We have suggested that both are based in misunderstandings. Also, both criticisms tend to emanate from sociologists with
very different theorectical commitments to those of ethnomethodology. What they amount to is the charge that ethnomethodology
does not conceive these matters in the ways that other approaches
do. To that charge, ethnomethodologists are apt to reply: of course
it doesn't!

Another common criticism is that, in comparison with the topics
conceptualized in other sociological approaches, ethnomethodology concerns itself with the study of microscopic social processes,
usually resulting in investigation of 'trivial' matters. Ethnomethodologists argue that this criticism also reflects 'perspectival bias'.
They emphasize that they have a thought-out rationale for their

studies, one which is just as intellectually defensible as that which informs other kinds of sociological investigations.

A more fundamental criticism concerns the means by which ethnomethodologists study members' methods and yet, on their own arguments, they simultaneously employ these methods. Critics point out that ethnomethodology is itself an organized social activity, and therefore can be viewed for how *it* is practically accomplished. This is sometimes referred to as the problem of 'radical reflexivity', that is, the study of the study of the study . . . etc. Ethnomethodologists acknowledge that this infinite regress is a logical possibility. They point out, however, that this is a problem for philosophers rather than sociologists interested in analysing the everyday world. They accept that an ethnomethodological study can be made of ethomethodological studies, and that a further ethnomethodological study can be made of the ethnomethodological study of ethnomethodological studies, and so on. They argue that nothing of fundamental significance *for sociology* is implied. Therefore it is not their particular interest to continue indefinitely along this chain. Moreover, the production of any account anywhere along this chain requires it to be accomplished by the use of members' commonsense methods of practical reasoning. Their interest is in these methods.

Conclusion

We end this chapter with a few remarks on the similarities and differences between symbolic interactionism and ethnomethodology. At a general level, they are similar in the emphasis they place on the qualitative investigation of social processes. They are also similar, of course, in their view of social life as constituted through meaning, and of sociology as an *interpretive* discipline. Both approaches have contributed to a re-evaluation of the centrality of language in social life. It is understandable, therefore, that students, coming to sociology for the first time, often have difficulty in seeing any real differences between them.

Yet on closer inspection the differences are not hard to recognize. Interactionist studies typically are concerned to identify 'social meanings' that some group of actors share and to explain these meanings in terms of the relation the actors have with one another and with other groups. Thus the interactionist is concerned with *actors*, their beliefs, actions and relationships. The ethno-methodologist, in contrast, is concerned with *activities* rather than actors. Ethnomethodological studies inquire not so much into meanings, as into the work which makes meanings possible. The ethnomethodologist asks about how such meanings are 'locally' managed and the methods by which members in the setting accomplish the here-and-now practical relevance of their under-standings. One could say that ethnomethodological studies *end* at the point where symbolic interactionist studies *begin*.

This difference could be characterized as a shift in *level of analytic focus* as one moves from symbolic interactionism to ethnometho-dology. This shift is manifest in the different concepts employed. Where the symbolic interactionist speaks of 'self' and 'other', of 'shared symbols' and 'joint actions', the ethnomethodologist speaks of the 'local production' of understandings and the methods by which members 'assemble the sense' of situational particulars. It is also marked by characteristic differences in 'style' between sym-bolic interactionist and ethnomethodological studies. The former typically are impressionistic and 'loose'; the latter tend to be far more technical and precise.

Perhaps the most notable difference, however, lies in their vitality as research programmes. As we stated earlier, symbolic interactionism seems to be past its most productive phase. Though some good empirical studies are still being done within the interactionist tradition, few new ideas of note have emerged in recent years. Ethnomethodology, on the other hand, appears still to be developing its ideas and finding new phenomena to study. And that, arguably, is the acid test of any sociological perspective.

Further reading

Button G., and Lee, J. R. E., *Talk and Social Organisation* (Multilingual Matters, 1987). A collection of studies in conversation analysis.

Grathoff, R. (ed.), *The Theory of Social Action: The Correspondence of Alfred Schutz and Talcott Parsons* (Indiana University Press, 1978). For Schutz's review of Parson's *The Structure of Social Action* and the correspondence which ensued between them on the nature of social action and socio-logical theory.

Heritage, J., *Garfinkel and Ethnomethodology* (Polity Press, 1984).

Livingston, E., *Making Sense of Ethnomethodology* (Routledge, 1987).

Lynch, M., *Art and Artefact in Laboratory Science* (Routledge, 1985).

Schutz, A., *On Phenomenology and Social Relations*, ed. H. Wagner (University of Chicago Press, 1970). A useful selection from Schutz's writings.

Sharrock, W., and Anderson, R. J., *The Ethnomethodologists* (Tavistock, 1986).

Sudnow, D., *Studies in Social Interaction* (Free Press, 1972). For Schegloff's 'Notes on a conversational practice: formulating place'; for Garfinkel's 'Studies in the routine grounds of everyday activities' which reports on disruptive 'experiments' in everyday life in order to display its routine, taken-for-granted features.

Turner, R., *Ethnomethodology* (Penguin, 1974). For Weider's 'Telling the code' which summarizes the study of the convict code; Sudnow's 'Counting deaths', showing members' practices for counting and describing deaths in a hospital; and Sacks's 'On the analysability of stories by children' which describes the organization and use of 'membership categorization devices' in story-telling.

Questions

1 What does Schutz mean when he calls the common-sense world of daily life an 'intersubjective' world? How does he analyse the nature of intersubjectivity?

2 Explain what Garfinkel means by 'the local production of order'. Does this idea deny the 'constraints' of social life upon individuals?

3 What is the 'documentary method of interpretation'? How does the work of suicide investigators display this method?

4 How does Weider's study of the 'convict code' differ from those of more conventional sociological approaches?

5 In what ways does CA demonstrate the detailed nature of the social organization of ordinary talk?

6 What are 'adjacency pairs'? How do conversationalists employ the adjacency pair structure to organize their speech activities?

7 How does Lynch's study of the activities of laboratory scientists demonstrate the practical construction of scientific knowledge?

8 How would you assess the merits and demerits of ethnomethodology as a sociological perspective?

7 Sociological perspectives and research strategies

Introduction

Previous chapters have compared sociological perspectives in terms of their conceptions of social organization but, as is well known, sociologists disagree as much about their methods as about anything else. The methodological disputes are intertwined with the substantive, sociological, ones. They do not interconnect thoroughly and systematically but there are affinities between some sociological views and some methodological positions. Here we give some introduction to the 'philosophy of science' background to recent arguments over sociological method and sketch the way these connect with research practice.

The key question put in this chapter is: what role does the sociological researcher play? Is the researcher, for example, someone who is finding out about the properties of an independent social reality? Or is he or she, instead, someone who is engaged in 'reconstructing social reality'? The typical discussion of method mostly says things about social surveys, fieldwork and other forms of inquiry. Although our discussion will briefly mention these forms of inquiry it will be designed to explicate the motivation behind the arguments over specific research techniques, rather than to describe these techniques in any detail. The questions we have posed may seem unclear at this stage, but a main point of the discussion will be to show just what is involved in them and just how fundamental they are.

Is sociology a science?

The very first question often put to beginning sociology students is: do you think sociology is a science? This is not a question that someone who has hardly even started the subject can begin to answer, but the fact that it is asked indicates how prominent it still is in the thoughts of sociologists. Much sociology *starts* from this question. In fact, its development depends on assumptions made about whether the study of social life can possibly be conducted in a truly scientific fashion.

If the question 'can sociology be a science?' is to be answered, then another question is prior to it: 'what does it take to be a science?' This is one for the philosophy of science. However, philosophers of science are no more in agreement with one another than are sociologists, so it is with some background on recent disagreements in the philosophy of science that we begin.

Positivism and science

At the centre of controversy has been the doctrine of positivism. This doctrine has long had great influence on sociology, at least as far back as the discipline's supposed founder, Auguste Comte. Emile Durkheim is a key figure because amongst other things he is regarded as providing one of the definitive demonstrations, with his study *Suicide*, that the positivist programme could work in sociology.

We acknowledge that the term 'positivism' as used here is something of a catch-all. Indeed, 'positivism' has now become an all-purpose term of abuse, indiscriminately lumping together thinkers who are not actually in agreement on many things. That said, positivism in general has two basic features. Firstly, it is convinced that there is only one *bona fide* source of knowledge, namely, scientific investigation. Secondly, it assumes that science is unified, that knowledge is acquired by a single method which is the same for all the sciences. Granting this second point (though only for the sake of argument) the obvious next question is: what is this method?

According to positivism, then, if sociology is to study and acquire knowledge of social life, it must be a science and must follow the standard method of the sciences. Could the supposed 'standard method' of science work in sociology?

Popper: science and pseudo-science

A key figure in the philosophy of science for more than the last half century, since the publication of his *The Logic of Scientific Discovery*, is Karl Popper (1902–89). Popper identifies knowledge with 'scientific knowledge' to the extent that all his arguments are designed to explain the growth in our knowledge by explaining how science has grown. Further, he calls his key, initial problem 'the demarcation problem', which asks: what do genuine sciences have in common? It is called the demarcation problem because another way of asking it is: what demarcates true science (like physics) from something that only looks like science (such as, in Popper's opinion, Marxist and Freudian doctrines)? In respect of these two assumptions, then, Popper conforms to our criteria of positivism.

Popper prefers to call his doctrines 'critical' and 'fallibilist'. The essence of science, he says, is mutual criticism. Human beings only learn about the world by forming ideas about its nature and testing them against reality itself. By forming and testing ideas they can discover that they have made mistakes and so can learn. People, however, do not necessarily verify their own ideas, but others may try to do so. The growth of knowledge is associated with a type of society in which people are free to criticize: he calls it 'an open society'. Popper's views are, therefore, associated with a political position, namely, classic liberal conceptions of the freedom of the individual and associated resistance to collective control. Hence he is a severe critic of Marxism, which he sees as having strong totalitarian inclinations.

The critical aspect is not arbitrarily inserted in his doctrines. It results from Popper's solution to the 'problem of induction'. The classic idea of induction is that science proceeds by accumulation of facts, and gathers them by making observations of events and drawing general conclusions from them. Suppose that we observe swans, and note that all the swans we see are white. On the basis of these consistent observations we may wish to venture the generalization: all swans are white. This is induction. The case of generalizing about swans serves as an example of scientific procedure in general; science builds up a mountain of such generalizations rooted in observation.

Popper observes, however, that in generalizing that all swans are white we can never be *fully* confident that our generalization is true. All the swans we have so far observed are white, but what about the next one? It might be black. Our generalization is very vulnerable as *one* counter example proves it false. But this is a good thing. We have an asymmetry between acceptance and rejection of a generalization. We can never conclusively prove a generalization true by observation because a generalization which covers *all* cases will cover cases we have not yet examined, but we *can* conclusively prove it false as it takes only one counter-example. Science actually proceeds by refutation, by the *disproving* of generalizations. Our best scientific generalizations are those which have (so far!) withstood our most determined attempts to prove them wrong. People put forward generalizations and others try to refute them, to prove them wrong, and any generalizations which have withstood our tests may yet be refuted. Popper's doctrine is not only 'critical'; it is also 'fallibilist' because it emphasizes that genuinely scientific theories are open to refutation and that we learn through making mistakes.

The difference between science and pseudo-science, then, is that between the making of generalizations which can be tested and those which cannot. Karl Marx's theories were scientific, in Popper's judgement. In Popper's view, Marx did make definite predictions that there would be a revolution by the working class in Western Europe in the late nineteenth century. No such revolution occurred. Marx predicted that something definite would happen and so made it possible to prove him wrong. If it did not happen, then his theory was rejected. Marxists, though, are not scientific, only pseudo-scientific. They say there will be a revolution, but, unlike their mentor, they refuse to put a date on it. They say there will be a revolution, there is no revolution, and then they go on to say that there are reasons why it has not yet taken place and that it *will* occur – sometime ... They cannot be proved wrong: the fact that no revolution has occurred or shows any sign of happening has no consequences for their theory because they simply say that the time is not yet ripe.

In stressing the importance of prediction, Popper also favours a conception of the scientific method which is widely favoured in positivist circles. This is the 'hypothetico–deductive' method, that is, the method of deducing hypotheses for producing scientific theory. An explanation of an event is derived, that is, logically deduced from generalizations. A scientific theory is a hierarchy of statements arranged in order of decreasing generality from the very general (such as 'All swans are white') to statements of a quite specific kind ('This is a swan'). If we hold that 'All swans are white' and are informed that 'This is a swan' then we can make a prediction: 'It will be white'. This very simple instance is the model for scientific theories of all kinds: by deduction from universal generalities we are in a position to make predictions about particular cases. These predictions are definite enough for us to tell if they are fulfilled or not. We predict that this swan is white. We know how to tell if it is white or black. If it is black, then our theory has been refuted. The hallmark of science for Popper is the capacity to make predictions which are open to refutation.

Popper rejects the view of scientific progress through steady accumulation of inductively based generalizations in favour of one which recognizes discontinuities through the refutation and replacement of whole theories by new ones. His view, however, still enables him to talk of scientific progress. We can say that our current theories are better than the previous ones because they have (so far!) withstood attempts at refutation better than their predecessors, which have been disproved.

Kuhn: scientific revolutions

Popper's views have been the focus of controversy. A key figure in the debate is Thomas Kuhn. Like Popper, he believes that change in science involves sharp discontinuity. One frame of reference is thrown out and a new one installed. The title of his main book, *The Structure of Scientific Revolutions* (Kuhn, 1962), emphasizes the way the overthrow of a whole system is involved in the change from one theory to another.

A mature science is dominated by a single, shared frame of reference: its scientists agree on fundamentals. The frame of reference, which Kuhn initially called a 'paradigm' and later termed 'the disciplinary matrix', provides an accepted setting within which research is done. He terms this research 'normal science', which is a kind of puzzle-solving. A researcher doing normal science has a problem but knows roughly what the answer to it will look like. The research will be done within the boundaries of the paradigm which tells what the solution ought to be and what methods will find it. However, as work under a given paradigm proceeds anomalies accumulate. There are results which just do not fit as they are supposed to, but they will be disregarded at first because the accepted way of doing things pays off so well and because it is assumed that, eventually, some way of fitting them into the received framework will be found. Some anomalies, however, will persist and their presence will eventually acquire a critical significance. The fact they do not fit the basic framework will now be taken to suggest that there is something wrong with the framework and that a whole new one is required. The bringing in of the new paradigm is the scientific revolution, transforming the way in which the discipline looks at things, reorganizing the way scientists go about their business, introducing new research technologies and techniques. The notion of 'revolution' is used by Kuhn to suggest that there are some closer parallels with political overturnings than might be imagined. The scientific revolution tends to involve a struggle between generations. Those who have been brought up on the old paradigm tend to adhere to it, whilst the young scientists who take up the new one only finally triumph throughout the discipline when the older generation retire or die off.

The pivotal importance of Kuhn's work for the argument here, though, is in his ideas about the relations between different paradigms. The conflict between generations shows something important, namely, that the members of the older generation do not accept that their paradigm has been refuted. They do not accept that evidence has shown that their framework is wrong and that a new framework is better. There is no evidence which *unequivocally* shows that a framework is wrong. Ajustments can be made to the framework to accommodate things which, on first sight, do not fit. As a simple example, if we have 'All swans are white' in place and someone finds a bird which looks like a swan but is black we can say, ' "All swans are white" is refuted' but we could in principle equally say that swans are white, so this bird is not a swan. In more serious and complex ways, the relation between two rival scientific theories (and their respective groups of supporters) is not clear–cut either, so the choice between them cannot be purely rational, that is, based upon decisive evidence which clearly refutes one of the two. Other considerations, possibly including the interests of scientists, will be involved. After all, if the paradigm in which they have invested their careers goes out, then the older generation lose more than just their favoured theories!

In this context, the importance of Kuhn is not in suggesting that scientists are base and self-interested (just like the rest of us), but in highlighting the point that the things we believe about the world are shaped also by social interests and not by evidence alone. It seems odd indeed to suggest that what we believe the world 'out there' to be like may depend not just on the evidence but on the internal politics of the scientific community. It seems natural to suppose that we believe the earth is a planet in the solar system because science has proved it to be the case, and much less natural to accept that our belief is the outcome of some kind of 'party political' triumph in a struggle amongst scientists who have no way of conclusively disproving the idea that the earth is, after all, the centre of the universe! If, though, we have not (as we thought we had) conclusively disproved previous theories, then our current theories are no better than their predecessors *because the latter have not been refuted*. Though possibly unintended by Kuhn, this interpretation of his ideas has had considerable influence on sociological thinking, not least in challenging Popper's view of science.

Positivism in sociology

Since positivism has provided a popular philosphy of science, it is not surprising that sociologists have often sought to shape their work to accord with its requirements: if science is what the positivists say it is, then to be scientific a sociology will have to match the criteria the positivists have identified.

Positivist doctrines have a first use as a critical instrument. Not much sociology satisfies Popper's primary criterion, namely, that a position be open to refutation. The sociological positions outlined in preceding chapters do not issue predictions precise enough to allow for refutation. They are not made up of the spelled-out, hierarchically organized systems of generalizations which enable the deduction of specific hypotheses (as the predictions are termed) which can then be tested. Sociology is not scientific, then, because it does not have testable theories. The positivists conclude that the way forward is to create the possibility of refuting theories. This move has two main elements: (1) the creation of true theories, that is, systems of propositions which can be ranked in order of generality and which imply specific, testable hypotheses; (2) the development of a methodological apparatus that will allow the testing of hypotheses, that is, the creation of measurement systems. Together, the two elements involve the mathematicization of sociology.

The classic theories of natural science are not really like our example of 'All swans are white', which can be tested by checking to see what colour a given swan is. The classic theories are, in fact, stated in mathematical equations. For example, one such theory states that there are definite relations between the temperature, volume and pressure of a gas, such that if one of these is varied by a certain amount, the others will change in known proportions. Hence we derive the testable hypothesis (= prediction): if the pressure is increased and the temperature remains the same, the volume of the gas will be changed. The law is usually stated as a mathematical equation: $P_1 V_1 = P_2 V_2$ (T is constant) where P_1 is pressure at time 1. P_2 pressure at time 2. V_1 is volume at time 1, V_2 volume at time 2 and T is temperature.

The law does not simply tell us that if the pressure changes and the temperature remains the same, then the volume will alter: it says that if the pressure is changed by a specific amount, then if the temperature is constant the volume will also change by a specifiable amount. The statement of the laws in this form, and their testing, both presuppose that we have ways of measuring the relevant 'variables' as these measurable properties are called. Access to scales stating temperature in degrees, volume in cubic units, and pressure per cubic units, together with appropriate instruments, such as thermometers and pressure gauges, allow us to specify and measure particular cases. From the law we can predict that, at constant pressure, a rise of so much in the temperature will result in a change of just so much in volume, and if we can measure the changes in temperature and volume we can see quite clearly if they come out as predicted. Only such measurement allows the law to take its precise, refutable, form. Hence, sociology needs to develop true theories which can be stated in mathematical equations and needs to develop measurement scales and instruments to enable testing of these theories.

It is now perhaps possible to see why Durkheim's *Suicide* is regarded as a leading model for the positivist approach. Though not stated mathematically his theories are set out in ways which parallel the form of mathematical laws. For example, as we saw in Chapter 2, he indicates that 'the greater the degree of integration of domestic society, the lower the level of suicide' and provides ways of measuring such variables as 'integration of domestic society' in terms of the proportion of married people in the population. He makes extensive use of statistics and their manipulation to test out his hypotheses, thus bringing a mathematical element into his theory. The fact, however, that *Suicide* remains to this day an exemplary study says something about the fate of the positivist programme. It has not been notably successful at building upon

Durkheim's supposed breakthrough. Far from turning sociology into a science with mathematically specified laws and developed measurement systems, positivists are still mainly advocating positivist views, calling upon sociology to develop testable theories (cf. Lenski, 1986) and worrying about the inadequacy, indeed incompetence, in its use of mathematics and its attempts at measurement (cf. Blalock, 1984). Although *Suicide* may be held up as a model, it is not one which is or has been easily and successfully emulated.

Positivists in sociology are not necessarily discouraged by their failure. For them, positivism is *the* way of obtaining knowledge and depends on using *the* proper scientific method. For they believe that a consequent outcome is the 'objectivity' of findings. In fact, from their point of view, the need to pursue positivist approaches originates in the need to achieve objectivity in sociological inquiries, and they cannot conceive any other way of doing so. The idea of objectivity has two main aspects:

(1) *Neutrality* For positivists, this aspect is about what we would ordinarily call objectivity and has to do with neutrality between positions. Impartiality with respect to the positions and interests involved in a dispute is often considered a basis for seeing the rights and wrongs of the matters at issue. Impartiality encourages a conception that the sociologist should be 'value free' – a term also favoured by Max Weber who was not by any means a positivist (Weber, 1989).

(2) *Mind independence* For positivists, the objective of science is to determine the character of the world of nature, the properties of something existing independently of us and subject to its own laws of behaviour, regardless of what we think about it. The way the world is and the nature of our thoughts about it are independent of each other. Our ideas of how things are can be quite removed from how they really are, as the history of science shows. For example, people thought that the earth was the centre of the universe, when in reality it was only a satellite of the sun. We need methods which (*a*) ensure that we get at how things really are without the intervention of our beliefs about them and (*b*) inhibit the involvement of the researcher's personal views and prejudices in order to allow the phenomena to reveal their own intrinsic character.

At the beginning of the chapter we asked: 'what is the researcher doing?' and can now give a first positivist answer: the researcher is giving nature the opportunity to reveal itself to us. The aim is to develop research methods which minimize any influence that the investigator might have on the collection of data, particularly anything that might allow the investigator's preferences or preconceptions to influence the process of data collection, potentially preventing him from truly perceiving the nature of the phenomena he is trying to identify and describe. These requirements have effectively been condensed into the demand for the 'reproducibility' of data, the insistence that each researcher ought to get the same results if he 'replicates', that is, goes through the same operations. The prime way attempts have been made to secure 'replication' in sociology has been through the creation of kinds of research in which explicit and standard procedures can be developed, so that one researcher can (notionally, at least) repeat or replicate, and thereby test, the work done by another. The sociological procedure which reputedly does so most effectively is the social survey.

The social survey and objectivity

The social survey collects data through the asking and answering of questions. The collection of data is usually done by several researchers, who ask members of the population they are studying a series of questions and record their answers. The questions to be asked are printed out so that each investigator will be asking the same questions and in the same order, thus preventing any variation in the questioning process. The researchers will also be trained in how to administer the procedure and how to record the answers, further to ensure that it does not matter who is asking the questions or who is writing down the answers. The people being asked the question, the 'respondents', will have been selected from the population being investigated. Opinion pollsters who study the voting dispositions of the whole electorate do not have to interview all its members. The questioning of a very small proportion, no more than a few thousand, is sufficient to allow generalization to the whole population of voters, itself many millions strong. The persons to be interviewed are, then, only a sample of the population they are to represent, but to ensure that they will represent that population they must be selected by strict rules. Typically, this means that the sample is to be chosen randomly, that is, by a method which ensures that one member of the population has exactly the same chance as any other of being chosen. The random nature of the process of selection is necessary for statistical reasons, for it is (usually) only from a randomly chosen sample that one can legitimately use statistical techniques to generalize to the whole population. For example, sociologists often choose people from the electoral lists according to a table of random numbers. This procedure of simply picking people out if their position on the list corresponds to some number from another list means that the personal inclinations of the researchers do not in any way enter into the choice of the people to be studied.

Once the data has been collected and the answers to questions written down, then these materials can be coded. Nowadays coding involves transforming the answers recorded in the interview into a form that can be handled on a computer. The transformation of the initial data into this other form is something that again ought to be done according to strict rules to ensure that the people doing the work are not deciding for themselves how different answers should be classified for translation into the coding scheme. All these procedures should have been worked out in advance and explicit guidance provided to minimize the judgement coders need to use. Indeed, the coders should have been trained and tested to ensure that two coders will classify the same item in the same way. Once the data has been coded, it can then be fed into the computer and there analysed. This analysis involves the manipulation of the data according to the strict and explicit rules of statistics. The social survey is a paragon of the virtues for positivist sociologists because there is (or ought to be) very little room for the idiosyncracies of individuals to affect the process.

By contrast, the bane of the positivist's life is field research, or, as it is more often called, participant observation. Sociology has rather a restricted repertoire of investigative techniques and survey research and participant observation are the main two. In fact, survey research is overwhelmingly the most widely used. Some years ago a study of major sociological journals showed that some 90 per cent of studies in them used data gathered in surveys as their primary source (Phillips, 1971). Survey research and fieldwork are usually (though not always) regarded as rival methods. Certainly, for someone who gives survey methods the virtues enumerated above, fieldwork must seem an unacceptable approach.

The typical field researcher spends some time observing the day-to-day life of a group of people. The researcher accompanies, for example, beat officers in the police, follows them around, makes notes of what happens as it goes on. What the fieldworker actually does will largely be dictated by circumstances but otherwise it will be up to him or her. There are no explicit rules to guide a worker in what to observe or how to write down the notes they keep. We cannot be sure that another researcher would notice the same things, or, if they did notice them, would see them the same way – people do often disagree about what they witness. Fieldwork cannot, in a close sense, be replicated, be done over again. If someone goes to live amongst a group which has been previously studied, then, in the period between the two investigations, much about the group will have changed, so the second researcher will not be studying quite the same situation. In any case, fieldwork is rarely repeated. It takes a lot of time and cannot be closely reproduced. In summary, then, the positivist objection to studies based on fieldwork is that they do not attempt to ensure the reproducibility of their methods, and, worse, they would probably be unable to do so if they tried.

Since there are only the two primary methods, the association of the social survey with the positivist outlook ensures that dissent from that outlook will involve rejection of its preferred method and that fieldwork methods will be used despite positivist objections. In any case, if positivist ideas are rejected so will criticisms of fieldwork emanating from them.

Reactions against positivist ideals of objectivity

Objections to 'value freedom'

The first objections to positivism in sociology can be made with respect to the notion of being value free. One source of such objections would be someone we have used as an example of positivism, Karl Popper. In Popper's view it is not necessary to seek objectivity *at the level of the individual scientist*. The objectivity of science is not achieved because the scientist is some kind of in-human creature, divested of feelings, values, politics, judgement or imagination through subjection to a rigorous disciplinary regime of investigative rules. The best science is not cautious, rule-complying work; rather it is bold, adventurous, inventive and speculative, throwing over the previous conventions. The objectivity of science is achieved *at the collective level*. It results from mutual criticism and in effect the cancelling out of individual biases. Indeed, far from being a handicap to the progress of science, the partiality of its participants is a benefit, for the very diversity of strongly held views will motivate the critical effort of trying to prove that other people's views are wrong.

The Marxists have doubts too, and not just about the ideal of value freedom within the positivist framework. They have doubts about the value freedom of positivist ideas themselves. Though we did not identify them as such there, we have already cited Georg Lukács as arguing that positivist type ideas of science stand in the way of a proper analysis of the 'social totality', and, relatedly, also cited the way the Frankfurt School condemn them for helping to maintain social regulation. The positivist approach *may* be all right for understanding nature, but it cannot be applied to social life, for there truth is not achieved through impartiality. In societies constituted through class struggle, understanding is distorted and falsified by the needs of that struggle, and the realities of a society's organization are concealed to serve the purposes of some classes in that struggle. Within a given social formation, only some classes are in a position to be able to grasp the true nature of the society. In the 'classic' Marxist conception, only the working class in capitalist society is capable of grasping it. The increasingly naked forms of exploitation, the growth of visible inequality and the intensified political struggle induced by the concentration of the working class in industrial plants and in urban communities – these realities will force themselves upon the working class. The truth about social organization is not found by being neutral in class struggle, nor is it learned by the pursuit of purely scientific inquiries. In talking of 'the unity of theory and practice' Marxists mean that the truth about social reality is learned through involvement in political struggle and through the attempt to make revolutionary changes in the social order. In such a context, attempts to appear 'objective' in the positivist sense are likely to result in ideological misrepresentations of the real nature of the society which is clearly class-divided and oppressive.

Marxists, though, do not dissent from the notion that objectivity involves the apprehension of a 'mind independent' reality. A keystone of the Marxist argument is the notion of 'ideology', which entails there being a difference between how social organization really is and how it appears in the thoughts of people in society. There are those, however, who do dissent from the notion of 'mind independence' and we now turn to their arguments.

Objections to 'mind independence'

Seen in positivist terms, the researcher is giving nature the maximum opportunity to reveal itself. The world is 'out there' and the purpose of science is to find out about it without our ideas, passions and preconceptions getting in the way. For positivists, the world's being the way it is regardless of our ideas about it is such an obvious and necessary truth that they cannot accept that it is an assumption on their part. They cannot, therefore, easily see how their critics can treat it as an assumption, let alone one that could be set aside. How can investigation proceed, except in the knowledge that the world being investigated exists independently of the activities and ideas of the investigator? None the less, there are those who do see the 'mind independence' of reality as an assumption, and one that may not even be necessary.

As we have said, Kuhn has played an influential part in challenging the assumption of mind independence. Popper relies upon a conception of reality as independent of our thoughts about it because we test our theories against reality itself. We make predictions and then observe to see what happens in reality. The observation of the real phenomenon is the key to the whole procedure. What, though, if the process of observation was itself 'theory laden', to use a term developed by N. R. Hanson (1962)? What if our capacity to observe something depended upon our theories about it so that without the theory we could not possibly observe the phenomenon? This is the thought that Kuhn has influentially developed. Consider the cloud chamber photographs physicists employ. These photographs provide observations on the creation and decay of atomic particles, but to someone without a great deal of knowledge of physics they look like an arbitrary assortment of meaningless lines. Physicists talk about observing these particles, but they can only make the sense they do of these pictures in terms of the physical ideas they accept: it is physical theory which tells us how these lines could trace the movement of particles and what they could possibly show about their life and death. The theory makes the observation possible and so, in a sense, the capacity to observe the particles depends on the theory itself. In such a case, perhaps the nature of reality is not entirely independent of our ideas about it.

The idea of the mind independent of reality can also be questioned in terms of arguments about the nature of social reality. The natural world may be 'mind independent' in the sense that Mount Everest does exist independently of our ideas of it and changing our ideas will not lead the mountain to grow larger, to get smaller, to move across the globe or disappear. Yet is our relation to *social* reality like that, does it exist quite independently of our thoughts about it?

Karl Popper now turns up on this side of the fence. In sociology, he is a 'methodological individualist', one who argues that society has no existence over and above the individuals who make it up. There is no 'state' or 'nation' save as the aggregate of its individual members. State and nation have no reality *save as ideas in people's heads*, ideas which organize their conduct. Though otherwise a vast distance from Popper, and even on this point in complex disagreement with him, Peter Winch (1958) has argued something that at least sounds the same.

Positivist ideas are often borrowed from the natural sciences, which serve as a model for treating the relations between people as if they were between natural phenomena. To use our example from Chapter 5, interactions between people might be conceived as comparable to the interactions between colliding billiard balls. Winch argues against adopting this idea because the relations between people are more like the interchange of ideas within a conversation than they are like the transfer of physical energy between two billiard balls. People interact in terms of their ideas. He uses the example of 'war'. People in a war shoot, stab and bomb each other. They interact physically all right, but their conduct is guided by their understanding of things. They are not just attacking each other out of explosions of mindless rage, but are guided by the idea, amongst others, that they are in a state of war and that people can be divided into those on 'our side' and 'the enemy', that their duty is to resist and kill the enemy. The organization of war is not, then, something independent of our ideas, but something which involves, indeed consists in, our very ideas of war.

These views are relatively recent expressions of ones which have been long been opposed to positivism in sociology and which can claim Max Weber as one of their main representatives, though they considerably antedate even his work. Again, we saw in Chapter 5 that this tradition is sometimes called the *verstehende* or 'understanding' approach. If we think of the study of collisions between billiard balls and the model for sociological investigation, as the positivist tradition invites us to, then the researcher's primary role is that of an onlooker observing events and looking for regular, law like relations between them. If, however, people, unlike billiard balls, respond to events as they see them, so to speak, then the sociological investigator has to be concerned to get some notion of how the people being studied see things, to understand their point of view. This concern significantly changes the conception of the researcher's role: instead of being a detached spectator, the researcher is now conceived as an involved participant, aiming to understand fellow human beings.

Symbolic interaction and fieldwork methods

Symbolic interactionists are notorious for the slogan we cited in Chapter 5: 'If people define situations as real, they are real in their consequences.' Note that this slogan does not involve denying that there is a difference between how situations are and how they appear to be to the members of society. It simply says that people react to situations as they perceive them and that if we want to understand the pattern of their reactions we need therefore to understand how they see the things they are reacting to. We need, that is, to appreciate their point of view.

The leading example of this point is the labelling theory of deviance. This theory is much misunderstood, but what it actually proposes is that *for our sociological purposes* it does not matter whether someone 'really did' the crime of which they have been found guilty. The *relevant* sociological point is that people treat others on the basis of the way they categorize them, and so if we categorize, that is, label, a person as guilty, then that label will affect the way in which we shall subsequently treat them. Being defined as 'deviant' certainly has real consequences for the people so defined. They will be restrained, transported to prison, denied their civil rights, have their career disrupted and destroyed, for example, and when they are released from prison they will be treated then as 'ex-convicts', people will not want them living next door, will not employ them, and so forth.

Because peoples' responses depend on their perception of situations, sociological research involves not simply the description of the situations in which people act, but the descriptions of those situations as they appear to the people who act in them. From the symbolic interactionist point of view, a prominent feature of research must be the identification of the actor's point of view. The researcher must find ways of perceiving situations from the standpoint of the actors involved. _It cannot be assumed_ that they will see things in the way the researcher does.

It must not be thought, though, that 'the actor's point of view' is kept privately within the heads of the relevant individuals. The task of identifying the actor's point of view is not a matter of psychological guesswork, with the researcher just speculating about what people think. From the symbolic interactionist point of view, social life is a process of communication between social actors. As part and parcel of social life, people communicate to one another how they see things, so the researcher can find out what these points of view are and must do so through participation in the process of communication. Clearly the optimal environment for the researcher to gain access to the expression of the actors' points of view is the world of their daily life. Thus, the basic method of inquiry is through fieldwork investigation, which provides the opportunity to develop intimate relations and candid communications with those being studied so that a full and detailed acquaintance with their view of things may be acquired. In this framework, the great weight of methodological concern is on self-consciousness about the management of social relations in the fieldwork situation. As communication is a two-way process, the researcher is inevitably, and often unconsciously, communicating his own point of view to those being studied. So there must be an appropriate 'presentation of self' (to use Erving Goffman's phrase) if the researcher is to be seen as someone acceptable, who can be allowed to hang around, who can be talked to and, importantly, confided in. Further, the communicational practices of different social groups are themselves varied, so the researcher must find out the conventions of the group under study in order to avoid misunderstanding. For example, he might inappropriately construe words or actions in the terms of his home culture. Moreover, the researcher is not conceived merely as participant, but also as _mediator_ for it falls to him to express the point of view of the group under study to people who are not aware of it, such as professional colleagues and other social groups.

Ethnomethodology and the organization of description

Many people (including readers of our previous editions) profess that they are unable to tell the difference between symbolic interactionists and ethnomethodologists. It is very difficult to make the real and substantial difference clear briefly and in simple terms. We began this task in Chapters 5 and 6 and now we develop it further.

The symbolic interactionists say that people respond to situations as they define them and the aim of research is to describe the actor's point of view. They point to the process of communication and the vehicle of language as means by which that point of view is expressed and can be identified. They therefore try to examine social relations as relations of communication.

Ethnomethodologists, though not contradicting what symbolic interactionists say, take a rather different tack. They note that there is something like an equivalence between how people perceive situations and the way in which they do (or would) describe them. As every sociologist knows perfectly well, the members of society are in possession of one or another natural language, hopefully English for readers of this text, which they use to talk to one another and to describe the things they themselves or others are doing. Most sociologists are interested in whether the descriptions that the members of society give of what they are doing are correct and often ask if they need correcting by them, the sociologists. Every sociologist must equally well presume that the ways in which the members of society use the natural language at their disposal will be socially organized. However, though the other sociological perspectives recognize that human beings are 'symbol-using animals', counting this an important fact, they do not give it much further attention. We have mentioned, for example, how Parsons solves the problem of communication between members of society by 'fiat'. His mode of analysis requires that the members of society can communicate between themselves and that they can communicate with the sociological researcher, but Parsons just takes it for granted that people have a common language and can talk to one another in it; he does not raise any questions about how this possibility is made available or what it consists in. In contrast, ethnomethodologists make the use of natural language a main focus of their inquiries. Rather than just taking it for granted that the ways in which people use language will relate to the organization of their relationships, they seek to make the social organization of the way people talk to one another a topic of sustained investigation and, as a main part of this endeavour, are concerned with the ways in which they describe their own and others' activities. Description itself is a socially organized activity, worthy of detailed study.

For example, take labelling theory. The symbolic interactionists are interested in the difference that being labelled 'deviant' makes in the relations between those who are labelled and those who so label them, especially the reactions of the latter, the labellers. Symbolic interactionists know perfectely well that the business of labelling someone a deviant is often the outcome (in our society) of finding them guilty in court and that someone cannot be labelled 'guilty' just any old how. They are more interested in the fact that the label is attached than in paying attention to all that is involved in arriving at a guilty verdict. Ethnomethodologists, however, probe into the business of having someone convicted, recognizing that it is a complex and extended process which involves all kinds of considerations, ranging from the organization of procedures whereby police decide whether to prefer charges and how to formulate these through to the involvement of lawyers, court hearings and jury deliberations. The capacity to *describe* someone as 'guilty as charged' is the upshot of this lengthy and elaborate process and it is to the organization of its inner workings that ethnomethodology pays attention.

The symbolic interactionists consider social relations from the point of view of communication, asking how the participants in them communicate to one another their mutual expectations and evaluations. For example, they have been much interested in the ways doctors, by wearing white coats, speaking in jargon and keeping the patient waiting, and so forth, impress upon those patients that they are the authority, are in charge. The title of Philip Strong's *The Ceremonial Order of the Clinic* (Strong, 1979) indicates how much he is influenced by Erving Goffman's view of social relations as ritual. In fact, he treats the relations in the paediatric clinic as having a substantial ceremonial element, describing relations between the doctor and the parents of the patients as ones in which the parties seek to convey the impression that they have confidence in one another, with the parents displaying confidence they may not actually feel in the doctor, and the doctor reciprocally showing that he regards them as good parents (though these feelings might not be genuine either).

Ethnomethodologists do not deny the merits of this approach. For them, however, it does not probe enough into what people actually *do*. Indeed, the analogy with ceremony and the use of metaphors and parallel concepts in parallel situations might well mask what people are actually doing. Instead of trying to conceive situations in general terms of (say) 'impression management' ethnomethodologists prefer to regard social relations as primarily *practical* and to ask how specific kinds of activities get done in practice. Social life involves people doing things and so a description needs to be made of the ways in which people actually carry out the practical business of whatever they are doing. For example, the business of charging someone with an offence in our legal process involves paperwork and the filling in of forms. Consequently, ethnomethodologists have shown interest in how people actually fill in forms. Similarly, the business of arriving at the verdict eventually falls into the hands of a jury, whose members reach their verdict by talking amongst themselves. Ethnomethodologists ask how, by talking amongst themselves, members of a jury can decide 'the facts' of a case: who really did what? who is to blame? what does the law require the accused should be found guilty of? Hence their task in this connection would be to produce a description of how people find 'matters of fact' by talking amongst themselves.

These examples from the legal setting demonstrate the connection ethnomethodology makes between how people give descriptions and how they make judgements and decisions. The way people describe things in their talk (or otherwise depict them, via diagrams, film or whatever) is connected with the ways in which they find out what are (for their purposes) matters of fact. The general programme of ethnomethodology therefore gives central place to the study of the ways in which people find what, as a matter of fact, is happening in a given situation. For example, how they find out whether someone is guilty as charged, whether a schoolchild is intelligent or not, whether a person is entitled to unemployment insurance, whether someone was being rude. They are concerned to examine how people make such findings in the practical environments in which they characteristically make them, so they want to examine how the finding of guilt is made in jury proceedings, how the intelligence of a schoolchild is determined in the classroom, how rudeness is detected in conversation. In its turn, this concern is very much tied up with the examination of the way people, through talk in juries, classrooms and informal conversations, describe things to one another.

This kind of approach calls for appropriate methods. A jury's guilty verdict results from people talking to one another in the jury room, and how actually the things they say lead to the finding they eventually make is an intricate matter, one which can only effectively be untangled if one has a good and detailed record of the events in question. The desire for close access to the actual, practical things people do calls for something like fieldwork access to social settings. To see how teachers are judging the abilities of their pupils requires access to the schools and classrooms where this activity is occurring. Such access, however, is not necessarily the same as that required by the symbolic interactionists, who want to get close to the people involved and to know them intimately. The aim is, rather, to get close to the details of the *activities* involved, to make as full a record of them as possible: just what things do teachers do to decide whether the children they are teaching are intelligent or not? The length of time spent 'in the field' may actually be quite short, perhaps only long enough to make some close observations on what, say, a police officer does when interviewing a suspect and filling in a form. As stated in Chapter 6, the focus is on activities rather than people. In aiming for a good close record, detailed field notes will do at a minimum, but preferably researchers will try for an audio- or video-tape recording which can subsequently be re-examined over and over in much detail.

Like the symbolic interactionists, the ethnomethodologists' method also calls for self-consciousness, but of a different kind. The symbolic interactionist requires self-consciousness because the point about social life being a matter of communication applies also to sociological research. In turn, the ethnomethodologists' point about fact-finding and description being socially and practically organized also applies to sociologists' research, as much as to any other work or activity. There is, therefore, a need for self-consciousness about the ways in which ethnomethodologists are able to examine and interpret materials and to find out what the people involved are doing. It is possible, since the ethnomethodologists themselves are members of society and consequently have the same capacity as anyone else, to find out what someone is doing or what is happening on a given occasion. Basically, they have the same 'common-sense' knowledge. Hence, the ethnomethodologists' self-consciousness is particularly directed toward the extent to which the investigations of sociological researchers are dependent not upon some distinctive, specialized, sociological method, but upon the 'common-sense' procedures of fact-finding and describing which are current amongst the (other) ordinary members of society. It is, therefore, directed to the extent to which sociological research itself employs methods of fact-finding and describing, which are those routinely in use in the society itself.

Post-structuralism and the text

The symbolic interactionists and ethnomethodologists both reject the positivist conception of research which essentially requires the minimization of the researcher's involvement. This requirement ignores the extent to which the research process is a matter of human activity and, in the case of studying social life, one which has a social character. For the symbolic interactionist, the researcher is engaged in a relationship with those being investigated: for the ethnomethodologist, sociological research necessarily involves drawing upon the common culture, the 'common-sense understandings', he shares with people in society. In each case, the concern for self-consciousness about these things means that there is a desire to make explicit just how the researcher goes about the research, just what things are done to produce the study.

What is going on may be compared to what was done by the architects of the Pompidou centre in Paris. Buildings, of course, require various services if they are to be usable – heating, lighting, ventilation, and so forth. Traditionally, architects have sought to conceal the means of delivery of these services, making them as unobtrusive as possible. Thus, they have hidden the heating ducts, the electrical cables and so forth in the walls and under the floors. The Pompidou centre, though, does not treat these services as matters of embarrassment and concealment, but puts them ostentatiously on display, out front where people can see them. Buildings need heating pipes and electrical conduits, so why pretend that they do not? Similarly, sociological research involves people doing things, so why try to conceal these necessities from view, why not put them on display, as an integral part of the research structure itself, and thus as an explicit part of the research report?

The post-structuralists, for example, do not treat these questions as rhetorical. They have an answer to why people have tried to conceal these things and it is in accord with their general view of the role of knowledge and domination. The primary role of such 'concealment' has been to create a false impression of objectivity thereby furthering the cause of one point of view, the supposedly scientific one, in the struggle for dominance.

The positivist researcher wants the research report to look almost as though it is the voice of nature itself speaking, as though what it says is not just the product of a mere person. By sounding as though it had the authority of nature behind it it presents itself as something others must accept. The author of a research report written in this way is trying to impose a point of view on others, almost to pass it off on people as though it were not a point of view at all, thus legitimizing *one* way of seeing things as the *only* way. We are verging here on the self-fulfilling prophecy, for if the authors of sociological research reports are successful in convincing others of their view, then there will only be one view because others will have been eliminated. However, if the sociological viewpoint triumphs in this way, it will have resulted from mis-representation rather than because sociologists have 'played fair'.

Sociologists in the positivist tradition wanting to convince others of their own point of view do not acknowledge that they are themselves necessarily involved in a persuasive exercise which requires use of the 'rhetoric' the positivist tradition has ostenta-tiously scorned. Rhetoric is the art of persuasion. Positivists conceive of science as something which eschews persuasive tech-niques in order to let the evidence speak for itself. Yet most thinkers now accept that the evidence is not independent of some scientific theory or other, it does not speak for itself. Scientists not only do, but must use 'rhetoric' themselves if they are to convince others. Hence it is important to be self-conscious about the rhetorical character of sociological research reports. The kind of techniques Derrida contrived for the 'deconstruction' of texts in general can be applied to traditional sociological or other scientific writings to show how they aspire to a unity and coherence they cannot have. They encourage future sociological writings to 'come clean' about their rhetorical character and self-consciously to adopt the techniques employed in novels and other writings.

In contemporary literary criticism, the current bane is 'realism', that kind of writing which is supposed simply to represent how things are in the real world. Such novels claim to avoid all literary artifices in order that they may represent reality itself, just as positivists ostensibly dispense with rhetoric. The counter-argument suggests that 'realism' is not only itself a collection of literary devices of a particular kind, it is also a potentially dishonest approach in trying to present itself as what it is not. Instead, novels must deliberately present themselves as novels, as constructions out of literary devices. Questions as to whether they represent how things are 'in reality' are irrelevant since the idea that there is any single, external reality to be represented is itself a false one, as the novels themselves may be designed to show. The novel should be treated and enjoyed as a text, as an artefact or construction, one which is overtly aware of its own character as the product of artifice. A mild example of this kind of exercise can be found in John Fowles's novel, *The French Lieutenant's Woman* (1969). Chapter 12 ends by asking about the French Lieutenant's woman: 'Who is Sarah? Out of what shadows does she come?'

Chapter 13 begins:

I do not know. This story I am telling is all imagination. These characters I create never existed outside my own mind. If I have pretended until now to know my characters' minds and inner-most thoughts, it is because I am writing in (just as I have assumed some of the vocabulary and 'voice' of) a convention universally accepted at the time of my story: that the novelist stands next to God. He may not know all, yet he tries to pretend that he does. But I live in the age of Alain Robbe-Grillet and Roland Barthes; if this is a novel, it cannot be a novel in the modern sense of the word...

So perhaps I am writing a transposed autobiography; perhaps I now live in one of the houses I have brought into the fiction; perhaps Charles (the main male character) is myself disguised. Perhaps it is only a game. Modern women like Sarah exist, and I have never understood them. Or perhaps I am trying to pass off a book of essays on you. (Fowles, 1969, pp. 97)

In other words, the author intervenes in the novel, interjecting to remind readers that they are readers and that it is a work of fiction they are reading, warning them against thinking of fictional characters as though they were real people. The reminder is given in a way which disrupts the convention that had hitherto been used to tell the story, thereby reminding the reader that the 'realism' of the novel is only the product of a convention, and that conventions can be broken. Indeed, the convention that had hitherto been followed – that of the omnipotent narrator – may once have been unquestioningly accepted but nowadays is impossible to respect. Further, reminders that the story is a novelist's construction give way to attempts to provoke doubts that it is a novel at all: perhaps it is only a game, or a collection of essays. Just to add further complication, it must be noted that we have been disregarding the passage's own warning by talking as if 'the author' was the real person, John Fowles. Consequently, we overlook the possibility that 'the author' may be another character in the novel, as much a fictional figure as Sarah and Charles. The features of Fowles's novel are strongly paralleled by the passage of sociological writing by Woolgar and Ashmore discussed below, which has the same tendency of the text to 'turn back' upon itself, to start worrying about what kind of text it is, thus raising doubts about its own status and raising the possibility it might be misleading its readers.

The general points apply not only to novels but to writing generally. Another feature of the opposition to realism is the denial that there is a necessary difference between fiction and other forms of writing. All forms of writing are literary, composed of literary devices, and the presentation of certain documents as 'factual' itself entails the employment of a battery of literary techniques. Hence, supposedly factual works should be examined for the ways in which they are constructed as 'factual' and can be subjected to the method of 'deconstruction' as contrived by (*inter alia*) Derrida, to show up the ways in which they undermine their own supposed difference from 'fictional' ones.

We require, therefore, a self-consciousness of sociological work as pieces of writing and of sociological studies as texts, with the relentless critique of any attempts they may make to deny their status as literary/textual productions. We have to make clear the written character of our own work by the explicit employment of obtrusively literary techniques. In the traditional novel, an omnipotent narrator often tells the whole story in an impersonal manner and knows everything about all characters and thoughts. This narrator has now been eliminated (or is retained only to be parodied or discredited – as in the quotation from Fowles) and replaced by a multiplicity of narrators, who are limited by their point of view, who may not be reliable and who may indeed be deliberately misleading us. Such novels are constructed to show us that *it is not really possible* to accept one single, overall point of view of the sort the novel has traditionally provided. Yet this single, overall point of view is just the one to which the sociological researcher has traditionally aspired. The introduction of novelistic techniques into sociological writing will be such as to make the sociological research report itself a composite of different (often discordant) voices and will thereby demonstrate to us that the god-like stance to which the novelist and the sociologist once aspired cannot be had. Instead, we will see that everything is related to some point of view, and that the sociologist's view is only one amongst a competing plurality, with abolutely no claim to uniquely authoritative status.

It is very difficult to provide a sociological example of the kind of thing that results from these arguments, especially if it is to be brief, but the following may serve as a sample. It is from the introduction (by Woolgar and Ashmore) to a collection of essays. The passage quoted comes at the end of a summary of the contents of the rest of the book:

> Finally, the 'introduction' by Woolgar and Ashmore is largely a conventional empiricist monologue occasionally enlivened with dialogic discussion – a form which the authors emphatically repudiate. Moreover, it includes several passages which attempt to propagandize the reflexive project as the most important development since SSK (the Sociology of Scientific Knowledge)! Obviously, such hyperbole has little place in an enterprise which justifies itself in terms of the abandonment of realism. The author's claim that all such passages are, in fact, ironic, is clearly a belated and transparent attempt to get themselves off the hook, and should not, therefore, be taken seriously, (Woolgar, 1988, p. 10)

In other words, as part of its summary of the book's contents, the introduction is now summarizing itself, and is criticizing itself at the same time. It is criticizing itself for being the kind of thing – a 'conventional empiricist monologue' – that the book is supposedly designed to get away from and also for attempting to present its own approach as making intellectual progress when the point of the book is to challange the idea of intellectual progress itself. Perhaps, though, the authors are adopting a familiar literary technique, irony, and are therefore parodying the 'conventional empiricist monologue' and the idea of intellectual progress. However, to present their approach as 'irony' might be merely to cover up the fact that the text is thoroughly inconsistent, making problematic what things it says should be taken seriously, raising the question as to whether *anything* it says can be taken seriously. These criticisms are, remember, part of the very text being criticized, and the problems they raise are not resolved. In fact, the text goes on to add further layers of ambiguity to its argument and further doubts about the sense of its own position. It ends up in paradox.

Clearly, this line of argument makes studies impossible as they have traditionally been conceived, but critics also suggest that it makes its own work pointless. If taken seriously, the argument means that any attempt to produce studies which tell us how things really are can be shown eventually to undermine itself, and, persumably, studies emanating from post-structuralist sources will also liquidate themselves. This criticism, however, has already been anticipated in the citation from Woolgar and Ashmore who are more than aware of the fact they are cutting the ground from under their own feet and continue to do so with enthusiasm. They would argue that they are merely bringing out the conditions which are common to their own and their critics' situation, but that the critics have not yet recognized that their own texts can be deconstructed and shown to be as ambiguous and self-contradictory as Woolgar and Ashmore's own. These critics continue to delude themselves that they are making unequivocal sense and reaching positive and progressive conclusions, but they are really holding on to outdated ideas (in the way that someone who nowadays *seriously* tried to write a nineteenth-century novel with the then conventional 'omnipotent narrator' would be doing). After all, the primary purpose of post-structuralist strategies is to undermine the whole 'modern' tradition. In particular, the strategies are intended to subvert a key supposition supporting the project of modernity (discussed in Chapter 4), the supposition that language can be a means of transparently representing reality, permitting the acquisition of knowledge and through it self-conscious control of social life. Clearly, holders of post-modernist views are willing to undermine themselves if, in the course of so doing, they can also liquidate the modernist project.

From positivism to realism

Views like those of symbolic interaction, ethnomethodology and, most dramatically, post-structuralism, all present challenges to the positivist idea of objectivity in sociology. We have presented them as specifically challenging the positivists' idea that reality is independent of our ideas, offering instead the idea that reality is a 'social construction' (to use one way in which this idea is sometimes expressed). The idea (at least for sociological purposes) is that reality becomes the same as that which people treat as real. Thus, symbolic interactionists see reality as that which people collaboratively define as real, ethnomethodologists see it as that which people identify as real through the situated use of socially provided 'fact-finding' methods. For them, the sociological researcher is engaged in 'reality reconstruction' in so far as he or she is trying to work out what the reality constructed by those being studied actually is. Post-structuralists are out to subvert the idea of 'reality' altogether, and promote the idea that there is a 'crisis of representation', that is, the notion has been eroded that the purpose of language and its products – reports, stories and texts – is to 'represent reality'. They sometimes identify themselves with the slogan 'there is nothing outside the text' to reinforce their position, stressing the extent to which anything that readers take to be 'reality' is merely an effect of specific literary devices and conventions. This point is intended to apply to the writings of natural scientists just as much as to those of novelists, bureaucrats or sociologists.

Accepting for the sake of argument the adequacy of these characterizations, many interpret such points of view as undermining all possibility of objectivity and, thereby, all possibility of knowledge. Consequently, it appears to involve the surrender of the confidence our civilization has reposed in the expansion of science, denying that it can achieve in respect of the social anything to match its accomplishments in the study of nature. Indeed, doubt is even being cast on the achievements of natural science, suggesting that these may be no more than convenient fictions. 'Realist' critics argue that with their particular methods the ethnomethodologists and post-structuralists particularly would liquidate their own conception of sociology. In this view, often deriving from the Marxist tradition, social reality shapes the lives of members of society; instead they are being offered the conception that social reality itself is created by the individual members of society. This suggestion that people's ideas shape reality seems to them to be getting things upside down when Marx had done so much to put things the right way up by arguing that socioeconomic realities shape ideas. Whatever the merits of these arguments, there has been some comfort for those who want to believe in the objectivity of sociology and the mind independence of social reality in the recent resurgence of 'realism' in the philosophy of science.

As usual, there is no necessary agreement amongst realists as to what realism is, so for our purposes we must select just one representative of this standpoint and have chosen Roy Bhaskar. He argues (Bhaskar, 1979) that the interactionists, the ethnomethodologists and their like are right to oppose positivism but are wrong to suppose that by doing so they are rejecting the idea that sociology can be a science. Such rejection derives from confusing a legitimate doctrine, 'naturalism', with an illegitimate one, 'scientism'. According to Bhaskar, naturalism 'may be defined as the thesis that there is (or can be) an essential unity of method between the natural and the social sciences' (1979, p. 3) whereas 'scientism' is a mistaken version of naturalism. Scientism denies what naturalism accepts, that there are any significant differences in the methods appropriate to studying social and natural objects. Bhaskar argues that sociology can be a science *in the same sense* but not *in the same way* as (say) physics. The differences in the nature of the objects physics and sociology respectively study mean that there will be differences between the methods appropriate for investigating them. The positivists had assumed that the same method unified the sciences, but Bhaskar rejects this view. If the same method unifies the sciences, then the positivists and their critics are agreed, sociology could not be a science if social phenomena consist in our ideas. For the methods of the natural science – which are the essential methods of science – make no room for the study of ideas. The positivists drew the conclusion that sociology could be a science by defining social reality differently, that is, seeing it as an independent reality which did not consist in ideas. The critics of positivism drew another conclusion, that sociology could only understand human conduct by taking note of people's ideas, and therefore it could not be a science because scientific methods are not geared to study such phenomena. If, though, we allow that sciences do not necessarily employ the same method *and* can accept that social reality is in significant part comprised of ideas, then we can claim that sociology can be a science. Bhaskar argues for this approach.

The key difference between postivism and realism is in their respective views of what scientific inquiries aim to do. The positivists think that scientists aim to establish the regularities that connect events. The examples we gave of Boyle's law involved establishing that there are regular connections between such events as a change in pressure and a change in volume of a gas (provided, of course, that the temperature does not change). If this was all that science did, realists argue, it would not be enough to give us a true understanding of nature. Knowing that increasing the pressure of a gas increases its temperature may be informative and useful, but it does not really enable us to understand this phenomenon. Genuine understanding of this regularity comes through learning something about the nature of gases, about the way they are composed of molecules and about the ways the motion of molecules is affected by compression. Science helps us understand because it investigates not only regular connections between events, but also, and more fundamentally, tells us about the nature and constitution of *things*. Thus, science investigates the nature of a gas and tries to find out what it is made up of and how the things it is made up of interact to make it behave in the ways that it does. Hence, positivists put great emphasis on 'laws' whilst the realists give prominence to 'mechanisms'. By mechanisms we refer to the way the organization of things can regulate their behaviour, in the way that the inner structure of the clock moves the fingers around.

The key to Bhaskar's position is the insistence that reality is 'stratified', that is, composed of different levels, some of which are readily apparent and observable to us in our own daily experience, others we can only gain access to through experimental methods or intrusion into the phenomena with instruments. According to the above arguments, the things we can observe, the regularities in behaviour, are to be understood in terms of the underying structures we cannot observe. They are the 'mechanisms' that cause the behaviour of the phenomena we can observe. For example, we can observe the regular pattern which is the maturation of the human organism, the growth from infant to adult, but we cannot observe in the same way the working of the genetic code embodied in DNA, although the genetic code is the mechanism producing the growth of the organism. The business of science involves, typically, the movement from the examination of the manifest, observably regular behaviour of phenomena to investigation into their deeper structures in order to discover how these structures act as 'mechanisms', that is, serve to make things work as they do.

Realists see no reason to suppose that social science need proceed in any different way. We should accept that people do act in terms of their ideas, that people respond to situations as they define them, but this does not entail that people are not implicated in complex (and *real*) structures of social relations of which they are unaware but which act as the mechanisms which cause people to have the ideas they have and to act in the ways they do. Bhaskar allows that his argument is meant only to establish the *possibility* of a social science, one which studies phenomena that are as real and independent as those of the natural sciences, namely, the underlying structures of social relations within which individuals acquire their ideas and perform their actions. The argument does not have direct implications as to what sociological researchers should do and how they should make their investigations. As suggested, however, it clearly has affinities with views like those of Marxists and Durkheimians, providing them with, at least, the defence that their theories are not faulty just because they presuppose the existence of a mind independent reality. They reassure themselves that there is indeed a world 'out there'.

Conclusion

These disagreements over method between the sociological standpoints are every bit as great and fundamental as those which divide them over substantive sociological issues. Indeed, in this chapter we have tried to show how the 'anti-positivist' positions, ranging from certain kinds of Marxism through symbolic interaction to post-structuralism insist that methodological conceptions cannot be considered as neutral with respect to sociological controversies. If knowledge is to be sought at all – a view questioned by the post-structuralists – then the understanding of what kinds of methods are needed is basically tied up with the conception we have of what sociology is trying to do. Unless we are clear on this point, all consideration of specific techniques of data-gathering are merely ritualistic.

Further reading

Bhaskar, R., *The Possibility of Naturalism* (Harvester, 1979). Outlines his own realist theory of science and discusses its application to the social sciences.

Blalock, H., *Basic Dilemmas of Social Science* (Sage, 1984). A critical reappraisal of the achievement of positivist research written from a sympathetic point of view.

Brown, H., *Perception, Theory and Commitment* (University of Chicago Press, 1977). Review of the change to the 'new philosophy of science'.

Cicourel, A., *Method and Measurement in Sociology* (Free Press, 1964). Classic assault on positivist method from an unsympathetic point of view.

Clifford, J., 'On ethnographic authority', *Representations*, vol. 1, no. 2, Spring 1983, pp. 118–46. Discusses the problem of writing (anthropological) ethnography and the authority of the ethnographer as a reporter of truth in the light of post-structuralist ideas.

Clifford, J., and Marcus, G. (eds), *Writing Culture* (University of California Press, 1986). Essays on literary and political aspects of describing social life.

Halfpenny, P., *Positivism and Sociology* (Allen & Unwin, 1982). Detailed and discriminating account of variety of positivist views.

Keat, R., and Urry, J., *Social Theory as Science* (Routledge, 1975). Accessible statement of realist views.

Kolakowski, I., *Positivist Philosophy* (Penguin, 1972). Historical background of positivist thought.

Kuhn, T., *The Structure of Scientific Revolutions* (University of Chicago Press, 1962).

Magee, B., *Popper* (Fontana, 1974). Sympathetic and lucid short account of Popper's ideas.

Marsh, C., *The Social Survey* (Allen & Unwin, 1983). Defence of survey tradition against criticisms.

_____, *Exploring Data* (Polity, 1988). Introduction to technicalities of data analysis in statistical terms.

Popper, K., *The Logic of Scientific Discovery* (Hutchinson, 1959). Classic source of Popper's arguments about science.

_____, *The Open Society and Its Enemies* (Routledge, 1962), especially volume 2. This features Popper's argument about the totalitarian implications of Marx's argument, plus, in Chapter 23, his argument that objectivity in science is not a property of the individual.

Schwartz, H., and Jacobs, J., *Qualitative Sociology* (Free Press, 1979). Comprehensive discussion of sociological research engaged in 'reality reconstruction' of the kind done by symbolic interactionists and ethnomethodologists.

Smith, W. H., *Strategies of Social Research* (Prentice Hall, 1975). Review of a range of methodological topics pertaining to measurement, survey field research and the practicalities of using these.

Winch, P., *The Idea of a Social Science* (Routledge, 1958). Classic contemporary statement of 'anti-positivist views' and subsequent focus of numerous controversies and a vast amount of discussion.

Woolgar, S., *Knowledge and Reflexivity* (Sage, 1988). A collection of papers which exemplify the 'reflexive' approach to sociological writing.

Woolgar, S., *Science, the Very Idea* (Horwood, 1988). Discussion of problems with the idea that science gives a representation of reality.

Questions

1 What are the leading features of positivism, and how are they exemplified by Popper's arguments?
2 In positivist terms, what is the role of the sociological reseacher?
3 What is the hypothetico–deductive method?
4 Why does Popper give such emphasis to the refutation of scientific theories?
5 From a positivist point of view identify the respective merits and demerits of survey research and fieldwork.
6 Why does Kuhn think that scientific change can best be described in terms of 'revolutions'?
7 What does it mean to say social reality is 'mind dependent'? Why should anyone argue that it is?
8 Contrast the methodological concerns of symbolic interaction and ethnomethodology.
9 What is the relation between positivism and realism?
10 Does the deconstruction of texts entail the destruction of methodology?
11 Does the approach of the post-structuralists deny the possibility of being objective about the social world?

8 Conclusion

At the outset, we opted to use the concept of a 'sociological perspective' as an organizing device for setting out the kinds of work going on in sociology. We suggested that the field could usefully be viewed as consisting of a number of distinctive though linked perspectives. We hope that it has proved to be a convenient and useful device.

Like analogies, such devices, however, have their limitations; they begin to creak and groan under the strain when pushed too far. Such strain is generated when either the differences or the similarities between approaches are stressed too much, resulting in categories that are either too rigid, too watertight, or so loose as to not be worth the bother. Clearly, we have to do some grouping or categorizing of like with like, but in choosing the relevant criteria for selecting similarities, we can underplay differences between members of a category and exaggerate differences between different categories.

For example, we decided to organize Chapters 2 and 3 under the general category of 'structuralism', thereby claiming that all the thinkers we considered paid considerable attention to the concept of society as a whole and how it holds together – in short, how 'the problem of order' is tackled. We then claimed that this problem is solved in two major ways: one way by focusing on the consensual, integrative elements, the other by emphasizing the impetus to change generated especially by the economic base. That these approaches cannot be held apart for very long was demonstrated as early as Chapter 2 where we saw how the 'neo-functionalists' tried to salvage what they considered to be the best features of structural-functionalism in a considered accommodation with conflict theory. Similarly, when we came to examine conflict theory in detail in Chapter 3, it soon became clear that 'consensual' elements featured prominently for explaining how society is held together, albeit they are presented pejoratively as 'ideology' rather than more glowingly as 'value consensus'!

Yet even within the organizational constraints of these two chapters, we saw in each of them a large, perhaps alarmingly large, variety of thinkers with differing though overlapping views. What a range is covered by Spencer, Comte, Durkheim, Parsons, Merton, Smelser, Erikson – even before we moved on to Marx, Weber, Dahrendorf, Hindess, de St Croix and the like. Furthermore, this range can be seen to be even more extended in Chapter 4. Here there seemed to be no holds barred in the range of considerations taken up by our chosen continental thinkers. They seem to incorporate the concerns of both kinds of structuralists and to raise even more issues in attempting new kinds of synthesis in their examination of how society works. We moved through concepts like alienation, hegemony, structures in dominance and repressive tolerance via the work of Lukács, Gramsci and Marcuse and the Frankfurt School and went on to consider attacks on the 'subject', on 'humanism' and on 'rationalization' by Althusser. Habermas seemed to move us even further away from our earlier concerns with his strong emphasis on communication rather than on the working class or value consensus as *the* element in the social structure. Yet all of these thinkers seemed in retrospect to be strongly rooted in mainstream structuralist concerns once we turned to an alternative version of the concept of 'structuralism', namely, that rooted in the underlying structure of language and ideas and associated with the work of Lévi-Strauss. In following this thread of language, we ended up in very deep waters indeed, as we moved on to Foucault's arguments about the oppressive nature of reason and then ended up with Derrida and his 'deconstructionism', which seemed to deny us the very tools for using reason.

By the end of Chapter 4, then, the organizational device of 'sociological perspective' has become very stretched. Nevertheless, all the thinkers are still involved with the overall nature and organization of society, albeit in very differing ways. Should we be alarmed by these differences? Should we be looking for better answers? Should we be looking elsewhere for answers? If our account fairly and reasonably shows the state of sociological thinking on these matters, what are we to make of it?

Perhaps the best approach to giving some sort of an answer to these questions is to remind ourselves of the kinds of problems and questions addressed by the thinkers we have considered. They are big questions, they are difficult questions; they are questions that transcend the boundaries of sociology as a mere academic discipline. For example, one former British Prime Minister advised us all that we were now a classless society. We feel we may have 'unpacked' that notion to some considerable extent, especially in Chapters 2 and 3. Another more contemporaneous Prime Minister has declared that there is no such thing as society. After examining, among other things, our discussion of Durkheim on the individual and society, Parsons on personality, culture and social relationships and, not least, Althusser on the 'individual' and the 'subject', the utter simplicity of adopting such a Hobbesian, atomistic view of society cannot be uncritically accepted. Similarly, to probe the role of unconscious forces, whether they be Marxian 'ideology', Lévi-Strauss's symbolic systems of meaning and understanding or the pressures created by 'rationalization', may stimulate novel insights into the working of our own society.

Perhaps, however, we may give ground to the second Prime Minister and, with Weber, concede that there is no such thing as society if it is conceived in terms other than the aggregation of individuals' relationships. If we do so, we are adopting the stance of methodological individualism. In so doing, we cannot avoid other and clearly related difficult questions, as we saw in Chapters 5 and 6. Of course, the biggest of these questions might well be how we move from everyday face-to-face interactions to talking about the social structures at the societal level which we, as individuals, inherit and have to cope with. And even if we move away from this 'micro-macro' problem, as it is sometimes oversimplistically known, there are plenty of other challenging, knotty puzzles, not least that of explaining how we derive or create our sense of orderliness in these mundane everyday transactions. Once we abandon trite, circular (tautologous) pseudo-explanations like 'we learn how to (= are socialized into) behave like this or that' it is difficult indeed to see how we sustain all our interactions in their full complexity and we have examined how symbolic interactionists and ethnomethodologists suggest solutions to this problem.

In so doing, we have raised another batch of extremely challenging questions which we attempt to pull together in Chapter 7. They are absolutely fundamental in that they concern how we can go about studying the world, what is involved in making a sociological study of it and how we can produce scientific knowledge. What sort of knowledge is it? Is it objective knowledge? It may be very sobering or even disconcerting to discover that sociology has only two major techniques, namely surveys and fieldwork for exploring the world and thereby attempting to provide data for answering some of these questions. It is possibly even more disturbing to realize that these techniques are worthless unless fundamental issued raised by philosophers of science are taken fully on board. Such issues include questions about the nature of science and the nature of its subject matter: can we make a scientific study of human beings who have minds and intentions as well as physical movements and physical properties? Can we produce convincing, even 'law-like' generalizations about such phenomena? And if we cannot do so, what is the alternative? Do perspectives in action and meaning provide such an alternative? Do we have to follow Derrida and the like into deconstructionism – an approach some consider no better than nihilism!

These are complicated and difficult questions and there are plenty of others in the book. Throughout, we have endeavoured to provide clear expositions of the various perspectives, stances and arguments. To do so, we have inevitably oversimplified, as any comparison with the original texts will reveal. Nevertheless, we have still ended up with some complex and difficult questions; simplifications can only go so far before we risk losing touch with the original problem.

For anyone wanting cut and dried answers, answers 'off the peg', sociology is certainly not the subject to take up. For it is a subject area best characterized by its lively disputatiousness, its conflicting approaches and versions and, vitally, by its questions. The quality of these questions must be decisive in making any kind of choice of area to study. Are they worth answering? Are they big enough? Are they important enough? Are better answers and approaches provided anywhere else? Our response is: yes, yes, yes and no!

References and selected bibliography

Althusser, L., *et al.*, *Reading Capital* (New Left Books, 1970).

Anderson, R. J., Hughes, J., Shapiro, D. Z., and Sharrock, W. W., 'Flying planes can be dangerous: work skills and traffic management in air traffic control', unpublished paper, University of Lancaster, Dept. of Sociology (1989).

Atkinson, J. M., and Drew, P., *Order in Court: The Organisation of Verbal Interaction in Judicial Settings* (Macmillan, 1979).

Avineri, S., *The Social and Political Thought of Karl Marx* (Cambridge University Press, 1969).

Baccus, M., 'Multipiece truck wheel accidents and their regulation', in H. Garfinkel (ed.), *Ethnomethodological Studies of Work* (Routledge, 1986).

Barthes, R., *Mythologies* (Cape, 1972).

Becker, H., *Outsiders: Studies in the Sociology of Deviance* (Free Press, 1963).

Blumer, H., *Symbolic Interactionism: Perspective and Method* (Prentice-Hall, 1969).

Bottomore, T. B., and Rubel, M., *Karl Marx: Selected Writings in Sociology and Social Philosophy* (Penguin, 1965).

Bredemeier, H. C., and Stephenson, R. M., *The Analysis of Social Systems* (Holt, Rinehart & Winston, 1967).

Cohen, G., *Karl Marx's Theory of History* (Oxford University Press, 1978).

Dahrendorf, R., *Class and Class Conflict in Industrial Society* (Routledge & Kegan Paul, 1959).

Davis, K., 'The myth of functional analysis as a special method in sociology and anthropology', *American Sociological Review*, vol. 24 (1959), pp. 757–72.

Derrida, J., *Writing and Difference* (Routledge, 1978).

Derrida, J., *The Post Card* (University of Chicago, 1987).

Dunham, H. W., and Faris, R. E. C., *Mental Disorders in Urban Areas* (Phoenix Books, University of Chicago Press, 1967).

Durkheim, E., *Education and Sociology* (Free Press, 1956).

Durkheim, E., *The Division of Labour in Society* (Free Press, 1964).

Durkheim, E., *The Rules of Sociological Method* (Free Press, 1964).

Durkheim, E., *The Elementary Forms of the Religious Life* (Allen & Unwin, 1968).

Durkheim, E., *Suicide* (Routledge and Kegan Paul, 1970).

Elster, J., *Making Sense of Marx* (Cambridge University Press, 1985).

Erickson, K. T., *Wayward Puritans* (Wiley, 1966).

Flavell, J., *The Developmental Psychology of Jean Piaget* (Van Nostrand, 1963).
Foucault, M., *The Order of Things* (Tavistock, 1970).
Foucault, M., *The Birth of the Clinic* (Vintage Books, 1973).
Foucault, M., *Discipline and Punish* (Allen Lane, 1977).
Fowles, J., *The French Lieutenant's Woman* (Cape, 1969).
Francis, D. W., 'Some structures of negotiation talk', *Language in Society*, vol. 15, no. 1 (1986), pp. 53–79.

Garkinkel, H., *Studies in Ethnomethodology* (Prentice-Hall, 1967).
Gerth, H. H., and Mills, C. W. (eds), *From Marx Weber: Essays in Sociology* (Routledge, 1967).
Goffman, E., *Asylums: Essays on the Social Situation of Mental Patients and Other Inmates* (Penguin, 1968).
Goffman, E., *The Presentation of Self in Everyday Life* (Penguin, 1971).
Goffman, E., 'The interaction order', *American Sociological Review*, vol. 48 (1983), pp. 1–17.
Goldschmidt, W., *Comparative Functionalism* (University of California Press, 1966).
Goldthorpe, J. H., *Social Mobility and Class Structure in Modern Britain* (Oxford University Press, 1980).
Goldthorpe, J. H., Lockwood, D., Bechhofer, F., and Platt, J., *The Affluent Worker: Industrial Attitudes and Behaviour* (Cambridge University Press, 1969).
Gramsci, A., *Selections from 'The Prison Writings'* (Lawrence & Wishart, 1971).

Habermas, J., *The Theory of Communicative Action* 2 vols (Heinemann, vol. 1, 1984; vol. 2, 1988).
Hall, C. S., *A Primer of Freudian Psychology* (Mentor, 1954).
Hanson, N., *Patterns of Discovery* (Cambridge University Press, 1962).
Heath, C., *Body Movement and Speech in Medical Interaction* (Cambridge University Press, 1986).
Hindess, B., *Politics and Class Analysis* (Blackwell, 1987).
Hollingshead, A. B., and Redlich, F. C., *Social Class and Mental Illness* (Wiley, 1958).
Hughes, E., *The Sociological Eye* (Aldine, 1971).

Jameson, F., 'Postmodernism, or the cultural logic of late capitalism', *New Left Review*, no. 146 (1984), pp. 53–92.
Jordan, Z. A. (ed.), *Karl Marx: Economy, Class and Social Revolution* (Michael Joseph, 1971).

Kolakowski, L., *Main Currents of Marxism – Its Rise, Fall and Dissolution: Volume I, The Founders* (Oxford University Press, 1978).

Lefebvre, H., *The Sociology of Marx* (Allen Lane, 1968).

Lemert, E., 'Paranoia and the dynamics of exclusion', *Sociometry*, vol. 25 (March 1962), pp. 2–25.

Lenski, G., 'Rethinking macrosociological theory', *American Sociological Review*, vol. 53 (1988), pp. 163–71.

Lévi-Strauss, C., *The Elementary Structures of Kinship* (Eyre & Spottiswoode, 1969).

Livingston, E., *The Ethnomethodological Foundations of Mathematics* (Routledge, 1986).

Lockwood, D., *The Blackcoated Worker* (Unwin University Books, 1966).

Lofland, J., *Doomsday Cult*, 2nd edn (Prentice-Hall, 1977).

Lukács, G., 'Reification and the consciousness of the proletariat', *History and Class Consciousness* (Merlin, 1971).

Lynch, M., *Art and Artefact in Laboratory Science* (Routledge, 1985).

Lyotard, J., *The Post-Modern Condition* (Manchester University Press, 1984).

MacBeth, D., 'Basketball notes: finding the sense and relevance of detail', in H. Garfinkel *et al.* 'Respecifying the natural sciences as discovering sciences of practical action', unpublished manuscript, University of California, Los Angeles, Dept. of Sociology, 1988.

Mehan, H., *Learning Lessons: Social Organisation in the Classroom* (Harvard University Press, 1979).

Merton, R. K., *On Theoretical Sociology* (Free Press, 1967).

Mitchell, W. C., *Sociological Analysis and Politics; the Theories of Talcott Parsons* (Prentice-Hall, 1967).

Parsons, T., *The Structure of Social Action* (Free Press, 1937).

Parsons, T., *The Social System* (Routledge, 1951).

Parsons, T., *Societies: Evolutionary and Comparative Perspectives* (Prentice-Hall, 1966).

Parsons, T., *The System of Modern Societies* (Prentice-Hall, 1971).

Parsons, T., 'The social structure of the family', in R. N. Anshen (ed.), *The Family: Its Function and Testing* (Harper, 1959).

Parsons, T., and Shils, E. A. (eds), *Towards a General Theory of Action* (Harper Torchbooks, 1962).

Phillips, D., *Knowledge from What?* (Rand McNally, 1971).

Rosen, G., *Madness in Society* (Routledge, 1968).

Sacks, H., Schegloff, E. A., and Jefferson, G., 'A simplest systematics for the organisation of turntaking for conversation', *Language*, vol. 50 (1974), pp. 696–735.

Scheff, T. J., 'The social reaction to deviance: ascriptive elements in the psychiatric screening of mental patients in a Midwestern state', *Social Problems*, vol. II (1964), pp. 401–13.

Schegloff, E., 'Notes on a conversational practice: formulating place', in D. Sudnow (ed.), *Studies in Social Interaction* (Free Press, 1972).

Schegloff, E., 'Identification and recognition in telephone conversation openings', in G. Psathas (ed.) *Everyday Language* (Academic Press, 1979).

Schegloff, E., and Sacks, H., 'Opening up closings', in R. Turner (ed.), *Ethnomethodology* (Penguin, 1974).

Schutz, A., *Collected Papers:* vol. I, *The Problem of Social Reality* (Martinus Nijhoff, The Hague, 1967).

Schutz, A., *The Phenomenology of the Social World* (Heinemann, 1972).

Smelser, N. J., *Social Change in the Industrial Revolution* (Routledge, 1959).

St Croix, G. E. M. de, *The Class Struggles in the Ancient World* (Duckworth, 1981).

St Croix, G. E. M. de, 'Class in Marx's conception of history, ancient and modern', *New Left Review*, no. 146 (1984), pp. 94–111.

Stafford-Clark, D., *Psychiatry Today* (Penguin, 1973).

Strong, P., *The Ceremonial Order of the Clinic* (Routledge, 1979).

Suchman, L., 'Representing practice in cognitive science', *Human Studies*, vol. 11, nos. 2 and 3 (April/June 1988), pp. 305–26.

Szasz, T. S., *The Manufacture of Madness* (Paladin, 1973).

Turner, R., 'Talk and troubles: contact problems of former mental patients', unpublished PhD dissertation, University of California, Berkeley, 1968.

Weber, M., *The Protestant Ethic and the Spirit of Capitalism* (Unwin University Books, 1965).

Weber, M., *Max Weber's 'Science as a Vocation'* (Unwin Hyman, 1989).

Weider, D. L., *Language and Social Reality* (Mouton, The Hague, 1974).

Westergard, J. H., and Resler, Henrietta, *Class in a Capitalist Society: A Study of Contemporary Britain* (Penguin, 1976).

Woolgar, S., *Knowledge and Reflexivity* (Sage, 1988).

Index